WHY PLANES CRASH

2001 AND 2002

BY
SYLVIA WRIGLEY

CONTENTS

WHY PLANES CRASH

CASE FILES
2001

ACKNOWLEDGEMENTS

THANK YOU, as always, to Cliff Stanford, both for introducing me to flying and for never balking when my enthusiasm overflowed. And also a belated thank you to Lee Dumbleton for teaching me to love everything about the Piper Saratoga, even when I was convinced it was trying to kill me.

I'd like to extend a special thank you to Simon Spruck, Yamaguchi Yoshiaki, contri, anynobody, Cybergothiche, Carrie Schmitz, Shahram Sharifi, Noel Jones, Dean Morley, Martin Varsavsky, Sören Karleby, Ken Elliot, Andres Rueda and Noel Jones for making their photographs and illustrations available as a part of this book.

A shout-out to PPRuNe and /r/aviation, my two favourite sources of aviation discussion, even if we don't always agree.

Excellent editing and production were provided by E-QUALITY PRESS. Any remaining errors are my fault and despite the careful ministrations and admonishments of the editor.

For more information on the *Why Planes Crash* series, please see *http://planecra.sh/2001*.

CONTENTS FOR
CASE FILES 2001

INTRODUCTION

WHEN I FIRST CONSIDERED this series, I knew I wanted to focus on modern failures. I'd been invited to London to speak on *Aircraft Confidential*, the Discovery television show highlighting famous aviation disasters. Many of the fascinating, frequently talked about aircraft failures like Aloha Airlines losing its hull or the fast spreading fire of Swissair 111 are lacking resonance for the flyers of today. They are historically interesting but not immediately pertinent to modern aviation. These are accidents which will not happen again, often as a direct result of the efforts of investigators of the time. I find them endlessly fascinating; however I am even more intrigued by real-world problems which we are still experiencing in aviation.

The question now is really: Why do planes *still* crash? By concentrating on modern crashes, we can focus on the issues of today and understand what can be done to continue to keep aviation safe.

It is often too easy to point at the pilot. He is a single point of failure who can be blamed without financial repercussion for the airline, without requiring lengthy legislative amendments by the governments, without requiring changes at manufacturing plants. A single reputation is destroyed, sure, but millions in man-hours and money are saved. That's the efficient answer and, thus, the one we should arrive at only when the other factors have all been investigated.

This is not to say that pilots don't make errors, or that those errors should be disregarded. However, when considering the incident, we should be asking ourselves what the reasonable repercussions of a mistake are. A pilot who gets lost in an airfield and queries his position should not be left to blunder forward onto an active runway. A passenger who insists that he must get in at all costs should not be able to pressure the pilot into reckless behaviour. And attending advanced training certainly shouldn't result in bad habits being taught which put the entire aircraft at risk. All of these accidents and more are covered in the pages to come. Some are more technical than others and require more time to explain, but I am hopeful that every analysis is interesting to pilots and passengers alike.

This book covers eleven accidents and incidents which took place over the course of 2001. Each section includes text quoted directly from the accident report. If you'd like to read the original accident report for more information and context, then simply skip to the end of the section where you'll find a link to the original report.

In each chapter, I cover the core chain of events which led to the accident rather than making a simple judgment. Accidents are invariably a combination of factors, and pilot decisions and (in)actions can be the result of a culmination of those factors. A strong investigation will not only consider the cause but the contributing factors: those actions or inactions which could have saved the day but didn't. The objective in accident investigations around the world is not to cast blame, but to understand every aspect so that we can stop it happening again. Unravelling the mystery from the wreckage is the most important step.

LOST IN THE FOG

Cessna Citation 525. Photo by Noel Jones.

THE CESSNA'S FLIGHT PLAN reported the crew as instrument rated for an approach down to a minimum visibility of 550 metres. At the time, the visibility at Milano Linate Airport was 100 metres with fog and overcast at 100 feet: much less than the flight crew required for a safe landing at that airport.

Despite this, the Cessna pilot decided to continue. The controller on the Tower frequency, having warned him of the low visibility, cleared him to land on Runway 36R, the *Pista principale*.

There are two aprons—the manoeuvring areas of an airport where aircraft are loaded/unloaded and able to park. At Milan, the North apron serves the *Pista principale* for large transport-category aircraft. The West apron, next to the *Pista turistica* is available for the smaller General Aviation traffic using the short runway. Until fairly recently, it was easy to keep the two types of traffic separate. But as General Aviation aircraft have become more powerful, it has become more common for "small" planes at the West apron to require the longer *Pista principale*.

The airfield has with two runways that run north/south: on the right is the large runway with taxiways that connect it to the North apron. On the left, is the small runway with taxiways at the top and bottom. These taxiways start at the West apron and carry on past the small runway to the large runway. The main taxiway runs parallel to the *Pista principale* for its full length. Four connecting taxiways are numbered clockwise starting from the north. R1, R2, R3 and R4 connect the main taxiway to the *Pista principale*. These are used by the large transport-category aircraft using the North apron and are not all that important to our story.

The remaining taxiways do not follow the clockwise convention. Next is R6, which runs from the West apron along the bottom (the south threshold) of the *Pista turistica* and then continues to the mid-point of the *Pista principale*. Finally, R5 is at the top of the airfield, passing the northern thresholds of both the *Pista turistica* and the *Pista principale* to the North apron.

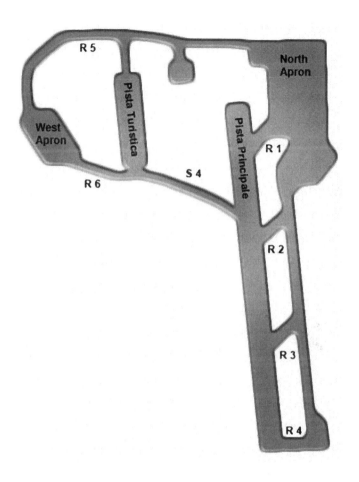

Illustration of the runways at Milan-Linate Airport. Photo by Simon Spruck.

The German Cessna landed on Runway 36R (northbound on the *Pista principale*) at 04:59:34. The aircraft passed the intersection for TWY R6, which connects to the mid-point of the *Pista principale*. The pilot requested permission to backtrack so he could use that taxiway to proceed directly to the West (GA) apron.

D-IEVX: EchoVictorXray on the ground, we could do a short back-track, to turn off to General Aviation.

Tower: DeltaVictorXray roger, on the ground on the hour, report runway vacated on Romeo 6.

D-IEVX: I'll call you on Romeo 6.

D-IEVX: DeltaVictorXray is entering Romeo 6, now.

So far, everything has gone well.

The Cessna had already submitted a flight plan for the next flight: 05:45 hrs from Milano to Paris Le Bourget with two passengers on board. Once clear of the runway, the Tower controller asked the Cessna to contact Ground Control, who are responsible for movements on the airport excluding the active runways.

About forty minutes after the Cessna made its request to backtrack, Scandinavian 686 (a McDonnell Douglas MD-87) contacted Linate Ground Control from the North apron, asking for engine start clearance. The commercial flight from Milan to Copenhagen had 104 passengers on board.
The McDonnell Douglas MD-87 was given a slot time for take-off at 06:16 hrs.

Scandinavian 686 commenced their ground operations. They contacted Ground Control, the air traffic controllers responsible for movements of aircraft around the airport, including taxiways and inactive airways. Scandinavian 686 received taxi-clearance at 05:54:23.

Scandinavian Airlines (SAS) McDonnell
Douglas MD-87. Photo by Dean Morley.

Ground: Scandinavian 686 taxi to the holding position Cat III,
QNH 1013 and please call me back entering the main taxiway.

Four minutes later, the Cessna at the West (GA) apron
requested start-up clearance and was given a slot time of 06:19 hrs
for take off.

For a few minutes, the two aircraft were on the same frequency
but then Scandinavian 686 contacted Tower, who control traffic on
the runway. From this point on, the two aircraft were unable to hear
each other's calls. They had no way to know what the other aircraft
was doing other than by looking out the front. In the early morning
fog shrouding the airfield, that was no help.

Milan Linate Airport had clear procedures in place for low visibility conditions in order to keep the aircraft safe. What they didn't have is an ASMI.

Normally, the key to tracking ground traffic at a large airfield is the Aerodrome Surface Movement Indicator (ASMI) radar which makes it easy to track the aircraft as they move around the airfield.

Milano Linate Airport was equipped with analogue ASMI radar but it was old and apparently was becoming unreliable. In 1994, the civil aviation Air Navigation Service Provider began planning for the installation of a new radar system.

The project became stalled in 1995, with concerns raised about the costs. The airport was advised to "avoid the acquisition of equipment that would become obsolete in view of the rapid technological development in this area." In other words, don't replace the unreliable system with a new one, because a newer new one in a few years might be better and then we'll have to buy another one. This is a common issue with new technology but most people go ahead and take that risk at the point when the need for a replacement becomes desperate.

In November 1999, a Notice to Airmen (NOTAM) was released that the ASMI radar was out of service. Two years later, on the 8th of October 2001, Milano Linate Airport *still* did not have a functioning Surface Movement Radar.

Airports not equipped with ASMI radar have three conditions of visibility for low visibility operations.

- **Visibility 1:** visibility sufficient to taxi and avoid collision with other aircraft/vehicles on TWY and intersections by direct visual observation, and for ATC operators to exercise visual control of all such traffic.

- **Visibility 2:** visibility sufficient to taxi and avoid collision with other aircraft/vehicles on TWY and intersections by direct visual observation, but insufficient for ATC operators to exercise visual control of all such traffic.

- **Visibility 3:** visibility not sufficient for pilots to taxi autonomously and for ATC operators to exercise visual control of all such traffic.

In Visibility 3 conditions, departing traffic should be assisted by a FOLLOW-ME vehicle. All traffic would halt when the runway was in use.

The aircraft would only taxi when landing traffic had reported arriving at the parking bay and departing traffic had already taken off.

In other words, if Milano Linate had declared Visibility 3, the Cessna would not have taxied to the runway until after Scandinavia 686 had departed and would have had a lit vehicle to show the way.

At the time, the decision to declare Visibility 3 conditions was based on reports from the pilots. The controllers had no other method for taking this step. Only when a pilot thought to report that visibility was so bad that he could not taxi safely would the airport declare Visibility 3.

The pilots didn't know this. There was no reason to assume that their reports were required. If the airport had not declared Visibility 3, then it must still be safe to taxi.

One report was received that morning: a concerned pilot said he thought he saw a vehicle moving near his aircraft while he was holding for Runway 36R. This was not considered sufficient to re-assess the current visibility situation.

On that foggy dark morning, the Runway Visibility Range (RVR) (measured at points with high intensity runway lighting) was less than 200 metres. At the West (GA) apron where the Cessna was starting its taxi, the visibility was half that value or even lower.

No one could see a damn thing.

Here's the instruction the Cessna crew were given:

Ground: DeltaVictorXray taxi north via Romeo 5, QNH 1013, call me back at the stop bar of the . . . main runway extension.

D-IEVX: Roger via Romeo 5 and . . . 1013, and call you back before reaching main runway.

This is what's called a "partial read-back". The Cessna did not repeat the full instruction and more importantly, refers to the main runway, rather than the main runway *extension*. It should have been corrected.

The controller didn't respond.

Here are the markings that the Cessna was expected to follow as it taxied from GA parking to the taxi-way:

Taxiway R5 and R6 both had a green lights centre line. Upon exiting the West (GA) apron, the two runways split, TWY R5 going left and TWY R6 going right. Even in bright conditions, the difference between the 5 and the 6 is minimal. The green lights for TWY R6 light started about 80 metres from the split. The TWY R5 lights did not start until about 350 meters from the split. Visibility even under the bright runway lights was less than 200 metres. For the pilots in the cockpit, squinting through the fog at the green lights in the distance, the TWY R5 lights could not have been visible.

Taxiway selection for TWY R5 and R6.

The Cessna was rated for CAT I landings: a precision instrument approach and landing with a decision height not lower than 200 feet (61m) above the touchdown zone elevation. This requires making visual contact with the runway. A CAT I approach requires an RVR of not less than 550 metres. The reason that many commercial flights can continue to function in bad weather is that they are rated for CAT III landings. CAT III landings are in circumstances where there are not sufficient visual references to allow for a manual landing. The aircraft must have an automatic landing system in order to land in CAT III conditions.

CAT IIIa is 250 metres RVR, CAT IIIb is 175 metres RVR. On the morning of the incident, Linate was in CAT IIIb conditions. If visibility had worsened at all, the airfield would have closed.

The important point is that the aircraft *must* be equipped for CAT III ILS operations and the aircraft crew *must* be certified. The

Cessna was not equipped for CAT III operations and neither of the crew was certified. They were attempting to get by visually in conditions that did not allow for it.

The fact that the aircraft was even out there in reduced visibility conditions should have alerted airport authorities. Someone should have at least checked with the crew to clarify. But no one noticed.

The Cessna crew were instructed to follow a route that had minimal signage and markings. There was no radar monitoring of ground movements because the ASMI had been out of service for two years. The West apron had inadequate signage and lacked proper markings. On top of all that, the lines painted on the ground for the taxiways did not match the taxiways in the AIP / Jeppesen maps.

And finally, although the visibility was so bad the airport was on the verge of having to close, there was no move to declare Visibility 3, which would have offered the aircraft a FOLLOW ME vehicle to show the way and restrict its movements during take-off and landings.

And so, into the fog, the Cessna began to taxi. Let's look at the controller's instruction again:

Ground: DeltaVictorXray taxi north via Romeo 5, QNH 1013, call me back at the stop bar of the . . . main runway extension.

D-IEVX: Roger via Romeo 5 and . . . 1013, and call you back before reaching main runway.

The yellow taxi line leads towards the south and then to the east, where it splits: left to Romeo 5 and right to Romeo 6.

The taxiway centre lights for Romeo 6 was located at about 80 metres from the split. The closest centre light for Romeo 5 was about 350 metres from the split. Visibility at that point was around 100 metres. Only one set of lights could possibly be visible in the fog. The Cessna followed the route for Romeo 6.

Now, the pilot correctly read back Romeo 5. However, his actions and decisions all imply that he believed that the aircraft was cleared for the same route he had followed to the GA apron a few hours earlier: Romeo 6. This is furthered by the readback: the pilot dropped every descriptive phrase which did not make sense if he was to taxi on Romeo 6: *taxi north*, *stop bar*, and *runway extension*.

Romeo 5 had all of those things. Romeo 6 had none of them. But no one corrected him when he dropped those phrases.

A second aircraft at the West apron, LX-PRA, was cleared to taxi the same route. Again, the stop bar and runway extension were mentioned as a part of the instruction. This exchange took place in Italian.

Ground: OK RomeoAlpha taxi north Romeo 5, QNH 1013, you must follow a Citation marks Delta IndiaEchoVictorXray who is also taxiing on Romeo 5. Obviously he is not in sight, and the clearance limit for you is the stop bar of the extension of the main runway on Romeo 5.

LX-PRA: We follow the German and the stop of the . . . on Romeo 5.

Again, the ground controller received a partial readback and again, he did not correct it.

As the controller and the flight crew spoke in Italian, it is unlikely that the Cessna crew took it in or had the chance to re-consider the key information repeated: stop bar, extension of the main runway.

There was not a single vertical sign indicating TWY R6 for the entire length of the taxiway. There were no markings to alert the crew that they were following Romeo 6 rather than Romeo 5 as instructed. The Cessna followed the green centre-line lights, which simply reaffirmed their belief that they were following the correct route.

As they passed south of RWY 18R, the *Pista turistica*, the pilots noticed two markings on the ground: S4 and S5. The pilots would not have found these location references on any maps: they were not marked in the AIP Italy, nor in the Jeppesen charts.

S1 and S2 were marked on Romeo 5. There was no S3. Instead there were two S5 markings and then an S6. The investigation found that there was no documentation whatsoever regarding these markings or their intended meanings. They appear to have been part of an abandoned project to increase parking stands on the West Apron.

The Cessna crew contacted Ground to give an unsolicited position report, possibly the last chance for anyone to recognise that the Cessna was on the wrong taxiway, heading directly for the mid-point of the main runway.

D-IEVX: DeltaIndiaEchoVictorXray, is approaching Sierra 4.

Ground: DeltaIndiaEchoVictorXray confirm your position?

D-IEVX: Approaching the runway . . . Sierra 4.

Ground: DeltaVictorXray, Roger maintain the stop bar, I'll call you back.

D-IEVX: Roger Hold position.

The controller did not have Sierra 4 marked anywhere on his map. He didn't know what they meant by that update. Instead of investigating further, he disregarded the information. The controller simply presumed that the Cessna was correctly north of the two runways on Romeo 5.

The Cessna crew, having clearly stated their location, presumed that the controller had confirmed they were on the correct taxiway and thus that they were safe to proceed in the fog.

The ground controller contacted another aircraft, asking his position at the North apron, near the beginning of the main taxiway. They spoke in Italian, so the Cessna pilots would not have been able follow the conversation. The controller was cautious in the low visibility, taking time to verify that the route was clear for the Cessna to continue its taxi north of the runway. But that's not where the Cessna was.

Ground: DeltaVictorXray continue your taxi on the main apron, follow the Alpha Line.

D-IEVX: Roger continue the taxi in main apron, Alpha Line the . . . DeltaVictorXray.

Ground: That is correct and please call me back entering the main taxiway.

The Ground controller still had not realised the significance of the Sierra 4 position report. He clearly believed that the Cessna was at the lights bar across Taxiway R5.

The Cessna crew were lost, but they reinforced the controller's presumption with their readback. They did not notice the inconsistency between the clearance received and their actual position.

At the same time, the Tower controller, on a different frequency, cleared Scandinavian 686 for take-off on Runway 36. The Cessna crew, listening to the Ground frequency, could not hear the call. The Cessna taxied on.

D-IEVX: I'll call you on the main taxiway.

The Cessna crew continued forward on Romeo 6 towards the *Pista principale,* the active runway. 180 metres before the runway, the aircraft passed a STOP marking painted on the black asphalt. The Cessna then crossed a yellow runway-holding marking. The crew did not react to any of these warnings.

Ahead of the Cessna was a unidirectional lighted red lights bar and a lighted vertical sign, which said CAT III in white on a red background. These lights were not controllable by ATC since 1998 so were permanently left on. These were all markers of an active runway.

Milan Linate also had an anti-incursion sensors system that alerted the controllers immediately in case of an unexpected aircraft crossing into the runway. However, the system was deactivated in 1998. The investigation was not able to find any documentation as to why the anti-incursion sensors system was deactivated and by whom.

Meanwhile, on the Tower frequency, Scandinavian 686 confirmed the instruction from the Tower controller.

SK 686: Clear for takeoff 36 at Scandinavian 686. When . . . airborne squawk ident and we are rolling.

The Cessna crossed the red lights and the final yellow runway-holding marking painted on the asphalt. The pilots were so convinced of their route that they somehow managed to blank out every piece of information which might have saved them.

The following cognitive elements were not sufficient to raise doubt in the pilot's mind:

- the clearance received from the GND controller, explicitly inviting to enter [sic] the **Main apron**;

- the absence of a clear instruction to cross the runway;

- the fact that they were tuned on the GND frequency instead of being instructed to switch to the TWR frequency to cross the runway.

The firm belief that they were on the right track did not allow the perception of evident warnings.

Furthermore, continuing on their taxi on TWY R6 along their path, the bar with red lights on was crossed, the **Stop** sign which was passed by the ICAO pattern B, then the ICAO pattern A markings that were crossed in succession, it is probable that the meaning of all these markings have been interpreted correctly by the crew and fitted with their belief to be on the right path and that they were cleared to enter the runway.

—From the English translation of the official report

That is to say, as they continued to taxi along Romeo 6, they encountered and passed the bar with red lights, a stop sign and two ground markings, all of which signify a runway. It is hard to believe that the pilots could not have seen these signs. The investigators believe that the pilots could not have misinterpreted this information and must have convinced themselves that they were clear to enter the active runway. It was the only route to the main taxiway from

Romeo 6. At that moment, the Scandinavian passenger jet was hurtling down the runway for take-off. In the thick fog, the Cessna followed the green lights that led to the runway centre-line, directly into the Scandinavian's path.

The flight crew of Scandinavian saw the Cessna at the very last moment: there was an unintelligible exclamation recorded in the cockpit and the flight data recorder registered a "large elevator nose-up command" one second before the collision. It was too late.

The Cessna was split into three pieces, scattered across the runway near the intersection. Scandinavian 686 lost its right engine in the collision. The aircraft managed to get airborne for 12 seconds when the left-hand engine ingested debris from the crash and lost thrust. Scandinavian 686 descended abruptly. The pilot reduced engine thrust immediately, deployed engine reverse levers and applied the brakes. The right wingtip dragged through the grass. Despite all of this, the aircraft slid over the runway end and impacted the airport baggage building at a speed of 139 knots (257.6 km/h).

The crew and passengers of the Cessna, the crew and passengers of Scandinavian 686 and four people in the baggage building were killed.

The deep fog wasn't finished with this disaster yet. With no visibility, it took some time for anyone to understand what had happened.

LX-PRA, the aircraft who was meant to "follow the German" down Romeo 5, realised something was wrong. He asked specifically where the Cessna was.

Ground: LimaRomeoAlpha are you confirming that you already are on Romeo 5?

LX-PRA: We were waiting to exit . . . to see the German coming out, we have not seen him, do you know where he is?

Ground: He is on the main apron, I should say that you can go.

LX-PRA: I should say so, we move.

As far as the Ground controller was concerned, he knew where all his aircraft are.

But odd reports were coming in. A number of people on the ground and in other aircraft reported having heard "a number of bangs" and he did not know what that could mean.

A police officer and a customs officer at Gate 5 behind the airport baggage handling area heard an explosion and ran towards it to find a workman on fire. They assisted the man and reported the Police Control Centre, who contacted the fire department. Two fire-fighting vehicles were sent to Gate 5 to deal with an unknown incident.

Meanwhile, the Tower controller was shocked to see that Scandinavian 686 was missing from his radar monitor. He phoned ACC Radar Control who confirmed that the aircraft had not made radio contract and was not showing on radar.

The Fire Station Control Centre received another phone call, stating that there was an aircraft involved in the fire. Four more vehicles were dispatched.

Tower contacted the fire station, which confirmed the fire and stated that fire vehicles had already been dispatched. The fire station did not elaborate, presuming that the Tower already knew that an aircraft was involved. Tower did not even know where the fire was located, let alone that an aircraft had crashed.

Aircraft I-LUBI was lined up on the *Pista principale* for take-off. Tower asked the aircraft to clear the runway and proceed to the holding bay, to make room for the fire vehicles. Tower then contacted the fire fighting vehicles, which were operating under radio code name VICTOR.

Tower: Victor you may enter the runway, from this moment the runway is clear, you may enter the runway. Make us a report for the whole length. We are missing an aircraft who should have taken off but at the moment it is not in flight so tell us what you may see on the runway, just in case.

Victor 10 responded by contacting the other vehicles.

Victor 10: To all Victor from Operations Control centre, you can enter the runway as well . . . for the time being it has been closed.

The request to search the runway for a missing aircraft (Scandinavian 686) was never passed on.

Presumably Victor 10 did not take in the implications of "there is an aircraft missing" as they knew about the MD-87. Certainly, Victor 10 dismissed the request to search the runway as non-urgent. Meanwhile, Tower still had not been informed that there was an aircraft involved in the fire.

I-LUBI vacated the *Pista principale* at TWY R4 and proceeded to the holding bay.

Five minutes after the collision, a doctor from the first aid centre thought to contact Tower to tell them that the Scandinavian Airlines aircraft impacted the baggage building.

In the midst of this chaos, however, it seemed the Ground controller may have had an inkling of what happened. He spoke to another aircraft in an upset voice, saying something about "probably a Scandinavian and a private". This was the first reference to the possibility of two aircraft involved in the accident.

At the same time, a Tower controller was frantically trying to make contact with the fire engines to find out what had happened. After five minutes of calling, Victor 1 responded.

Victor: Go ahead who is calling for 1, TWR.

Tower: OK Victor I want to know the exact position where you are operating. Is the runway clear? Or is it occupied? How many vehicles are on the runway?

Victor: Just in front of the infirmary, let's say, in the vicinity of the infirmary.

Tower: Understood. Then you do not have equipment on the runway?

Victor: Nothing.

A different Tower controller called the Air traffic services Reporting Office (ARO) and explained that Scandinavian 686 had not been able to take off "for his own problems", that is, he believed Scandinavian had experienced some sort of technical fault and aborted take off leading to the runway overrun. Tower still had no idea that two aircraft had collided on the *Pista principale*.

However, again the Ground controller makes a revealing statement to another aircraft that wished to taxi back to the North apron:

Ground: Sorry, which aircraft? There are two of them unaccounted for.

Then again, in a separate exchange the same controller referred again to the Cessna as still taxiing on Romeo 5. The Cessna had been burning on the *Pista principale* for almost 20 minutes now but no one had noticed.

Tower contacted I-LUBI, which had been holding at the bay, giving him clearance to enter the runway and taxi to Romeo 6 to return to the West (GA) apron.

Tower then contacted Victor to ask if they could see two aircrafts involved in the fire but received no response.

I-LUBI entered the runway and discovered the burning Cessna at the Romeo 6 junction. I-LUBI immediately contacted Tower, the first to report that there was a fire on the runway.

I-LUBI: I have Romeo 6 in front of me, we vacate the runway the first on the right since there is a fire on the runway . . . Romeo 2.

Tower: BravoIndia copied, then you will hold on Romeo 2 because we have other aircraft on the taxiway.

I-LUBI: Copied, we maintain . . . on Romeo 2, there is fire on the runway, things that are burning, wreckages in flames.

Tower: Received . . . thank you.

It seems odd that there was no immediate reaction but as far as Tower knew, the runway had been inspected by the fire vehicles. The controller may have assumed that this was debris from Scandinavian 686, part of the technical problem that caused the runway overrun. He certainly had reason to believe that the fire vehicles were already dealing with the issue.

There was, as yet, no real evidence of further on the TWR frequency (yet) but the Ground controller had clearly had time to think through the sequence of events. He spoke to LX-PRA, to try to find out what happened to the Cessna.

Ground: RomeoAlpha, excuse me, we are trying to understand
what might have happened, and . . . you were . . . you had
been instructed to taxi following the German, right? the DeltaIndiaEchoVictorXray.

LX-PRA: Yes, right, I confirm, but when we started taxi, as we
reported on. . . , it was not in sight, therefore we started taxi
for Romeo 5, but we have not seen the German.

Then the Tower received a phone call from the Airport handling
and service provider, which confirmed that the Cessna had not
returned to the parking area.

It was 23 minutes since the initial impact when the Tower
controllers finally realised that the Cessna was not where they
believed it to be. They followed up on the I-LUBI report.

Tower: Yes this is Tower, listen, I need to talk . . . to talk with one
of your vehicles because there is a small aircraft missing, a
private plane. Somebody has reported things . . . wreckages
in flames, on the runway. Therefore . . . I want to know if
earlier on firemen entered the runway, yes or no?

Fire station: earlier on firemen went directly to Gate n. 5, they
did not enter the runway, they went through . . .

Tower: But we . . .

Fire station: . . . the peripheral.

Tower: . . . but we had cleared them to enter the runway.

Fire station: Hmm we do not know . . . maybe they did not see it
because of the fog, they went directly to Gate n. 5.

Two officers from the traffic office immediately volunteered to inspect the *Pista principale* and report.

The fire station also requested vehicles to look for "a missing aircraft on the runway" but Victor 1 responded that no vehicles were free. Tower enquired again regarding the state of the runway and this time Victor 1 confirmed that definitely no fire vehicles had entered the runway since the initial report of a fire.

The traffic officers, operating under callsign DELTA 2, drove down the runway. 26.5 minutes after the collision, they reported what they found.

DELTA 2: TWR from Delta 2 . . . There is an aircraft on the
runway . . . ah, what . . . what remains of an aircraft, TWR
from Delta 2.

The Cessna, and thus the cause of Scandinavian 686's overrun, was discovered nearly 27 minutes after the collision.

After analysis of evidence available and information gathered, it can be assumed that the immediate cause for the accident has been the runway incursion in the active runway by the Cessna.

The obvious consideration is that the human factor related action of the Cessna crew, during low visibility conditions, must be weighted against the scenario that allowed the course of events that led to the fatal collision; equally it can be stated that the system in place at Milano Linate airport was not geared to trap misunderstandings, let alone

> inadequate procedures, blatant human errors and faulty
> airport layout.
>
> —From the English translation of the official report

The report concluded that the visibility was low, the traffic volume was high, and visual aids were lacking. The crew used the wrong taxiway and entered the runway without clearance but they should have been able to rely on the airfield charts, maps, markings and signs, which was not the case at Milan Linate.

Air Traffic Control gets a few mentions, as well. Their chart should obviously have reference to all markings on the aerodrome, but having failed to identify S4, it was unreasonable for the controller to continue to give clearance when the reported location of the Cessna was meaningless. They did not use standard phraseology and disregarded incorrect readbacks. Finally, the standard of the aerodrome was called into question, with the phrase "in dismal order" used to describe the markings, lights and signs.

> The combined effect of these factors, contemporaneously
> present on the 8th of October 2001 at Milano Linate, have
> neutralized any possible error corrective action and therefore
> allowed the accident.
>
> —From the English translation of the official report

The Cessna should not have been flying in the low visibility conditions, that much is clear.

The airport had the flight plan and really should have asked the flight crew to clarify whether they were aware of the visibility conditions and the operational requirements. If the controller was unhappy with the response, he could have contacted the local aviation authority to report the situation. He could have refused clearance to taxi, but this would have been a non-standard response. The responsibility for safe flight rests with the pilot, not with the controller.

However, the airport categorically should have been reporting the correct visibility level and offering the correct assistance to allow for safe conduct across the airfield. The airport's procedure for declaring visibility was amended a fortnight after the accident so that it no longer relied on pilots reporting problems before responding.

Chapter IV paragraph 4.1 conditions of visibility 3: substitute:

visibility which is not sufficient for the pilots to taxi autonomously . .

with the words:

RVR visibility of 400 meters or less.

—From the English translation of the official report

This was followed with a new procedure that in visibility of less than 200 metres, only one movement at a time would be allowed, and that, only with the assistance of the FOLLOW-ME. On the morning of the accident, the visibility was well below this level at the GA apron, which shows just how ludicrous it was that the planes were taxiing autonomously around the airfield.

The flight crew knew the visibility was below their minimums. They chose to take unnecessary risks and continued forward despite the fact that they were not sure where they were. There were plenty of clues that things were not as they should be. At the very least, they should have known to *never* enter the

were not in contact with the Tower Control

    Having said that, taking a wrong tu

common event. It should not result in a trag

the ineffective safeguards at the airport th

Bluntly put, the situation at Milan Linate wა   დent waiting

to happen. The Cessna crew gave a position report for Sierra 4 and at that point, *at the very latest*, the controller should have stopped them to verify where they were and what they were doing. Instead, the controller told them to continue, disregarding critical information that the plane was not where he thought it was and that the readbacks were not correct. The lack of basic organisation at the airport was further underscored by the chaos of the emergency response. It's horrifying to consider that if the accident had been survivable, the passengers and crew would have been trapped for twenty minutes in a burning plane on an abandoned runway.

    The aftermath of the accident led to the Milan Linate airport finally getting a long overdue overhaul. Although the lion's share of the blame was heaped onto the Cessna pilots, getting lost in an airfield in itself isn't a major failure. In the 21st century, it should not require the deaths of 118 people for a commercial airfield to ensure that basic safety guards remain in place, for the protection of everyone.

...l Documentation

- Original accident report:
  *http://www.ansv.it/cgi-bin/ita/
  RELAZIONE DINCHIESTA A-1-04.pdf*

Other References

- Accident report translated into English:
  http://www.ansv.it/cgi-bin/eng/FINAL REPORT A-1-04.pdf

Photography
Unattributed photographs are taken directly from the accident report.

- llustration of the Runways at Milan-Linate Airport by Simon Spruck

- *Cessna 525 CitationJet* by Noel Jones

- *Scandinavian Airlines (SAS) McDonnell Douglas MD-87* by Dean Morley

USING PROPELLERS AS AN AIR-BRAKE

ST. BARTHÉLEMY IS a beautiful Caribbean island, just 22 square kilometres (8½ square miles) with a small airport on the north coast by the harbour. The final approach path takes aircraft just a few metres over a hill directly before descending steeply to the paved runway of 650 metres (2,100 feet) with an overrun onto the beach. St. Barthélemy airfield (and St. Martin, the nearest commercial jet airport for the island) is regularly the subject of viral videos showing aircraft coming in low over the beach or overrunning into the sand. The location allows for stunning aviation photography. The History Channel's *Most Extreme Airports* ranked the airfield as the 3rd most dangerous airport in the world.

As any pilot will tell you, much of aviation is routine. Although flying has become more and more automated over the past century, the problem is not new; in WWII they were already quoting the catchphrase: *Flying is hours and hours of boredom sprinkled with a few seconds of sheer terror.* A risk of the trade is that it becomes easy for flight crew to slip into bad habits and push limits. It should come as no surprise that at an unforgiving airfield like St. Barthélemy, what seems like a simple shortcut can have tragic results.

Runway 10, taken from the beach at St Barthélemy. Photo by Martin Varsavsky.

Surprisingly, despite the challenges of landing at this small
airfield, there was not a single public transport accident reported at
St. Barthélemy from 1991 to 2001. All of the fifteen reported
accidents (including one fatal accident and eleven runway overruns)
were general aviation.

That was until the 24th of March, 2001.

F-OGES was a De Havilland DHC-6-300 operated by Caraïbes
Air Transport. The DHC-6-300, also known as a Twin Otter, is a
high wing aircraft equipped with two turboprops and capacity for
twenty passengers. If you take a look at the Twin Otter page on
Wikipedia, you'll find it features a lovely photograph of the aircraft
coming in to land at St. Barthélemy. It's a popular aircraft for island
hops.

On the 24th of March, Flight TX 1501 was a scheduled flight carrying seventeen passengers from St. Martin to the smaller island of St. Barthélemy.

The Captain was no newcomer. He'd received his Commercial Pilot's Licence in 1987 and received his type rating on the DHC-6 aircraft in 1988. He had 9,864 flying hours, 6,400 of those as captain.

St. Barthélemy aerodrome requires a site rating: pilots must have logged at least 2,000 flying hours and do the landing with an accredited flight instructor before being allowed to fly into St. Barthélemy. The Captain received his site rating for St. Barthélemy in 1991, a decade before the fatal crash.

His co-pilot received his Professional Pilot's Licence in 1999 and his type rating for the DHC-6 in December 2000, just three months before the accident. He had 670 flight hours with only 15 of them on the DHC-6. His manager considered his flying to be "average". He also had put in some 4,000 hours as a flight engineer. At the end of the month, he was leaving Caraïbes Air Transport to join another operator to return to this role. The week before the accident, he did line flying under supervision in the local area. His instructor performed several take-offs and landings at St. Barthélemy.

The two men flew together for the first time on the 22nd of March. The day before the accident, two passengers on the scheduled flight to St. Martin reported the Captain remonstrated with the co-pilot at take-off and again after a hard landing at St. Martin, in a "notably reproachful tone".

On the 24th of March, Flight TX-1501 was an hour delayed as a result of passengers arriving late from a connecting flight. When they were finally able to start-up, an issue with the rear cargo hold door held them up for a further ten minutes. The mechanic who fixed the door reported a stormy conversation between the co-pilot and the Captain after the repair was complete. The Captain sent a message to the Caraïbes Air supervisor to say he would open the door himself after landing, implying that he felt the co-pilot had done something wrong.

F-OGES finally departed St. Martin for the nineteen-mile trip to St. Barthélemy, their fifth flight to the island that day. This was the last scheduled flight of the day, after which the Captain would ferry the aircraft back to St. Martin and participate in a football match. He was going to be late.

They cruised towards St. Barthélemy at 1,500 feet and as they passed abeam of the island of Fourchue, the co-pilot contacted St. Barthélemy Information frequency. A few minutes later, he reported passing the *Pain de Sucre* reporting point for final approach to runway 10. That was the last communication heard from flight TX-1501 inbound to St. Barthélemy.

The Aerodrome Flight Information Service (AFIS) at St. Barthélemy is very basic. There are no radio-navigation aids. There are no radar recordings. There's no view of aircraft on approach until the last minute when they have passed over the La Tourmente pass. On the day of the accident, the radio communications recorder in the tower had been out of order for a year and a half. The agent said that when F-OGES reported *Pain de Sucre*, he gave them the latest wind and told them the runway was clear. Everything was normal, he said. Then he looked towards the pass and saw the aircraft turning left, belly visible, at low altitude. He immediately invoked the emergency procedure.

The aircraft never recovered from the steep left bank. It crashed next to a house on the Corossol road, about six hundred metres (less than 2,000 feet) from the threshold of runway 10. All of the occupants and one person on the ground were killed in the violent impact.

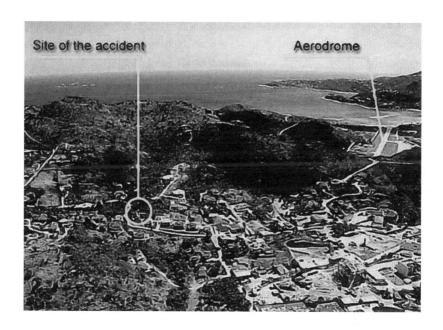

Aerial view of the accident site and St Barthélemy aerodrome.

The investigators arrived the following day and soon found they
had a problem. The St. Barthélemy AFIS had no recordings of any
kind and the investigators discovered that the aircraft's age and low
take-off weight meant it was not required to be fitted with flight
recorders. F-OGES had neither a cockpit voice recorder nor a flight
data recorder. The only hard data that the investigators had to work
with was the wreckage, which was spread over an area of nine
hundred square metres (ten thousand square feet).

The initial investigation was able to dismiss a number of
possibilities. The weight and balance sheet was erroneous; however
the aircraft was within the weight and balance limits set by the
manufacturer. There were no deferred defects logged, in fact, the
only issue in the technical log was the issue with the cargo hold
door, which was found still attached to the aircraft by the hinges.

There were no relevant wind or other weather phenomena reported. There were no traces of a bird strike. Both turboprops were operating and producing significant power at the time of impact. There was no evidence of a structural break-up in flight. The autopsies revealed no medical issues. With no flight data recordings, it seemed impossible to uncover the mystery of the crash.

There was one crucial find in the wreckage: two video cameras. One was so damaged by the impact and subsequent fire that it could not be played back. The other, though, had footage of the flight. The film started during the initial climb out from St. Martin, with views from the cruise and finally showing the approach to St. Barthélemy, ending just one minute before the crash. The final scene, a horizon with veiled clouds through the right side, shows that the aircraft was not turning.

The investigators analysed the film in order to understand the precise position and attitude of F-OGES that day, as well as the operation of the propellers and the engines. Once they determined what seat the footage was filmed from, they recreated the video on an aircraft of the same type to gain more information. Over the course of six commercial flights, they were able to prove that the engines were running normally from take-off up to the last image, with an increase in the propeller speed at the beginning of the descent towards the aerodrome.

The videos also allowed investigators to confirm the exact positioning and height of the aircraft, including the fact that it was slightly right of the approach path.

The investigation team also spoke to the people in the local area who saw and heard the aircraft before the accident.

The people living west of the La Tourmente pass heard a loud engine noise and saw F-OGES with its "nose up" go into a left turn. A Caraïbes Air Transport flight instructor, with 1,500 flying hours on the aircraft, watched from his terrace as it came in.

On the day of the accident, he saw F-OGES arriving on a track which seemed normal to him at the beginning but a bit low on short final compared to normal practice. For him, this track could be explained by downdraft winds which the aircraft can be subjected to at that place. He heard thrust being increased but at a much higher rate than for a simple correction, sufficient on approach. The aircraft then adopted a nose up attitude then turned slowly to the left before banking at about 60° to the left. The left wing then stalled and the aircraft dived towards the ground just before the La Tourmente pass.

—From the English translation of the official report

This was followed by an explosion as F-OGES crashed into the ground.

Between the film footage and the eyewitnesses, the team were able to recreate the final phase of flight. However, this did not offer any answers as to why F-OGES crashed the way it did. The video did not show any malfunctions or anomalies during the recorded duration of the flight. Sudden incapacitation in flight could not have happened simultaneously and suddenly to both pilots with no external reason. The witness descriptions proved that it was neither a sudden change in weight and balance nor a passenger intervention in the cockpit, both of which would cause an erratic track. The description of a sudden loud engine noise before the crash could mean that the aircraft had stalled and was in a recovery; however it seemed unlikely that the experienced pilots would fail to notice the aircraft's speed decay below approach speed on short final.

A Caraïbes Air Transport pilot said that he'd spoken to the Captain of F-OGES after his hard landing at St. Barthélemy that morning, saying that he recommended an initial approach at 1,500 feet and then keeping the descent path until touchdown. The Captain responded that he preferred to take a lower approach path.

Then a breakthrough came when the investigators spoke to the Caraïbes Air Transport mechanic who was on F-OGES for the earlier flight to St. Barthélemy. He had a front row seat in the cabin and told investigators that the landing was quite hard. He said he joked with the Captain about the hard landing, and the Captain responded that he still didn't have a feel for the aircraft, as he had only been flying it again for two days. The Captain then told the mechanic that he had previously used "beta" on approach to slow down and he planned to try that method again.

A propeller in alpha mode governs the RPM using the angle of the blade. In beta or reverse beta, the angle of the propeller blades is such that the propellers direct their thrust forward instead of back, effectively a reverse thrust. This is generally used in order to slow the aircraft down on the ground or in some instances to cool the engine on descent. A propeller-driven seaplane, for example, has no brakes and is dependent on changing the angle of the propellers in order to slow or stop on water. In flight, the effects can be unpredictable and De Havilland states that beta mode and reverse beta mode should *only* be used when the plane is on the ground. The power lever assembly has a mechanical stop that prevents the pilot from accidentally entering beta mode and passing below flight idle.

The mechanic was shocked that the Captain would consider such a thing. He immediately responded that beta mode was prohibited during flight. The Captain snapped back that he was not going to teach him how to fly the plane.

De Havilland DHC-6-300 flying over La Tourmente pass into runway 10 at St. Barthélemy.
Photo by Sören Karleby.

The Caraïbes Air Transport manager confirmed that he believed
that certain pilots used "beta range" for steep approaches, despite
the manufacturer's ban.

A retired pilot from the airline also admitted that sometimes
he'd used "the beta range" to keep the airspeed low while on the
steep approach path to St. Barthélemy, even though he knew it was
prohibited.

A Caraïbes Air Transport DHC-6 Captain stated that one of the problems of the DHC-6 was the fact that, to follow steep approach paths like that of Saint-Barthélemy, pilots quickly find themselves with the control column fully forward, even when the power is fully reduced. The problem is even more critical when the aircraft CG is to the aft. This is one of the reasons why some pilots use the "beta range" during the approach. In this case, it is possible to pass under the path with a low airspeed. If the power levers are mistakenly pulled beyond the "beta range", the propellers pass into "reverse" mode in a more or less symmetrical way. It is then necessary to increase power and a possible propeller unfeathering asymmetry can end up in a loss of control.

—From the English translation of the official report

The scenario began to come clear. The Captain had made clear his decision to use beta mode (by which he likely meant reverse beta mode) as he was having difficulty coming into St. Barthélemy. Selecting reverse beta range for the propellers would reduce the airspeed and allow him to regain the descent path. The propeller effectively acts as a powerful brake.

It was the last landing of the day and a go-around would add extra time to the already late flight. The co-pilot was inexperienced and had already been told off by the captain, so he was extremely unlikely to interfere. Once the propeller pitch offered reversed thrust, the airspeed dropped right down, as intended.

Now, the Captain needed to shove the levers back to their normal-use range. This would increase the thrust, which explains the change in engine noise that witnesses described. If the levers weren't moved perfectly in line with each other, it would cause asymmetry between the engines. And that's what the investigation concluded: he shoved the levers back into the correct position for in-flight but the movement wasn't perfectly aligned. This led to the violent yaw movement seen as a sharp roll to the left.

That close to the ground, the Captain had no chance to regain control of the aircraft.

As a result of the impact, it was not possible to determine the pitch of the propellers or the position of the levers. The lack of flight recorders and radar track made it impossible to prove categorically what happened, but this is by far the most likely explanation.

3.2 Probable Causes

The accident appears to result from the Captain's use of the propellers in the reverse beta range, to improve control of his track on short final. A strong thrust asymmetry at the moment when coming out of the reverse beta range would have caused the loss of yaw control, then roll control of the aircraft.

—From the English translation of the official report

The results of this investigation pointed to a company culture that allowed for shortcuts and risks: the captain was out of date, the management wasn't paying attention, multiple pilots referring to the use of beta mode in the air, the lack of support for the captain's hard landing when he stated directly that he was struggling to "nail the landing" at the airfield. The Captain was in a bad mood. The flight was already running an hour late and he was in a hurry to get home. He used the side effect of a propeller setting that was meant to be used only on the ground. His first officer was an inexperienced first officer who had already been told off once that day, thus unlikely to argue.

Combined with the challenge of flying into St. Barthelémy, it starts to look inevitable that something was going to go wrong. The critical factor is not how to stop pilots taking shortcuts, but rather how to keep those shortcuts from becoming standard and, most importantly, how to stop them from becoming fatal. In this instance, we have a clear failure of the airline's safety culture.

As a result of this specific accident, La Tourmente pass has been lowered by six metres (20 feet) in order to allow for a safer approach to runway 10. A new tower has been built and the AFIS agents now have access to updated radio equipment. However, how long aircraft should be allowed to run commercially without compliance to recording requirements (which would have made the sequence of events trivial to investigate) remains an open question.

Official Documentation

- Original accident report:
  http://www.bea.aero/docspa/2001/f-es010324/pdf/
  f-es010324.pdf

Other References

- Accident report translated into English:
  http://www.bea.aero/docspa/2001/f-es010324a/pdf/
  f-es010324a.pdf

Photography
Unattributed photographs are taken directly from the accident report.

- *Gustav III airport on St Barthelémy* by Martin Varsavsky.

- *De Havilland DHC-6-300 flying over La Tourmente pass* by
  Sören Karleby.

Nose Down into the Runway

THE AIRBUS 321 WAS a breakthrough, the first commercial aircraft to use digital fly-by-wire and a sidestick control. The controls in an aircraft are usually directly connected to the parts of the plane but with digital fly-by-wire the controls are disconnected, so the movement of levers and the stick are sent as data to the computers, which decide what to do with the movement. The computers consider the flight parameters as well as the pilot inputs to determine the changes required in the flight control surfaces.

Compared to traditional controls, the digital fly-by-wire system is lighter and more cost-efficient to manufacture. More importantly, the Airbus fly-by-wire system provides *flight envelope protection*. The pilot at the controls is not directly controlling the flight control surfaces of the aircraft. Instead, his input is sent to the flight-control computers, which interpret his actions and control the aircraft accordingly. Abrupt movements that would put the aircraft outside of its ability to fly safely are dampened, which prevents the pilot from exceeding structural and aerodynamic limits of the aircraft. For example, if the pilot pitches the aircraft nose up, the flight control computer will ensure that the aircraft does not pitch up beyond a safe value. The intent is to allow the pilot the freedom to pull back on the controls without worrying about whether he will put the plane into a stall, as the flight computer will ensure the climb is at the maximum safe rate.

A320 Cockpit. Photo by Shahram Sharifi of the
Iranian Spotters.

On the 7th of February, EC-HKJ, an Airbus A-320-B operated by Iberia, departed Barcelona as Flight IB-1456—a scheduled domestic night flight to Bilbao. The A320 held 136 passengers, 3 flight crew and 4 flight attendants. The expected flight time was 53 minutes. The aircraft was new, manufactured in 2000 and with a total flight time of 1,149 hours. The last (and only) annual inspection had been on leaving the production line.

The pilot flying was a commercial pilot with 423 hours. He completed his type rating course for the Airbus A-320 just over a month before. He was flying under the supervision of the Captain, who had spent over 10,000 hours flying, almost ten times the flight time of the aircraft that he was in charge of. The skies were fairly clear at Bilbao, with scattered clouds and a 10-knot wind gusting up to 25 knots.

As the Iberia flight passed over Pamplona, cruising at 15,000 feet, the flight crew were warned of possible light turbulence. 25 nautical miles out from Bilbao at 7,500 feet, the aircraft began to experience strong turbulence.

Bilbao Airport. Photo by Andres Rueda.

Bilbao Airport is close to the coast and is surrounded by mountains. South of the airport, there are peaks up to 4,839 feet which produce turbulence when the wind comes from the south. Eddies and whirlwinds are a hazard in stable atmospheric conditions.

8 minutes prior to landing, as they descended through 6,000 feet, the flight crew expressed surprise at the strength of the turbulence and commented on the 55-knot winds that they were facing.

The controller also discussed the wind conditions with Vitoria tower, specifically that although the wind at ground level seemed to be light, at higher levels it was "quite bad", with low to moderate turbulence and severe wind shear.

Bilbao Tower cleared IB-1456 to land on Runway 30, informing them of current winds of 8 to 15 kt at 240°, with light turbulence. The crew continued their approach at a stable ground speed but the gusting winds meant that the calibrated airspeed was fluctuating by +/- 6 knots. The aircraft appeared to be speeding up and slowing down as the wind gusted past.

Five minutes before landing, the overspeed warning sounded, caused by the strong winds gusting both horizontally and vertically.

At the time, Iberia had the following warning regarding Bilbao airport in their operations manual, quoted in the accident report:

1. Caution:

"When there is wind between 160° and 230° higher than 15 kt, expect turbulence and wind-shear during approach and landing.

"It is recommended that, when the intensity is higher than 20 kt and there are no reasonably positive pilot reports on conditions, no operations are to be carried out at this airport."

—From the English translation of the official report

"The current wind on the ground was just below this level; however the wind that the crew were experiencing as they came down to land appeared to be much stronger. The Terminal Aerodrome Forecast (TAF) released at 19:04 also warned of a 30% probability of winds up to 25 knots with gusts up to 40 knots.

However, both the current meteorological report and the information from Tower advertised only weather of lower intensity with winds under 15 knots, well within the limits of a safe landing. The plane shook with turbulence and the overspeed warnings continued as the crew continued into Bilbao.

The crew disconnected the autopilot as they descended through 400 feet. At a decision height of 247 feet, conditions were visual and IB-1456 continued the approach to land.

Runway 30 is 2,600 metres (8,530 feet) long with a stopway at the end of the runway with a glide slope lightly steeper than standard at 3.35°. The aircraft descended on the glide slope. One minute before touchdown, tower informed the crew that the wind conditions were 240° 8 knots.

At 200 feet, they flew into a tailwind. Before they reached 100 feet, a sudden up draft hit the plane, registering as a 1.15 g acceleration. This is not a lot of g-force, unless you are trying to land an Airbus. At just a hundred feet over the threshold, the sudden extra speed from the tailwind followed by the strong updraft makes for a tricky landing.

The Pilot Flying pushed his sidestick forward to counter the draft but the gusting hadn't stopped. Five seconds before the touchdown, a down draft struck. The Pilot Flying and the Captain both pulled back on their sidesticks. The two sidesticks work independently from each other and if both pilots use their sidesticks at the same time, an alarm sounds and the flight control system considers the algebraic addition of both sidestick inputs.

The dual input alarm sounded. Either pilot could have (and should have) cancelled the other pilot's sidestick input by pressing the override button but neither did. They both continued to pull back. The combination of the dual input exceeded a pitch-up rate of 10°.

The angle of attack increase, the high approach speed and the combined input of both sticks was interpreted by the computer as dangerous. The flight control system activated the Angle of Attack (AOA) protection.

The Angle of Attack is a critical aspect of aircraft performance and handling. An aircraft wing has a limited range of Angles of Attack that allow for efficient flight. If the Angle of Attack gets too high, the wing loses lift and the aircraft will stall. The aircraft becomes hard to control and is at risk of entering a spin.

The Airbus A320 flight envelope protection includes sophisticated Angle of Attack analyses to prevent the aircraft from entering a stall when overly forceful manoeuvres are requested. In an Airbus, a pilot cannot suddenly pitch the plane's nose up and risk stalling the plane; the elevator deflection is limited. The pilot does not have to concern himself with precise movements because he knows the flight computer will use the maximum safe value. The aircraft is protected from abrupt changes in configuration by the pilot.

This Angle of Attack protection is done using an algorithm which defines a safe value for the angle of attack and a maximum value for the current circumstances. The algorithm predicts the change made to the aircraft's attitude, based on the current angle of attack and the position of the sidestick. The AOA protection is activated when the sidestick is pulled fully backwards and there is a very high angle of attack or a fast-increasing angle of attack. Once AOA protection has been activated, the sidestick input is reduced. The flight control system ensures that the angle of attack remains between the safe value and the maximum value. The aircraft is *prohibited* from exceeding a safe angle of attack.

On this day in Bilbao, the unexpected increase in the angle of attack, combined with the high approach speed and the combined input of both sticks was interpreted by the computer as dangerous.

The flight control system activated the AOA protection. The aircraft was protecting itself against pilot error. But the pilots knew exactly what they were doing.

Once the AOA protection activated, the flight control system limited the possible angle of attack. Pulling back violently on the sidesticks had no effect—especially not with both pilots pulling at once.

In order to land, the pilots *have* to be able to raise the nose. An aircraft doesn't touch down nose-first. When landing, the aircraft flares: the pilot reduces the descent rate and pitches the nose up and the aircraft sinks gently to the ground, landing firmly on the landing gear.

The Ground Proximity Warning System sounded twice: SINK RATE. SINK RATE. The AOA protection made it impossible to flare. The Captain took control from his first officer and attempted to break off the landing. He put full power on, attempting a touch and go. His only hope: get the aircraft back into the air where they could work out what was going wrong. Throughout this, both pilots continued to desperately pull back on the the stick as they were still trying to regain control of the aircraft's pitch.

As a result, the AOA protection remained active. They could not pitch the plane up in order to land safely. They could not go around.

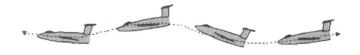

Phugoid Movements

There's a further aspect to the AOA protection. In order to avoid oscillations (known as phugoid movements), the AOA protection will limit the possible angle of attack even further if the airspeed is diminishing, exactly as it should be when landing. The pilots needed to slow down and pull the nose up. However, the flight control system will actually pitch the aircraft nose *down* if the airspeed decreases too suddenly.

For our pilots in Bilbao, things were about to get even worse. Four seconds in, the engines finally had enough power to recover straight and level flight, which would allow them to fly straight over the runway.

That's when the tailwind struck. The aircraft was just 80 feet over the ground when the calibrated air speed dropped dramatically. This triggered the protection against phugoid movements in a high angle of attack scenario.

The pilots were still frantically pulling back on their sticks. Instead, the flight control system pushed the nose down.

They were just a few feet over the runway when the nose pitched down. The plane hit the ground hard, undergoing g-force pressure of 4.75 g—a normal landing is just above 1 g. The nose gear tire marks on the runway lasted for just 10.5 metres (34 1/2 feet) before turning into deep metal scrapes.

The AOA protection de-activated after the aircraft hit the runway and the nose finally lifted.

The Captain continued the landing (to be fair, he had no choice) and slowed the aircraft along 1,100 metres of the runway. The nose dipped down again, scraping the engine nacelles along the pavement. The nose leg, or what remained of it, cut deep grooves into the runway. The aircraft veered violently to the left as the four main gear tires burst.

It finally halted at a 60° angle across the runway.

The Captain ordered an immediate evacuation using all exit doors and slides. The passengers panicked, injuring twenty-four passengers and one cabin crew member in the resulting stampede. Seven trampled passengers were taken to hospital.

3.2. Causes

The cause of the accident was the activation of the angle of attack protection system which, under a particular combination of vertical gusts and windshear and the simultaneous actions of both crew members on the sidesticks, not considered in the design, prevented the aeroplane from pitching up and flaring during the landing.

—From the English translation of the official report

As a result of this accident, Airbus Industrie modified the logic for AOA protection in case of turbulent conditions, inhibiting the activation of the AOA protection as triggered by wind gusts and deactivating the protection in flight at low height.

The National Meteorological Institute began a study of the meteorological phenomena of Bilbao, researching the development of turbulence, gusts and windshear in the vicinity of the airport.

The aircraft was written off.

Official Documentation

- Original accident report:
  http://www.fomento.gob.es/NR/rdonlyres/
  92DDBB9A-E936-42FC-A353-A2C7F39CE860/22834/
  2001_006_A2.pdf

Other References

- Accident report translated into English:
  http://www.fomento.gob.es/NR/rdonlyres/
  8B514392-B79A-46DC-A7C8-DC1BA137D076/
  23171/2001_006_A_ENG1.pdf

Photography
Unattributed photographs are taken directly from the accident report.

- *Bilbao Airport* by Andres Rueda

- *A320 Cockpit* by Shahram Sharifi of the Iranian Spotters Aviation Photography Team

  Iranian Spotters website is at:
  http://www.iranianspotters.net

Snow in the Engine

Human memory is fallible, especially in times of stress. Flight crew have manuals and printed checklists to hand so that they can deal with a wide variety of issues and remain confident that no critical items are forgotten. In this tragic accident, seemingly trivial items in the operations manual led to a fatal situation.

A double engine failure is a very rare occurrence. For both engines to fail at the same time, it can't simply be a mechanical fault. There are two main causes of double engine failure: severe fuel mismanagement and ingestion of foreign matter.

When G-BNMT departed from Edinburgh on the 27th of February, they had plenty of fuel. They were flying in clear weather. And yet, both engines failed within a third of a second of each other.

Double engine failure is so unexpected that at the time of the accident, the operating manual for the SD3-60 twin turboprop had no procedure for a correct response. And as a result, it took the lives of two competent crew who were running a Royal Mail service from Edinburgh to Belfast.

The sequence of events that led to the fatal crash started at the very beginning of the day, at three minutes after midnight.

G-BNMT, a Shorts Brothers SD3-60 Variant 100 operated by Loganair, arrived at Edinburgh airport. G-BNMT was a high wing monoplane with retractable landing gear and two turboprop engines.

It was a cold winter night when the aircraft arrived at Edinburgh just after midnight. The first crew taxied the aircraft to the stand, refuelled it and left the airport without securing the aircraft, as it was scheduled for a further flight.

G-BNMT SD3-60 in July 2000. Photo by David Unsworth.

The second crew arrived less than half an hour later for the next flight scheduled from Edinburgh to Belfast for 00:40. It was freezing cold. G-BNMT needed de-icing in order to fly but so did every other aircraft on the field. The flight crew were told it would take a few hours to get to them. They waited in the crew room.

Just after 2am, Edinburgh Airport closed as a result of severe weather conditions, "of a nature not routinely experienced in the UK." The flight was cancelled.

The second crew stayed on site in the crew room, hoping that the weather might clear. At 6am, they gave up. They returned to the aircraft, fitted propeller straps to each engine, put the pitot head covers on and went home.

The SD3-60 turbo-prop has air intake blanks ("bungs"), which are fitted into the engine intakes to prevent debris, dust and snow from entering the engine intake area. These intake bungs were routinely fitted by the engineers when the aircraft stopped overnight at the operational bases (Glasgow, Kirkwall and Inverness). At Edinburgh, there was no engineering personnel and no engine intake bungs.

The Operations Manual stated that *Engine covers and bungs should be fitted as available.* They were not available at Edinburgh that night and thus not fitted.

Meanwhile, in Glasgow, the accident crew arrived at 8am for a planned flight to Islay at 09:10, but the flight was cancelled as a result of the weather. The crew was rescheduled to fly G-BNMT from Edinburgh to Belfast—the plane whose midnight flight had been cancelled in the early hours as the weather deteriorated.

The snow and weather made it impossible to get to Edinburgh by road. Edinburgh Airport finally re-opened at 11:30 and the crew hitched a ride on another flight to pick up G-BNMT.

By the time the accident crew arrived at Edinburgh, the weather was much improved and the Captain did not feel that the aircraft required de-icing. Very little evidence remained of the wind and snow conditions that the aircraft had been exposed to.

At 15:03 they requested clearance to start, which was given. However, at 15:12, the crew advised ATC that they were shutting down due to a technical problem. The right engine driven generator would not come on line and the crew requested engineering assistance from the company.

An engineer transiting through Edinburgh tested the connections and asked the crew to run both engines for about 15 minutes. He then returned the connections to their original positions and the crew ran the engines again for 15 minutes. The original fault could not be reproduced.

The Commander asked the engineer to check the oil and confirm that the upper surfaces of G-BNMT were free from ice and snow.

The engineer found only a small slush deposit on the windscreens, which he cleared.

The crew restarted the engines and remained on the stand with engines running for about another 20 minutes.

At 17:10 the First Officer requested taxi clearance and the aircraft taxied to depart from Runway 06. The crew completed their "first flight of the day engine checks", including an *autofeather* test. This test feathers the propeller—that is, rotates the propeller blades, aligning them with the direction of the plane—and the anti-ice vanes are driven to the full anti-ice position.

The *Operations Manual* states that the engine ignition should be set to EMERGENCY setting when taking off on runways contaminated by snow or slush. In the EMERGENCY position, the ignition system operates continuously, which allows the engine to automatically relight if there is an engine flameout caused by ingestion of snow or slush during the take-off run.

There was still some slush residue on the taxiways but not on the runway. Conditions were "WET"—that is, surface soaked but with no significant patches of standing water. Thus, the engine ignition systems were set to NORMAL not EMERGENCY.

After take-off the crew retracted the landing gear and then released and retracted it again, to ensure that it was free of snow and slush. After this, the Commander called for after take-off checks to be completed. They were in clear weather but expected to fly into cloud. The Commander asked the First Officer to select the anti-icing systems ON.

Edinburgh Tower asked G-BNMT to change frequency to Scottish Control. The First Officer acknowledged the frequency change and the Commander selected the new frequency while the first officer selected the anti-icing systems to ON. The aircraft was at 2,200 feet above mean sea level.

The first engine flamed out. The second engine failed 0.37 seconds afterwards. The aircraft was experiencing a double-engine failure.

The most likely cause for a double engine failure in this scenario is foreign objects ingested by both engines at the same time, for example hail, ash or birds.

If this happens, it is often possible to rapidly restart the engines as the foreign objects clear. However, there was no procedure for an emergency engine relight within the Operations Manual. In fact, there were no procedures at all in either the Operations Manual or the Aircraft Flight Manual for a forced landing without power. The possibility of a double engine failure was simply not acknowledged.

The Commander declared that it was a double engine failure and initiated a descent while reducing the airspeed and turning towards the coastline.

Meanwhile, the First Officer notified Scottish Control. It was their first call on that frequency.

G-BNMT: MAYDAY MAYDAY MAYDAY THIS IS LOGAN SIX SEVEN ZERO ALPHA WE'VE HAD A DOUBLE ENGINE FAILURE REPEAT A DOUBLE ENGINE FAILURE.

The Controller responded with position and heading information.

Scottish Control: Roger er Loganair six seven zero alpha roger your mayday. Turn er left on to heading of er two five zero. The airfield is three miles to the northeast of your present position.

G-BNMT: Say again Loganair six seven zero alpha

The message was truncated at the last syllable. The air traffic controllers received no further communications from the aircraft.

Inside the cockpit, the Ground Proximity Warning Sensor alerts changed to a warning of TERRAIN, TERRAIN, followed by a continuous warning of WHOOP, WHOOP, PULL UP. The Commander increased the pitch attitude of the aircraft and correspondingly reduced speed. The accident investigation came to the conclusion that the commander probably achieved the best possible speed and attitude combination for the ditching.

But the water was rough and the impact too strong.

The final transmission from the aircraft, advising of a ditching, was never received. In the cockpit, the CVR recorded one further warning of TERRAIN, TERRAIN and then the recording ceased.

The training that they'd received for a ditching could not have helped them: the manuals had no proviso for escaping from a submerged aircraft. The Operations Manual specifies that *it is essential that the aircraft alights on the water with all exits closed.* The crew's only possible escape was the overhead hatch, which would have been difficult or impossible to open underwater.

The aircraft, or what remained of it, came to rest on the sea bottom, trapping the crew within. It is unlikely that the crew could have survived more than a few minutes in the cold seawater.

The time from the first engine flame out to the impact on the water was 62 seconds.

When they found the aircraft, the tide had receded. The flight deck was destroyed and the aircraft was firmly embedded in the sand. On initial investigation, there was no evidence of any technical failure or defect that could account for the double engine failure. At the same time, there was no crew action that could explain why both engines lost power at almost exactly the same time.

G-BNMT at Low Tide.

Through much testing, they were able to reconstruct the sequence of events that caused the flameouts.

G-BNMT arrived at Edinburgh at midnight and was parked facing into wind until its taxi to the runway at 17:10.

That night at Edinburgh, there was a sustained strong northeasterly wind, up to 43 knots, and light to moderate snow fall until 09:52 that morning, conditions strong enough that, as per the Maintenance Manual, the bungs must be fitted.

In the Maintenance Manual, it said that the bungs must be fitted in severe weather condition, which was certainly the case that night in Edinburgh. However, the Operations Manual made no mention of this, and stated only that the engine intake bungs must be fitted if the aircraft was parked for any length of time, for example an overnight stay. The pilots would have referenced the Operations Manual. G-BNMT was never meant to stay at Edinburgh and so no one reported the lack of bungs.

For eight hours, it was snowing and the wind was blowing hard. The temperature remained between freezing and +1°C. The snow entered the plenum chambers of the engine where the large snowflakes would easily have flowed upwards in the local airflow, landing on the top and sides of the engine.

When the plane was first parked, the engine casings would have been warm enough to melt the snowflakes but the storm continued as the engines cooled and the wet snow froze onto the casings. Within this now frozen area, there were plenty of surfaces where the snow could accumulate. Fresh snow rapidly built up on the frozen snow and by morning, it probably occupied "a significant proportion of the available volume within the plenum chambers."

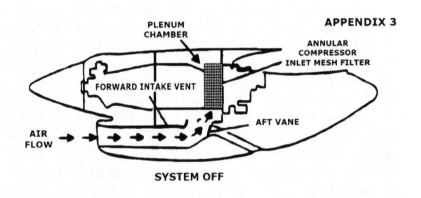

Cross Section.

Each time the engines were run, they would have warmed rapidly. Snow, slush and water would have fallen to the bottom of the plenum chambers, resting at the bypass doors of the anti-ice vanes. As the engines continued to run, the intake air drawn in ranged from frozen to +2°C, cold enough to refreeze the slushy deposits. This kept the material in place.

At first sight, the snow/slush lying against or adjacent to the bypass doors would be expected to melt during the periods of idleness of the hot engines. In practice, however, the continuous feed of cold air produced by the wind and temperature drop created by its flow over the melting ice/slush would have ensured that the warm engine had little or no chance to further melt the slushy or possibly re-frozen material.

—From the official report

But when the accident crew arrived at Edinburgh, most of the snow and slush had been blown away or melted. The captain did not know the extent of the weather that the aircraft had been exposed to. By the time the final crew did their pre-flight checks, there was no snow or ice to be seen on the aircraft frame. The engineer found only a small amount of slush deposited in the window.

Checking the engine intakes is not a part of the pre-flight procedure and in order to do so, the crew would have needed steps to see up there. Even if they had climbed up to check inside the intake cowl area, the snow/slush in the plenum chambers would not have been visible. The Air Accident Investigation Branch conducted tests and concluded that the slush/snow could only be spotted with the use of mirrors or by actually removing the engine cowlings.

The forward intake vane and the aft vane shown above are part of the anti-ice system, which was activated shortly before the flameouts. The anti-icing system on the aircraft is turned on through a series of switches on the panel. The final pair of switches that were activated set the anti-icing vanes into motion.

The forward vane is a deflector, hinged at its forward surface. The aft vane is a bypass door, hinged along the upper edge. The vanes were operated at least once on the ground and then again as a part of the autofeather tests. But as the vanes returned to their starting position, the airflow was such that the snow/slush slid back towards the bypass doors. The engines were idle and the much lower compressor demand meant that very little of the snow/slush/water was ingested by the engines.

The original crew prepared G-BNMT ready for an immediate flight, leaving it parked, facing into wind, for much longer than intended. The final flight crew may not have known of the snowstorm that had blown into the plane during the previous night and certainly could not have known that the plenum chambers had filled with snow and slush. All pre-flight checks and procedures were carried out as normal.

Once in the climb, the accumulated snow, ice and slush was disturbed by the movement of the anti-ice vanes and was ingested by the engines on climb power, causing the flameouts.

The AAIB cited six causal factors, starting with the lack of a practical procedure regarding the installation of intake bungs in adverse weather conditions. The next few factors refer to the snow entering the engine intake system as a direct result of unprotected engine intakes facing directly into strong winds. The large volumes of snow, ice or slush melted, re-froze and continued to rest in the chambers. Finally, the movement of the intake anti-icing vanes and the presence of the snow *altered the engine intake airflow conditions and resulted in the near simultaneous flameout of both engines.*

The final causal factor cited is that *the standard operating procedure of selecting both intake anti-ice vane switches simultaneously, rather than sequentially with a time interval, eliminated a valuable means of protection against a simultaneous double engine flameout.*

Modern training for adverse weather conditions now includes turning the anti-ice systems on one at a time, acknowledging the risk of ice being ingested as a result. Standard operating procedure has changed as a direct result of this accident.

Official Documentation

- Original accident report:
  http://www.aaib.gov.uk/publications/formal_reports/2_2003_g_bnmt.cfm.

Photography
Unattributed photographs are taken directly from the accident report.

- *G-BNMT* photographed by David Unsworth.

  You can see more of his photography at:
  http://www.flickr.com/photos/daviduair/.

CAN YOU SEE WHAT I SEE?

ASPEN AIRPORT (ASE, also known as Sardy Field) is known among pilots as one of the most challenging approaches in the US. The single runway is at an elevation of 7,820 feet (2,383 metres) and surrounded by mountains. The minimum decision altitude (MDA) is 10,200 feet and incoming aircraft must make staggered steep descents to safely reach the threshold.

Aspen/Pitkin County Airport (ASE). Photo by
Carrie Schmitz.

On the 29th of March in 2001 a private jet, a Gulfstream III, crashed into sloping terrain on final approach, killing three crew members and fifteen passengers on impact.

The Captain and the First Officer were both properly certificated and qualified with thousands of hours of experience. Neither was fatigued. The aircraft was properly certified and equipped. The navigational aids and airport lighting systems were all functioning as intended.

And yet the $10 million Gulfstream jet crashed 2,400 feet (730 metres) short of the runway threshold, killing all the occupants.

On the morning of Thursday the 29th, the Captain and his First Officer arrived at Burbank airport around lunchtime for a charter flight taking fifteen passengers to a dinner party in Aspen. Note: All times are given in Mountain Standard Time, which was the local time in Aspen.

As a part of the pre-flight planning, the First Officer discovered that the approach procedure at Aspen had been updated two days previous. On the 27th of March, two days before the flight, the FAA had released a Notice to Airmen (NOTAM) stating that circling was not authorised at night, as the FAA had concluded that instrument approaches into the airfield in the dark were dangerous. There is no straight-in approach to Aspen. The high terrain on all sides means that the glide slope would be too steep for a stable approach in instrument conditions.

The Captain expected a visual approach and stated early on that they would only try the approach once. If they weren't able to get in on the first attempt, they would divert to their alternate airport in Rifle, Colorado. The Gulfstream departed Burbank with three crew at 15:38 for the eleven-minute flight to Los Angeles International where they planned to pick up their passengers and take them to Aspen. However, the passengers were late.

While waiting at LAX, the Captain discussed Aspen's nighttime landing restriction with another pilot and the First Officer. Aspen ASE required aircraft to land "no later than 30 minutes after sunset" to comply with local noise restriction legislation. Sunset on the 29th was at 18:28, so the aircraft needed to land by 18:58 to comply with the restriction. It's not known whether the First Officer mentioned the NOTAM; however it is clear that the flight crew planned be on the ground before night fell.

The Gulfstream eventually departed at 17:11, forty-one minutes later than the First Officer had scheduled. The flight was expected to be one hour thirty-five minutes, for an estimated arrival at 18:46: twelve minutes before the curfew. The Cockpit Voice Recorder recovered from the accident makes it clear that the flight crew were keeping tabs on the time.

18:37:04 The First Officer calls for an approach briefing. The Captain responds, "We're . . . probably gonna make it a visual . . . if we don't get the airport over here we'll go ahead and shoot that approach . . . We're not going to have a bunch of extra gas so we only get to shoot it once and then we're going to Rifle."

18:44:22 The Gulfstream changes frequency to ASE Approach Control and makes contact with the controller.

18:44:43 A Canadair Challenger 600 contacts the controller to request another approach. The approach controller clears the aircraft to continue on the missed approach procedure.

18:45:00 First Officer states, "I hope he's doing practice approaches."

A missed approach is initiated when the approach is unstabilised or unsafe and cannot be completed to landing. The approach plates for an airport include a decision height or missed approach point, by which time the runway must be in sight. If it isn't in sight by that point, or there is any other reason that a safe landing might not be possible, the missed approach procedure is initiated. The aircraft will climb away on a specific heading and, once the procedure is completed, can initiate another approach attempt at the same airport or divert to an alternate airport, depending on the conditions and reasons for the missed approach.

A missed approach is a demanding situation and often pilots will deliberately request the missed approach procedure as a part of their training. This was what the First Officer was hoping for, because if it wasn't a practice missed approach, then it was likely that visibility at the airport was uncomfortably close to minimums.

At the time, the cloud tops were at 16,000 feet and the aircraft was in and out of cloud after descending past this level.

About 3 seconds later, the captain asked the controller whether the pilot of N527JA was practicing or had actually missed the approach. The controller replied that the pilot had missed the approach and indicated that he had seen the airplane at 10,400 feet. The controller also informed the captain that two other airplanes were on approach to ASE.

—From the official report

18:45:45 The Captain says, "Where's that . . . highway? Can we get down in there?"

18:45:56 The Captain asks, "Can you see?" The First Officer replies with, "I'm looking, I'm looking. . . . no."

18:46:26 The Captain says, "I got it," followed by "Can't really see up there, can ya?" The First Officer replied with "Nope, not really. I see a river but I don't see anything else."

18:47:19 The First Officer says, "I see . . . some towns over here and the highway's leading that way but I'm not sure."

18:47:30 The Approach controller makes a general broadcast that the pilot of a Cessna Citation saw the airport at 10,400 feet, 200 feet above the minimum decision altitude, and was making a straight-in approach. The First Officer says, "Ah, that's good."

18:47:41 The Captain tells the controller, "I can almost see up the canyon from here but I don't know the terrain well enough or I'd take the visual."

Aspen (ASE) Approach Path and Accident Site

Aspen has a *VHF omnidirectional range / distance measuring equipment* (VOR/DME) instrument approach which does not include straight-in minimums because the descent would be too steep. The instrument approach is a non-precision approach. After you pass the Red Table VOR (the initial approach fix), you reduce your altitude at specific intervals (called step-downs), which ensure that you are clear of the terrain. As you approach the airfield, you should have the runway (and surrounding terrain) in sight and be able to finish your approach visually.

These "step-downs" are staggered descents based on your DME distance. Reducing your altitude in steps ensures that you remain at a safe altitude as you approach the runway.

As you calibrate your height based on your distance from the runway, you can continue the descent to the *minimum decision altitude* (MDA) for the non-precision approach. At Aspen, the MDA for the non-precision approach is 10,200 feet. Once you reach this altitude, you *must* stop your descent unless you have the runway in sight and can continue the landing visually. You can continue your approach at (but not below) the minimum decision altitude until you reach the *missed approach point*, which is a specific distance, by DME, from the runway. If you cannot see the runway once you have reached the missed approach point, you *must* break off the approach and climb away.

18:48:04 The First Officer says, "Remember that crazy guy in this Lear[jet] when we were . . . on the ground in Aspen last time and he [stated that he could] see the airport but he couldn't see it." The Captain doesn't respond.

The visual approach into Aspen follows parallel to a highway which can be seen from the distance, clearly visible in the above aerial photograph.

18:48:51 The Captain says, "There's the highway right there."

18:49:28 The Captain asks the First Officer if he can see the high-way. The First Officer can't. "No, it's clouds over here on this area I don't see it." The Captain responds with, "But it's right there."

18:49:34 The Captain then says, "Oh, I mean, we'll shoot it from here, I mean we're here but we only get to do it once." He commented again that if the approach was not successful, they would need to divert to Rifle as it was too late in the evening to try again.

He doesn't seem confident that he has the highway in sight, let alone the airport. However, he did not brief the missed approach procedure, which meant that the crew weren't prepared for a missed approach even though it was seeming more and more likely that visibility was too low.

18:53:57 The flight attendant asks whether a male passenger can come into the cockpit and sit in the jumpseat. The cockpit voice recorder records the flight attendant asking a passenger to ensure his seatbelt is on, followed by the clunk of a seat-belt buckle being closed.

18:55:05 The Canadair Challenger 600 transmits his intention to execute another missed approach. The Captain comments, "The weather's gone down, they're not making it in." An uni-dentified male voice in the cockpit responds with, "Oh, really."

Flight crew members can't engage in "any activity which could distract them from their duties" including non-essential conversation once the aircraft has descended below 10,000 feet msl. However the Gulfstream was above that altitude when the passenger came forward.

18:56:06 The Approach controller clears the flight crew for the VOR/DME approach and instructs them to cross the VOR at or above an altitude of 14,000 feet. The flight is five miles from the Red Table VOR, which is the initial approach fix.

18:56:23 The First Officer says, "After the VOR, you are cleared to twelve thousand seven hundred."

18:58:00 The Approach controller asks the Canadair Challenger 600 whether he had the airport in sight, to which he replied, "Negative, going around."

18:58:13 The unidentified male voice in the cockpit says, "Are we clear?" The Captain replies, "Not yet. The guy in front of us didn't make it either." He asks the First Officer for the next step-down altitude and the First Officer responds with the information.

For this segment of the approach, they needed to maintain 12,200 feet until they passed a point known as ALLIX, which is 6 DME (6 miles south of the Red Table VOR by DME), at which point they can descend to 10,400 feet. They actually passed ALLIX at 12,100 feet, 100 feet below the minimum specified altitude for that step.

18:59:30 The Captain calls for the landing gear and landing flaps. The First Officer states that the step-down fix at 10,400 feet is 9.5 DME (9.5 miles south of the Red Table VOR). He calls Three Greens (confirming that the nose and main wheels are down) and then that the missed approach point is 11 DME (1.5 miles further).

The missed approach point is the point at which they were required to break off the approach and follow the missed approach procedure unless they had the runway in sight.

19:00:08 The unidentified male voice says, "Snow."

The aircraft was at 10,400 feet and about 4.4 miles north of the airport. The Captain said, "Okay, I'm breaking out," the first clear statement that he could see the ground. However, about 5 seconds later, he asked the Approach controller whether the runway lights were all the way up. The controller said, "Affirmative, they are on high."

19:00:43 The Captain asks the First Officer whether he can see the runway. The First Officer's response is unintelligible.

The aircraft has been descending at about 2,200 feet per minute but then levelled off at 10,100 feet, about 300 feet below the specified altitude for the step-down and also below the 10,200 foot minimum descent altitude, without any indication that the runway was in sight for either of the flight crew. The Captain neither corrected the descent nor initiated a missed approach. The First Officer did not challenge the Captain. The Captain asked if he could see the highway and the First Officer said, "see highway," but it wasn't clear if this was a statement or a simple repetition.

The descent continued about 10 seconds later. The Approach controller noticed that they have descended past the step-down altitude and the minimum decision height and asks them if they have the runway in sight. Within the cockpit, the First Officer said

"Affirmative," and the Captain said, "Yes, now we do." The First Officer confirmed to the controller that the runway was in sight. At this point, they were at an altitude of 9,750 feet.

19:01:13 The First Officer says, ". . . to the right is good" and the aircraft turns slightly to the right as they continue their descent. They are now 900 feet below the minimum altitude. The First Officer should be monitoring the altitude and calling out the altitude deviation as they descend, but he says nothing about the altitude.

According to the radar data taken after the fact, the airport was actually *to the left* of the aircraft at that moment. The descent continued at a rate of 2,200 feet per minute.

19:01:21 A configuration alarm sounds to indicate that the spoilers have been deployed after the aircraft is configured for landing. The engine power is reduced at the same time, which will increase the aircraft's rate of descent. The Captain likely is still trying to get under the snow showers so he can see, but on the Gulfstream the spoilers shouldn't be extended when the aircraft is configured for landing, and the lower power setting does not meet the minimum power required for going around.

19:01:28 The Flight Profile Advisory unit announces 1,000 feet, their current height above the ground. The First Officer calls out, "one thousand to go." Over the next few seconds, the unit announces 900 and 800 feet callouts.

19:01:36 The Gulfstream passes the missed approach point at an altitude of 8,300 feet, 485 feet above the airfield elevation, rather than the specified 2,385 feet above the field that it should be.

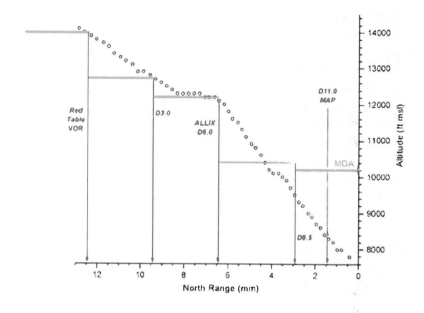

Aspen approach step-downs with the Gulfstream flight profile in blue.

The First Officer should have called out that they had reached
the missed approach point and whether the runway was in sight.
The Captain should have announced his intentions. Instead, as they
passed through the missed approach point, the Captain said,
"Where's it at?"

The Flight Profile Advisory continued its count down: 700 feet,
600 feet. They were below the minimum descent altitude, past the
missed approach point, close to the ground, in mountainous terrain.
It was insane to continue.

19:01:42 The First Officer says, "To the right." The Captain
repeats his words. The aircraft continues to bank gently to

the right. The aircraft is flying over a low valley so the Flight Profile Advisory does not call out 500 feet. The terrain dropped over 700 feet lower than airport elevation and then rose again as the Gulfstream continued its ill-considered descent.

The radar data is clear: the runway was still to the *left* of the aircraft.

19:01:47 The aircraft stops turning to the right and begins a turn to the left. This is the first clear indication that the Captain had seen the airport.

The local controller saw the Gulfstream for the first time as it emerged from a snow shower and banked steeply to the left. It was west of the runway and at low altitude. She immediately reached for the crash phone.

19:01:49 The Ground Proximity Warning System sounds: SINK RATE, SINK RATE. The Flight Profile Advisory calls out 400 feet. The Gulfstream is banking to the left at 10° and the bank angle is increasing.

19:01:52 The engines are increased to maximum power. The Flight Profile Advisory unit calls out 300 feet. The Ground Proximity Warning System and Flight Profile Advisory unit both sound alerts at 200 feet above ground level.

19:01:57 A few seconds later, the Ground Proximity Warning System sounds the bank angle alert: the aircraft is banked about 40°, left wing down. Then the Cockpit Voice Recorder data ends.

The Gulfstream crashed into terrain 2,400 feet short of the runway 15 threshold, 300 feet to the right (west) of the runway centre-line and, at the point of impact, 100 feet above the runway threshold elevation. A 72-foot ground scar showed that the left wing touched the ground first, with the aircraft in a 49° left-wing-down attitude. The aircraft crushed up like an accordion. The three flight crew and fifteen passengers all died on impact from massive blunt force trauma.

On the surface, the cause is clear. The flight crew persisted in an unsafe approach in bad weather in mountainous terrain long after they should have turned back. However, as far as the FAA was concerned, Aspen was *closed at night*. A critical issue for the investigation was why the aircraft was cleared for the approach in the first place.

The problem came back to the Notice to Airmen (NOTAM) that had been released two days previously. A recent flight inspection led the FAA to decide that the areas of unlighted terrain could conflict with traffic patterns and thus it was unsafe to allow an instrument approach procedure at night. However the NOTAM stated that circling was not authorised at night, which was meant to imply that the instrument procedure was not allowed at night, as there are no straight-in minimums published for Aspen. With this vague wording, however, the First Officer may have understood that an approach was still authorised so long as no circle to land manoeuvre was done. Worse, the controllers at Aspen had not seen the NOTAM at all. As a result of human error, the Denver Center had never sent a copy to Aspen. The controller should have notified the flight crew about the NOTAM and it should have been included on the ATIS (recorded airfield and weather information) that the flight crew had listened to shortly before their approach. The controller did warn all aircraft on frequency that the visibility had dropped to 2 miles but he did not know about the NOTAM.

On top of this, night was early. The crash took place 34 minutes after official sunset, 7 minutes after the beginning of official night. However, in mountainous terrain, darkness doesn't watch the clock. The Safety Board calculated that the sun had set below the mountainous terrain about 25 minutes before the "official sunset", with civil twilight ending around 18:30 rather than 18:55. In addition, a dark shadow from a westerly ridge crossed the accident 79 minutes earlier than the official sunset. A controller commented that it was "very dark" previous to the accident.

Those issues are all safety nets. None of these issues explain why the flight crew continued this ill-fated approach in borderline conditions as night fell.

The flight crew were both experienced pilots who knew the local terrain and had done CRM/human factors training. Yet they continued on below the minimum decision height and past the missed approach point, despite the snowstorms and rapid darkness that blocked their view of the mountains surrounding the airfield.

The crew coordination wasn't brilliant. The First Officer did not keep up with the callouts required on an instrument approach. The Captain didn't go over the instrument approach procedure and more importantly didn't go over the missed approach procedure, even when he was aware that the aircraft in front of him were having to execute it. Perceived pressure to land is generally associated with inexperienced pilots who manage to convince themselves that they must land the plane at all costs. And yet, they'd started the flight in clear agreement that they would attempt to get into Aspen once and if it wasn't visual, they would divert to Rifle. So why did they suddenly fixate on getting into Aspen at all costs?

Initially, the Captain and his first officer discussed the location of the runway and the highway, both clear that they do not have it in sight. In retrospect, the First Officer's comment is chilling: "Remember that crazy guy in this Lear[jet] when we were . . . on the ground in Aspen last time and he [stated that he could] see the airport but he couldn't see it."

A few minutes later, a passenger enters the cockpit and sits in the jumpseat. From this point on, there is no active discussion about how difficult it is to see the airfield, other than the Captain asking the controller if the runway lights were turned all the way up. They pass the missed approach and the minimum decision altitude and there is no evidence that they have visual contact with the runway. The controller noticed that they had descended past the step-down altitude and asked if they had the runway in sight. The two flight crew agree that they do, without any discussion as to *what* they've seen (the lights, the highway, or any other visual reference point). Neither crew member said anything about seeing the runway until directly asked, at which point they agreed in unison that it was there. The controller reported later that she could not see the aircraft when the First Officer reported that they had the runway in sight. Most damning, however, is that the aircraft turned to the right, when a left turn was required to align with the runway.

It's not clear whether the jumpseat passenger was the client or one of his guests. The client had chartered the jet to take his guests to a party he was hosting in Aspen. The cascade of events that led to the crash actually started that afternoon when the flight crew arrived at Los Angeles International Airport but could not find the passengers. At 16:30, the charter company phoned the client's business assistant to say that the passengers weren't there. During that conversation, the business assistant was told that the latest time that the aircraft could depart was 16:55.

The business assistant discovered that all but two of the passengers were in the airport parking lot. The two missing passengers included his employer, the client. The flight crew collected the passengers who had arrived and boarded them onto the plane, explaining that if the other two did not arrive shortly, they would be too late to be able to land at Aspen. One of the passengers relayed this conversation to the client. The client told his business assistant to call the charter company and relay a message to the pilot that he should "keep his comments to himself."

The business assistant told his employer that the flight might have to be diverted to Rifle and said that his employer became irate. The business assistant said that his employer told him to call the charter company and tell them that the airplane was not to be diverted. The employer told the business assistant to tell the charter company that he'd flown into Aspen at night before and he was going to do it again. The business assistant stated that he then contacted the charter company to express his employer's displeasure about the possibility of not landing at Aspen.

The Gulfstream departed Los Angeles Airport at 17:11, forty-one minutes later than scheduled and 15 minutes past the latest time for departure given to the client. At 18:30, the Captain spoke to the scheduler at the charter company and told the scheduler that it was important that they land at Aspen because "the customer spent a substantial amount of money on dinner."

That conversation was just half an hour before the crash.

The National Transportation Safety Board determines that the probable cause of this accident was the flight crew's operation of the airplane below the minimum descent altitude without an appropriate visual reference for the runway.

Contributing to the cause of the accident were the Federal Aviation Administration's (FAA) unclear wording of the March 27, 2001, Notice to Airmen regarding the nighttime restriction for the VOR/DME-C approach to the airport and the FAA's failure to communicate this restriction to the Aspen tower; the inability of the flight crew to adequately see the mountainous terrain because of the darkness and the weather conditions; and the pressure on the captain to land from the charter customer and because of the airplane's delayed departure and the airport's nighttime landing restriction.

—From the official report

The day after the accident, the FAA issued a revised NOTAM from "circling not authorised at night" to "procedure not available at night". Within the next fortnight, the charter company distributed a memorandum to state that airport operations at Aspen and three other airports were prohibited between sunset and sunrise. The memorandum, quoted in the official report, stated:

. . . if you cannot accomplish a landing and be on the ground at one of these airports before sunset you must divert to a suitable alternate. All passengers for one of these destinations must be informed of this policy. Flight crew members must report any violation of this policy or pressure from passengers to violate this policy to the Director of Operations or Chief Pilot.

—From the official report

New internal regulations were also put into place that only crew members, check airmen or FAA observers could use the jump seat. Under no circumstances are passengers allowed to move forward.

In the end, the poor cockpit resource management in the final minutes of the flight is the critical factor. The flight crew were staring out the window searching for the runway, rather than focusing on the flight. The Captain continued to descend past the minimum decision altitude in hopes of locating the airfield and the First Officer did not challenge the Captain's actions nor call out the altitude as they descended into mountainous terrain.

However, understanding the contributing factors are what helps us to keep this from happening again. The FAA had already determined that night flight into Aspen was dangerous but the NOTAM was ambiguous and did not make the issue clear. The pressure from the client on the other hand, was clear and unambiguous: if the Gulfstream did not make it into Aspen, he was going to be very unhappy. Three other missed approaches were reported on the frequency and the weather was snowy and dark. Long after the Captain should have abandoned the approach, he continued to search for the runway, knowing he had only one chance to get into Aspen. The presence of the passenger in the jumpseat, especially if it was the charter client, could only have increased the pressure to get in. Rather than accept that they were going to have to abandon the approach and divert to Rifle, he and his First Officer kept trying to spot the runway, desperately attempting to come in safely after dark at one of the most demanding airport approaches in the country.

Traditionally, pilots are seen as confident and courageous. This tragic evening, the Captain was challenged to perform and he did his best to deliver, despite the adverse conditions. In modern aviation, we are finally acknowledging that cautious good judgement is a much more useful trait in pilots than confidence and courage.

Official Documentation

- Original accident report:
  http://www.ntsb.gov/investigations/fulltext/AAB0203.html

Photography
Unattributed photographs are taken directly from the accident report.

- *Aspen/Pitkin County Airport (ASE)* by Carrie Schmitz.

TURNING INTO THE DEAD ENGINE

THE TWO PILOTS WERE co-owners of VH-CNZ. She was a commercial pilot with over 10,000 hours, 600 of them on type. One blog post at the time said that she was a flight instructor. He was a private pilot with just over 2,500 hours and 120 on type. VH-CNZ was a Piper Twin Comanche which had just had a new propeller governor fitted on the left side. They were at Archerfield airport near Brisbane, taking the aircraft out to test the governor.

The Piper Twin Comanche is a very fuel-efficient twin, with four tanks: a tip tank and an auxiliary tank on each wing. The fuel tank fillers are on either side of the engine nacelle.

When the aircraft refueller arrived, the commercial pilot was sitting in the cockpit and the private pilot was doing the preflight checks. Conditions were good but it was late afternoon and the sun was low in the sky. The pilots may have felt under pressure to hurry before the sunset. After the plane was fuelled, the aircraft taxied to Runway 10 right for take-off.

The plane departed at 17:15. It impacted the ground at 17:16.

17:14 CNZ Archer Tower Twin Comanche Charlie November Zulu is ready Runway 10 right departing to the southeast (male voice).

17:14 Tower Charlie November Zulu Tower runway right cleared for takeoff.

17:14 CNZ Runway right cleared for takeoff Charlie November Zulu (male voice)

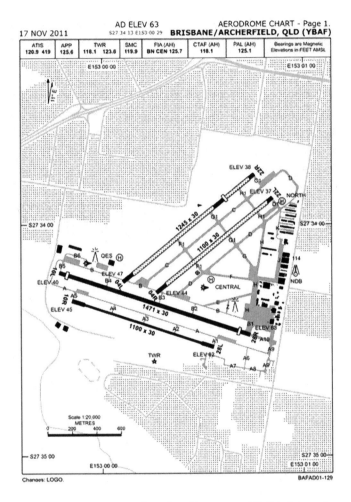

Archerfield Plate showing Runway 10 Right and
the position of the Tower.

Immediately upon take-off, the Tower controller spotted a cloud of "greyish black smoke" coming from both sides of the left engine. He contacted the aircraft immediately.

17:15 Tower Charlie November Zulu there is smoke coming from one of your engines (pause) it's the left engine.

17:15 Tower Charlie November Zulu did you copy?

The aircraft passed the tower. There was sufficient runway and overrun to land the aircraft and "decelerate significantly" before reaching the boundary fence. They probably would not have stopped the plane in time; however it is likely that they would have only caused minor damage.

17:15 CNZ Charlie November Zulu affirm. We're shutting it down and request a left turn back for landing (female voice).

17:15 Tower Charlie November Zulu left turn approved.

17:15 CNZ Charlie November Zulu (female voice).

17:16 Tower Charlie November Zulu clear to land.

17:16 CNZ Clear to land Charlie November Zulu (female voice).

Shutting down the engine in a twin propeller aircraft causes a thrust imbalance. The plane will yaw towards the inoperative engine. When turning into the dead engine, there's a tendency to over-bank. The pilot must consistently counteract this imbalance.

In a conventional twin-engine propeller plane like the Piper Twin Comanche, the left engine is considered the "critical engine". Shutting it down has a larger effect than shutting down the right engine, as a result of the asymmetric blade and disc effects. An example of this effect in a single engine plane is that the aircraft will tend to yaw to the left when using a clockwise turning propeller. In a multi-engine propeller aircraft, the engine with the down-moving blades produces more yaw, which in this case is the left. The shutdown of the left engine requires more pilot input to maintain straight flight than the right engine would.

The loss of the engine obviously also affects the flight performance of the aircraft. Initially, it is important to "clean up" the plane: to retract the landing gear and flaps, feather the inoperative propeller and ensure that the airspeed is maintained. This is especially critical at low altitude.

The flight crew shut down the left engine and the aircraft yawed sharply left and then to the right before commencing a left-hand circuit at 100 feet above the ground. The landing gear was extended throughout. The left engine was shut down but the propeller was not feathered.

The control tower cabin at Archerfield is 20 metres (65 feet) above ground level. The controller reported that as the aircraft flew past the tower, it appeared to be slightly below the tower cabin.

As the aircraft approached the western boundary of the airport, the aircraft turned left again. As it turned, the angle of bank suddenly increased. The Piper Twin Comanche was nose-down, inverted and rolling left when it impacted, 250 metres (820 feet) from the threshold of Runway 10. Both pilots were killed.

There was no evidence of fire. The left engine showed no signs of damage other than from the impact. No pre-existing fault of the propellers could be found. Based on the ground contact marks, the right engine was developing significant power at the point of impact. The left propeller was rotating but the engine was not developing power.

Archerfield Tower. Photo by Cybergothiche.

The left-wing fuel filler flap covers were open and both filler caps were missing. The caps were discovered on the runway and the adjoining clearway. The ground was wet under the inverted left wing where the fuel had poured out of the left tanks on impact.

The aircraft refueller recalled that the private pilot who was doing the pre-flight checks said that he would secure the caps after re-fuelling, as they were non-standard. Checking that the fuel caps are secure is a part of the standard pre-flight checks. The refueller stated that he filled the right tanks first and as he moved to the left side of the aircraft, he saw the pilot move towards the right tank. The refueller filled both the main and auxiliary tanks on the left side and placed the caps in the filler port of each tank. He did not secure the caps, as requested, and he left the flap covers open.

As the aircraft refueller finished, he saw the pilot lying beneath the fuselage, apparently conducting a fuel drain check. He told the commercial pilot, who was in the cockpit, that he had added 179 litres of fuel to the tanks and reminded her that the fuel caps were not secure.

The open flap covers were visible from the cockpit. The dark underside of the flap covers should have been clearly visible against the white upper surface of the wing. In any event, it is clear that the caps on the left wing were not secured and it is unlikely that the flap covers were closed.

They might have been in a rush, as the sun was setting and they wished to complete the test that afternoon. The pre-flight inspection may not have been completed. In addition, as a result of the failing light, the open flap covers on the wing may not have been as obvious.

As the aircraft rumbled down Runway 10 right for take-off, the caps fell from the left-wing filler ports. As the Piper Twin Comanche took off, the fuel vented from the open tank filler ports on the left wing. In the deteriorating light, the venting fuel from either side of the engine nacelle appeared as smoke to the tower controller and witnesses on the ground.

There's no evidence that the pilots had any indication in the cockpit of a malfunction. It is unclear whether the pilots saw the "smoke" or recognised that the fuel flap covers were open. It appears they shut down the left engine based solely on the traffic controller's report of smoke.

The aircraft should have been "cleaned up" before any manoeuvres were started. Instead, the pilot or pilots—it is not clear who was in control or that they were acting in a coordinated fashion—turned directly into the dead engine. The left engine propeller was not feathered, the landing gear was not retracted and, from the beginning, the aircraft was low and slow.

As they entered the third and final left turn, the cascading errors caused them to lose control completely.

SIGNIFICANT FACTORS:

1. The left wing fuel tank filler caps were not secured before takeoff.

2. Fuel vented from the left wing fuel tanks and had the appearance of smoke coming from the left engine.

3. The pilot(s) did not take the appropriate actions to maintain aircraft performance after shutting down the left engine.

4. The pilot(s) were unable to maintain control of the aircraft.

—From the official report

Both pilots had the training and experience to deal with such an emergency. The Piper Twin Comanche is capable of flying on one engine. We don't know who was flying the aircraft and this may well have been a contributing factor if it was not agreed between them who was the pilot in command and making the decisions.

Even so, it's hard to understand why the pilots reacted to a non-emergency in such an uncoordinated manner. In flight, all decisions have to take into account risk vs benefit. In this accident, the pilot(s) gave up all the benefit for increased risk and no gain.

The chain of events started with the fuel cap, which neither pilot took responsibility for. A pre-flight checklist includes checking that the fuel caps are secure but they were apparently in a rush. The sun was setting and the lighting was bad. When they received the incorrect report of smoke, they probably considered the recent work on the left engine propeller, making both pilots swift to presume a major fault. And as part owners of the Comanche, they may have been overly concerned about causing damage to the aircraft. They could have landed immediately, causing minor damage to the aircraft.

Having taken off, they could have flown on long enough to clean up the configuration and turn back safely.

Instead, clearly reacting under pressure, they turned off an engine that was still delivering full power, rather than taking the time to gain altitude and analyse the situation. They then compounded this error by turning back into the circuit without preparation.

The sad result is that a simple problem, a fuel cap not secured properly, turned into a tragedy.

Official Documentation

- Accident report:
  *http://www.atsb.gov.au/publications/investigation_reports/
  2001/aair/aair200102253.aspx*

Other References

- General summary:
  *http://www.comanchepilot.com/Tech_Articles/Safety/
  It_Should_Not_Happen_To_You/IT_SHOULD_NOT_HAPPEN_
  TO_YOU_PA/It_Should_Not_Happen_To_You_Pa/
  it_should_not_happen_to_you_pa.html*

Photography

Unattributed photographs are taken directly from the accident report.

- *Archerfield plate.*

- *Archerfield Tower* by Cybergothiche.

COLLISION COURSE OVER TOKYO

O**N THE 31**sт **OF JANUARY,** in 2001, two aircraft, a Boeing 747 and a DC-10, were flying over the sea near Yaizu City, in Japan's Shizuoka Prefecture.

At 15:55 JST (Japan Standard Time) the pilots in both aircraft saw the impossible: an oncoming aircraft on a collision course. Understanding how this could happen in controlled airspace outside one of the busiest airports in the world takes some explaining.

There were four aircraft. The two flights directly involved in the incident, JAL 907 and JAL 958, are referred to by type: a Boeing 747 and a DC-10 respectively. The other two aircraft, JAL Flight 952 and American Airlines Flight 157, added to the confusion but were out of the way of the near miss and are only referred to by flight number. We'll focus on the incident aircraft first.

Flight JAL 907 was a Boeing 747-400, registration JA8904, departing Tokyo and travelling to Naha.

15:36 The Boeing, carrying 16 crew and 411 passengers, departs Tokyo International Airport.

There were four flight crew on deck.

The Captain was in the left seat and in the role of Pilot Flying. In the right seat, a co-pilot trainee was the Pilot Not Flying (monitoring and offering support). The first officer and a copilot trainee were in the observer seats. The flight was departing and climbing.

JAL Boeing 747-446D JA8904 over Toyko International airport. Photo by Yamaguchi Yoshiaki.

15:41:16 The Boeing 747 passes 11,000 feet climbing to Flight Level 350 (35,000 feet).

The accident report includes detailed interviews with the flight crew that were taken directly after the incident, quoting their direct recollections from the event.

Boeing 747 Captain: "Our aircraft departed from Tokyo International Airport's runway 34R at 15:35. The aircraft and engines were normal. I engaged the autopilot when we had accelerated to 250 knots at an altitude of about 5,000 feet. Before crossing MIURA point, we were instructed to turn right and were cleared 'Direct YAIZU'."

MIURA and YAIZU are waypoints that are used to route flights through the controlled airspace.

Boeing 747 Pilot Under Training: "There were no problems with the weather, which was extremely fine with good visibility and smooth air."

Three air traffic controllers were on duty at the Kanto South C Sector of the Tokyo Area Control Centre. At the radar controller's console was a trainee controller undergoing on-the-job training with an ATC watch supervisor. The radar coordinator console was manned by an air traffic controller.

ATC Trainee: "At 14:30, I entered the IFR room for the shift change and from 14:40 I received on-the-job training at the Radar AG console of the Kanto South C sector. I think my current proficiency is about four out of ten. The traffic volume at the time of the on-the-job training was at about the level I could handle."

15:42:12 The ATC trainee instructs the Boeing to fly direct to Yaizu NDB, which is confirmed.

A further aircraft, American Airlines Flight 157, was cruising at Flight Level 390 above Izu Oshima towards Kushimoto.

15:42:25 The ATC trainee controller instructs the Boeing to maintain flight level 350 (35,000 feet).

ATC Trainee: "I instructed [the Boeing] to maintain FL 350 until further advised. That was because there was the possibility of it converging over the Pacific Ocean with [the American Airlines flight] which was at FL390."

15:46:38 The Boeing 747 continues to climb through flight level 216 (21,600 feet). The ATC trainee instructs the Boeing to climb to Flight Level 390. The Boeing confirms.

Meanwhile, Flight JAL 958, a Douglas DC-10-40 registration JA8546, was en route from Pusan to New Tokyo International Airport (Narita).

Japan Airlines DC-10.

15:46:51 The DC-10 is handed over from Kanto South Sector B, an adjacent sector. The letters HND flash over the DC-10's data block on the South C sector radar display.

The flight had been uneventful so far, but in just a few minutes the DC-10 would pass within metres of the Boeing.

The DC-10 was carrying 13 crew and 237 passengers.

There were three crew on deck. In the left seat and in the role of Pilot Flying was a Captain trainee (an experienced co-pilot preparing for an upgrade to command). In the right seat, the Captain was the Pilot Not Flying. A flight engineer was in the flight engineer seat. The flight was near its final destination of New Tokyo International Airport and so was flying level / descending.

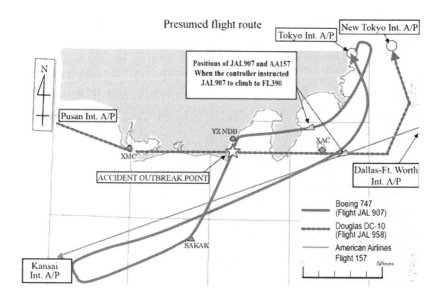

Presumed Flight Route of JAL 907, JAL 958
and AA 157.

15:47:02 The ATC trainee instructs American Airlines Flight 157 to descend to flight level 350, so that it is not at the same flight level as the Boeing. American Airlines Flight 157 doesn't respond.

This was because American Airlines Flight 157 was not on frequency. The controller at South B Sector did not instruct the American Airlines flight to change frequency even though he had completed its hand-off to South C Sector.

Meanwhile, at South C Sector, the supervisor decided that the altitude separation between the Boeing and the American Airlines flight needed to be established quickly and so the ATC trainee was attempting to establish radio contact early.

Now, it gets a little bit confusing, but bear with me.

15:47:14 A fourth aircraft, JAL Flight 952, requests clearance to fly directly to a fix near New Tokyo International Airport (Narita). The ATC trainee asks the aircraft to stand by.

15:47:47 Someone at South C Sector inputs the command to receive the hand over of control of the DC-10.

In the cabin of the Boeing 747, the cabin crew turned on the TV news and prepared the drinks trolley. A few minutes later, when turbulence had died down, the cabin crew started the drinks service.

The ATC Trainee at South Sector C attempted again to call the American Airlines flight, with no response. He also speaks to the fourth aircraft, JAL Flight 952, which has a similar flight number to the DC-10.

The two flight numbers may have become conflated in his head. In any event, it appears that he forgot the presence of the DC-10 entirely.

So did his supervisor.

The Boeing 747 followed the instructions and turned left over the YAIZU waypoint. It was now at FL370 (37,000 feet) and flying directly towards the DC-10.

Computers don't forget. In the control room, a conflict alert flashed on the display, showing the collision path of the Boeing 747 and the DC-10. Usually, a conflict alert would display *at least* three minutes before the predicted loss of separation. But because the Boeing 747 was turning, it was not clear that they were on a collision course. The conflict alert was issued a mere 56 seconds before the predicted collision.

The ATC Trainee saw the flashing conflict alert with only seconds to go. He decided that the DC-10 needed to descend to avoid the conflict. That was a logical decision: the Boeing 747 was climbing and could continue to climb. The DC-10 was level and ready to descend for its approach into New Toyko International Airport. Requesting it to descend should have ensured the vertical separation between the two aircraft.

So, the DC-10 needed to descend and the Boeing could continue its climb and the collision course would be averted.

Unfortunately, the ATC Trainee got his flight numbers confused. He tells the Boeing to descend to FL350, instead of the DC-10. From this point on, everything happens too fast to be able to effectively follow the timestamps.

ATC Watch Supervisor: "At around the end of my explanation, the conflict alert was flashing in the data blocks of [the Boeing 747] and [the DC-10]. I was in a flurry because I had forgotten about the presence of [the DC-10]. At that point in time, I deemed that the best decision was to descend [the DC-10], and so even though the trainee actually made [the Boeing 747] descend, I was convinced that he had issued the instruction to [the DC-10]. When the trainee had issued the descent instruction—which I later realized had been for [the Boeing 747] — when [the Boeing 747] read back the instruction, I heard something like the sound of an alert in the background."

That alert that he heard in the background was a traffic advisory from the Traffic Collision Avoidance System in the Boeing 747.

A Traffic Collision Avoidance System (TCAS) is installed into all modern commercial transport aircraft . It interrogates the transponders of all nearby aircraft, receiving their altitude and distance. The TCAS offers traffic advisories to alert the flight crew of nearby aircraft. When the flight crew receives a traffic advisory

(TA), they are not expected to perform avoidance manoeuvres, simply to be aware that there is the possibility of a conflict, in which case the TCAS will offer a resolution advisory (RA). It gives the flight crew a chance to locate the other aircraft visually and prepare for the next instruction.

TCAS predictions are based on the assumption that aircraft are flying straight. In this instance, as the Boeing turned onto the flight path of the DC-10, the TCAS triggered late.

DC-10 First Officer (Pilot Flying): "While we were flying from XMC to XAC, around about the time an RA went off, I couldn't make out whether it was for "907" or "957" but I heard a 'Descend' command in a fairly faint voice. It was after that, I believe, that I became aware of the TCAS display showing traffic at 12—13 nm at FL370 without an arrow pointing upward or downward. At the same time I sighted the traffic at 10—11 o'clock. I wondered why the traffic was at the same altitude as us."

Boeing 747 Captain: "After the left turn, as our aircraft was approaching FL370, we were instructed by Tokyo ACC to 'DESCEND FL350'. I understood that this was to maintain separation from the traffic, and thought that the controller intended to have our aircraft pass below the traffic because the situation was not yet critical. Since the controller handles multiple aircraft with a grasp of the whole traffic situation, we followed the instruction to descend."

The Captain disengaged the autopilot and the autothrottles for a manual descent. The momentum of the aircraft takes it up to FL372 (37,200 feet) at which point it begins to descend. The Boeing 747's descent starts just a few minutes after the drinks service has begun. A passenger in the back of the Boeing 747 stated, "it occurred around the time I was starting to relax, looking at Mt. Fuji from the right-side window."

DC-10 Captain (Pilot Not Flying): "As we saw the other aircraft turning over YAIZU, a TCAS 'TRAFFIC, TRAFFIC' TA sounded while we were about 10 nm distant at FL370. The other aircraft's altitude was also displayed as FL370. The PF disengaged the auto-throttles in anticipation of a resolution advisory."

Both aircraft were now at the same level (37,000 feet) and flying directly towards each other.

If the TCAS determines that there is a real risk of collision, and if the other aircraft is also TCAS-equipped, the TCAS will send a coordination signal to the other aircraft in order to resolve the encounter.

In this way, the evasive manoeuvres are coordinated: one TCAS system will select an "upward sense RA" (instructing the pilot to climb) and the coordination signal to the second TCAS means that the second system will select a "downward sense RA" (instructing the pilot to descend), thus resolving the conflict immediately.

The DC-10 flight crew saw the Boeing 747 turning over YAIZU. They received a traffic advisory (TRAFFIC, TRAFFIC) to alert them to the presence of the Boeing 747, which had been climbing and was about 10 nautical miles away. The First Officer (Pilot Flying) disengaged the auto-throttles, expecting a resolution advisory from the TCAS. For the avoidance of doubt, a TCAS display shows an arrow next to the other aircraft to show whether it is climbing or descending.

The Boeing 747, which had been climbing, followed the instruction from the ATC Trainee and now was descending. The TCAS resolution advisory alerted the crew to the conflict with a clear instruction: CLIMB, CLIMB, CLIMB.

The Captain, having already begun his descent, stated, "I will continue to descend." The Boeing 747 continued its descent, contrary to the direct instruction received from the TCAS.

Boeing 747 First Officer: "I did not think that the 'DESCEND FL350' instruction [from ATC] was smart but I considered it plausible. We had already made visual contact with the other aircraft, so I thought that the instruction would have been to avoid it. After the TA alert, the RA 'CLIMB, CLIMB, CLIMB' sounded, but I don't exactly remember the time interval between them. At that point in time, however, as the descent had already been initiated following the 'DESCEND FL350', with the thrust levers closed and aircraft already at descent pitch, the captain continued manoeuvring to descend while stating 'we're already descending, so we'll descend'. At that time, following the TCAS RA, reapplying maximum power and pitching up to comply with the RA command, at an altitude of what I thought was around 37,000 ft, would have been extremely dangerous."

Boeing 747 Captain: "At that time, I observed the other aircraft approaching from the forward right at about the same altitude, but I had already initiated a descent and judging that the best way to avoid a collision at that altitude would be to continue descending contrary to the TCAS command, I continued descending to FL350. Further, I also considered the risk of stalling if we pitched up given the insufficient thrust, leading to an even more dangerous situation. The other aircraft appeared to be about in level flight at FL370.

This was a completely unexpected decision. When you receive a resolution advisory from your TCAS system, you must follow it. The TCAS coordination with other aircraft is based on the assumption that both aircraft will comply with the instructions. It's clear that the flight crew were concerned about going directly back into a climb; however, at the very least the Captain should have *stopped his descent* which was in clear opposition to the resolution advisory of CLIMB, CLIMB. There's a clear training issue here. The Captain of the Boeing 747 did not appear to understand that the TCAS of the DC-10 would be given a corresponding advisory. If he was receiving the instruction to CLIMB then the conflicting aircraft would receive the instruction to DESCEND. He seemed to hope that the DC-10 would remain in level flight. He should have known that it would descend.

At South Sector C, the supervisor and trainee had not noticed that they told the wrong plane to descend. They did not know that TCAS resolution advisories had kicked in, which overrode their instructions. In this situation ATC transmissions should be kept to a minimum to avoid conflict and confusion . . . but the controllers needed to know that the aircraft had been issued resolution advisories.

The Boeing 747 continued to descend in line with the direct instruction from ATC. As the flight crew had not complied with the TCAS instruction to climb, they may not have seen it as important to inform the controllers that a resolution advisory had been issued. Pilots are taught set phrases in order to quickly inform ATC of TCAS resolution advisories. There is no procedure in place for an aircraft that is following ATC instructions contrary to a resolution advisory. The Boeing 747 had already confirmed its compliance to the instruction to descend, so no further call was made.

Meanwhile, the DC-10 flight crew *had* complied with the resolution advisory from the TCAS but had not informed ATC.

The Aeronautical Information Circular, quoted in the official report, states that:

Pilots who deviate from an ATC clearance in response to an RA shall promptly return to the terms of the previous ATC instruction or clearance when the conflict is resolved and they shall notify the appropriate ATC unit by use of the following phraseologies as soon as possible on the radio frequency."

—From the official report

"This implies that ATC can be notified once the conflict is resolved, as opposed to when the resolution advisory is received, which in fact is what the DC-10 did. During the incident, no radio calls were made.

Thus, ATC still considered itself responsible for avoiding the conflict. Also, neither the ATC trainee nor his supervisor had realised that the trainee mistakenly told the Boeing 747 to descend. The aircraft continued on their collision path.

The ATC trainee instructed the DC-10 to change heading to 130°. He did not receive a response as the DC-10 was completely focused on following the TCAS and looking for the traffic. The primary concern now should have been to provide *vertical* separation between the aircraft, but the supervisor decided against correcting the trainee's heading instruction. The DC-10 continued descending in response to the resolution advisory. It did not change heading and did not respond. The trainee then instructed the DC-10 to fly heading 140° and again received no response.

At this point, the supervisor took over the radio communications. Unfortunately, she made things worse.

The supervisor conflated the flight numbers (JAL 907 and JAL 958) and instructed Flight JAL 957 to descend. As Flight 957 did not exist in her airspace, she did not receive a response.

There were a total of six radio communications from South Sector C. All six messages either involved errors or were not received/understood. *Not a single communication* actually helped to avoid the collision rapidly approaching.

Boeing 747 First Officer: "I did not hear a TCAS 'increase' RA command. ATC was communicating something but I was too busy to understand the communications. I felt that the distance from the other aircraft at the closest point was around 10 meters."

The First Officer, who was Pilot Not Flying, should have been monitoring the TCAS traffic display, which would have made it clear that the DC-10 was descending with a large, downward facing arrow.

Instead, his statement, and the statements of every crew member in the Boeing 747 all described in detail the approach of the DC-10. No one was monitoring the instruments. Everyone was looking outside.

DC-10 Captain (Pilot Not Flying): "Before long, the TCAS 'DESCEND, DESCEND, DESCEND' RA activated and the PF disengaged the autopilot, set power to idle and lowered the nose little by little. Since the descent rate at this time was less than 1,000 ft/min, I exerted forward pressure on the control wheel while advising 'Lower it further. ' Immediately thereafter, the TCAS 'INCREASE DESCENT, INCREASE DESCENT' sounded. Judging that we had to descend rapidly, I called 'I'm pulling speed brakes' while pulling the speed brakes to full. The PF lowered the nose further. I switched on the seat belt sign."

The DC-10 Captain was supporting his first officer with advice ("lower it further") as well as fulfilling his responsibilities as Pilot Not Flying (speed brakes, seat belt sign). He wasn't staring out the window in horror, he was reacting.

Boeing 747 Captain: "As the relative distance to the other aircraft remained unchanged, I thought that without further action we would collide and pitched down even further. After that I saw the other aircraft appear to pass from right to left at about eye level. I indicated in the Captain's Report that the closest vertical separation from the other aircraft was approximately 10 meters. While we were manoeuvring to pass just below the DC-10, it appeared to fill the forward right window but we were able to avoid a midair collision."

The Captain of the Boeing 747 increased his descent, insistent on flying beneath the DC-10. The aircraft were within metres of each other and both were trying desperately to dive beneath the other.

The Boeing 747 pitched down abruptly in response. The cabin attendants flew to the ceiling, striking the ceiling panels, and then crashed down to the floor. One galley cart smashed through the ceiling panel and became lodged between the air conditioning ducts and a supporting beam. Seven passengers and two cabin attendants were seriously injured and 81 passengers and ten cabin attendants received minor injuries, including burns from the hot beverages.

DC-10 Captain (Pilot Not Flying): "Glancing outside at that time, I saw the other aircraft approaching from the forward right. Finally it appeared to be approaching rapidly. It appeared to be descending in the same way as us, I could visually see the top of the fuselage, and I judged that it was increasing its descent rate, so I felt that the situation was extremely dangerous. I think the PF felt the same, but we had no time to communicate and we both pulled back on the yokes almost simultaneously."

The DC-10 passing just above the Boeing 747.
Re-creation by "anynobody".

Honestly, I think both the Captain and the First Officer (Pilot Flying) deserve an award for gauging the situation and pulling out of the dive to allow the Boeing 747 to pass beneath.

DC-10 First Officer (Pilot Flying): "It felt as if the other aircraft was rapidly rushing toward us, and I wondered why since our aircraft was following the TCAS descent command. Subsequently, I saw the other aircraft become larger and lower its nose when it was just off the tip of our left wing or a little bit inward of that. At that point in time, judging that the attitude of the other aircraft was around 10–15° nose down, at the same altitude as us, and descending, I quickly applied power and pulled the control wheel. The other aircraft was so close that I thought its tail would snag our aircraft."

DC-10 Captain (Pilot Not Flying): "I knew that it was nose down, because I could see the top of its fuselage. I had the impression that the other aircraft was descending at the same altitude as us and was considerably nose down. Seeing that situation, I judged there was nothing that could be done but to pull."

The investigation report is not quite as effusive as I am and simply states that as the flight crew of the DC-10 consisted of a Captain, a Captain in Training and a Flight Engineer, they may have had *a higher level of judgement compared with a regular flight crew complement.*

You can say that again.

It is considered that the accident was caused as follows:

A Conflict Alert (CNF) was issued at Tokyo ACC warning of the proximity of Japan Air Lines flight 907 (Aircraft-A), which was making a climbing left turn, and Japan Air Lines flight 958 (Aircraft-B), which was cruising in level flight. While responding to this conflict alert, Tokyo ACC mistook the flight number of Aircraft-B for that of Aircraft-A, and instructed Aircraft-A, which was climbing at the time, to descend.

Immediately after Aircraft-A initiated a descent in response to this instruction, its Traffic Alert and Collision Avoidance System (TCAS) issued a Resolution Advisory (RA) to climb, but Aircraft-A continued the descent in compliance with the ATC instruction. Both Aircraft-A and Aircraft-B which descended in response to its own TCAS RA, came to abnormal close proximity while maintaining mutual visual contact, and just before their closest point of mutual approach both aircraft made evasive maneuvers to avoid a collision based on visual judgment. Aircraft-A made an abrupt descent intending to pass under Aircraft-B just before their flight paths crossed, and as a result passengers and cabin attendants (CA) of Aircraft-A rose from the cabin floor or seats, floated, then dropped and sustained injuries.

—From the English translation of the official report

The Boeing 747 levelled off at FL350 and reported to Kanto South Sector C that it was clear of the conflict. It was a few minutes later before it reported a near-miss with a DC-10.

DC-10 Captain (Pilot Not Flying): "Subsequently, while returning to FL370, I informed ATC that 'We have descended following a TCAS alert. We are now climbing through 35,500 ft for FL370'. This was the first radio communication we made after the two aircraft crossed. ATC replied only 'Roger'."

How did they get so close in the first place?

The near-miss took place at an altitude between 35,000 and 36,000 feet. The DC-10 was in level flight, ready to descend. If the Boeing 747 had been above 36,000, there would never have been any risk of a collision.

At the beginning of the incident, the Boeing 747 was climbing. If it had continued to climb without further instructions, it would have reached an altitude of approximately 38,100 feet. The initial ATC call mistakenly telling the Boeing 747 to descend put the aircraft on a collision course.

Aircraft testing showed that the swift change in direction would have caused buffeting but there was no risk of a stall and the altitude would have easily increased by 1,400 feet. So in the worst-case scenario, if the Boeing 747 had responded to the ATC instruction to descend but then reversed the descent once the TCAS display showed the DC-10 as descending, it would have safely climbed to approximately 36,200 feet.

In every instance, there would have been sufficient vertical separation to avoid the collision without further evasive manoeuvres.

The Probable Cause from the official report could be stronger, in my opinion. Note that Aircraft A is the Boeing 747 (Flight JAL 907) and Aircraft B is the DC-10 (Flight JAL 958).

The Captain's decision to disregard a resolution advisory from the TCAS is completely unacceptable. His response at the time and his explanations afterwards make it clear that there is a training issue; he was quite simply unaware of the consequences of his decision to continue the descent against the resolution advisory. This is furthered by the fact that the rest of the crew (which was overall less experienced than the crew of the DC-10) equally did not see it as odd that the Captain ignored the resolution advisory and were busy staring out of the window rather than monitoring the TCAS, which would have told them exactly what the DC-10 was doing.

The number of errors in the ATC handling of the incident is frightening; however it does seem clear that the ATC Trainee was out of his depth, which again, I would class as a failure of the system, rather than assign blame to the trainee. He clearly tried to deal with the emergency to the best of his ability, which quite simply wasn't good enough. The supervisor relieved him late and compounded the error, which is indicative of a greater failing within the ATC training at Kanto.

Nevertheless, in 2004, the ATC Watch Supervisor and the ATC Trainee were charged with professional negligence in causing injuries to passengers in the aircraft. They were later cleared, as their instructions were not the direct cause of the accident, because the pilots should have followed the Resolution Advisory rather than the controllers. However, the Tokyo District Public Prosecutor's Office filed an appeal and in 2008, a higher court overturned the decision and found both guilty, sentencing the trainee to one year and the supervisor to 18 months. Both sentences were suspended for three years.

This is a sad example of the fact that when systems and processes fail, it is far easier to blame individuals at the end of the line, rather than improve the environment and training that led to the failure.

Official Documentation

- The original accident report:
  http://jtsb.mlit.go.jp/jtsb/aircraft/download/pdf/02-5-JA8904.pdf

Other References

- Accident report translated into English:
  http://www.mlit.go.jp/jtsb/eng-air_report/JA8904.pdf

- Presentation by the Investigator-General:
  http://www.asasi.org/papers/2005/Hiroaki%20Tomita%20-%20near%20collision%20in%20Japan.pdf

Photography
Unattributed photographs are taken directly from the accident report.

- *JAL Boeing 747-446D JA 8904 over Toyko International airport* was taken by Yamaguchi Yoshiaki.

- *Japan Airlines DC-10-40* was taken by contri.

- *Artist's conception of JA8904 (below) diving under JA8546 (above)* by anynobody.

All times are in Japan Standard Time to coincide with the report. JST is UTC+9.

UNEXPECTED SPIN

THE 12TH OF MAY in 2001 was a fine day in the south of England. Stapleford Aerodrome in Essex had blue skies with a surface wind of 10–12 knots from the northeast: a perfect day for flying. That's what made it all the more surprising when G-ARIE, a Piper PA-24-250 Comanche (a popular four-seater, single engine plane), entered a steep spiral descent and crashed into the ground during a standard flight.

G-ARIE. Photo by Ken Elliot.

The pilot was a part owner of G-ARIE. He'd been flying since 1992 and this was simply a check ride. The Joint Aviation Requirements dictate that pilots revalidate their licences every two years and his last revalidation for single-pilot, single-engine rating was in July 1999. So he organised a one-hour dual flight in the G-ARIE with a qualified flight instructor. The instructor sat in the right seat but, for the purposes of a check ride, he is considered to be the commander. He had been a qualified flying instructor since 1991.

The pilot had taken G-ARIE out the previous week and the flight was uneventful. When he started up the plane that day, there was a single backfire but no other unusual events were reported. The pilot and his instructor took off at 15:15.

The two men seemed in normal spirits prior to the flight.

The radar recordings showed that after take-off, the aircraft flew east and then northeast, directly towards the area of Osea Island. There were two brief deviations where the aircraft turned approximately 60° to the right before turning left back onto track. The plane's ground speed was approximately 120 knots for the first six minutes of the flight and then decreased to 60 knots for about four minutes. The speed increased to 140 knots over the next minute and then decreased again to 60 knots.

That's when radar contact was lost.

The aircraft was last seen over Osea Island where there were other aircraft doing aerobatics and a jet aircraft flying past at low-level.

Two witnesses said they saw G-ARIE carrying out manoeuvres before entering a steep spiral descent. Others said it had been flying straight and level before going into the dive. The check flight should have consisted of general airwork: climbing at best angle and best rate; straight and level cruising flight, steep turns, recovery from stalls and recovery from incipient spin.

The Piper PA 24-250 Comanche is not cleared for aerobatics or intentional spinning; however all of the standard manoeuvres were well within the tolerances of the aircraft. The flight controls of the Comanche remain effective down to stalling speed and stalls are gentle and easily controlled. In addition, it is standard procedure to do clearing turns before carrying out stalls and there was no evidence of any such precaution prior to the spin. It did not appear that the spiral dive was the result of intentional manoeuvres.

A pilot flying a Yak 11 in the local area saw G-ARIE go into the spin to the right. He originally thought it was part of a training routine but then became puzzled as it continued to spin. He flew towards the plane and said that it did four to six complete turns before impact. The pilot called emergency on 121.5Mhz but there is no evidence of any emergency call from G-ARIE.

The eyewitnesses agreed that they saw the aircraft spinning continuously until it hit the ground. They heard little or no engine noise as it descended towards the earth and there was neither fire nor explosion when it struck the ground.

Examination of the accident site showed that the aircraft had struck the ground in a very steep nose-down attitude, estimated to be 70/75° to the horizontal. There had been no significant translational movement of the aircraft after the initial impact, consistent with an essentially vertical descent, and the relative lack of fragmentation of the wreckage indicated a relatively low vertical speed of, probably, between 60 and 80 kt. There was a clear impression of where the wing leading edges had struck the ground, the imprint of the right wing being slightly lighter and curved whilst that of the left, was straight and heavier.

—From the official report

In addition, the three blades of the propeller had folded straight backwards with only slight signs of "circumferential scuffing". This indicates that the propeller had been rotating at the time of impact but with very little power applied. Thus, the wreckage and ground marks told the same story as the eyewitnesses: the aircraft was slowly spinning in a steep nose-down attitude with little engine power when it impacted the ground.

But how had the two pilots let the plane get into such a state?

The postmortem examinations showed raised CO levels in both pilots, higher than would be seen in even the heaviest of smokers. Both men had inhaled an extremely large amount of carbon monoxide.

Carbon monoxide is colourless, odourless and tasteless—it is impossible to detect using your senses. It is in the smoke and fumes emanating from the exhaust systems of aircraft engines and combustion heaters.

If you inhale CO, it combines with the haemoglobin in your blood, which causes oxygen starvation in the body and the brain. The initial symptoms are subtle: mild tiredness, a feeling of warmth, tightness across the forehead. Later symptoms include headaches, dizziness, nausea, tiredness, confusion and shortness of breath or difficulty breathing. A form of hypoxia, CO poisoning causes confusion and impaired judgement. As the poisoning continues it causes problems with balance, vision, memory and eventually loss of consciousness and death.

The pilots hadn't put the plane into an intentional spin and lost control, as might have been originally been presumed. Much more likely was that both were incapacitated and unable to fly the plane.

It's quite possible that the pilots themselves, confused and disoriented, mishandled the controls as they succumbed to the poisoned air in the cockpit. Or G-ARIE might have entered the spin as the result of wake turbulence: the radar returns showed that a minute earlier, another aircraft had flown past the location where G-ARIE appeared to go out of control. Regardless of what caused the initial upset, it is clear that the pilots were not able to recover.

Carbon monoxide can enter the cockpit in a number of ways: cabin heaters may use the engine exhaust pipe as a heat source or the gases can enter from the outside. However, a sudden high onset such as this is generally caused by a leakage in the engine exhaust system which finds its way into the aircraft through ineffective seals, access panels, skin joints or through cabin fresh-air intakes. Any ineffective seals in the plane can result in reduced cabin pressure, which means that if there is a leak, the exhaust gas is drawn into the cockpit through the lower fuselage.

The investigators turned their attention to G-ARIE's engine exhaust system.

There, they found that although the No. 5 manifold stub pipe was severely twisted from the crash, there was clear evidence that the flange and the stub pipe wall had cracked right through prior to the impact. They found both fatigue fractures and evidence of tearing overload.

The remaining owners of G-ARIE stated that the exhaust manifolds had been changed relatively recently but there was no evidence in the aircraft log books for this. The owners produced an invoice, dated 22 January 1999, which apparently related to the right-hand manifold. This invoice was the only documentation associated with the fitting of the new manifold. The invoice stated that the manifold had been manufactured and inspected in accordance with airworthiness regulations. However, the manifold part number on the invoice was not listed in the aircraft parts catalogue nor does it relate to any other design of manifold approved for the aircraft.

Investigators discovered that the failed manifold did not conform to the design of the approved parts. The exhaust manifold stub pipes from cylinders 1, 5 & 6 had reinforcing doubler plates welded over the basic stub pipes. Piper Aircraft stated that the changes made to the exhaust were likely to cause localised and unpredictable thermal stress cycles. The reinforcing doublers welded on would also have changed the thermal and stress cycles in the pipe and doubler, especially at engine start-up. As a result, the single thickness part of the pipe was subjected to undue and unexpected thermal expansion and stress effects. In addition, the doublers protected the fracture from sight, allowing it to develop to a critical length before it was possible to detect the fracture with a visual inspection.

The maintenance records for the aircraft showed that G-ARIE had an annual inspection in June 2000 and had recently undergone a 50-hour/6-month check. Examination of the exhaust system is a requirement for both of these inspections; however as there was no record of the new manifold in the aircraft log books, there was no evidence that a new one had been wrongly fitted. There was no way of knowing that there had been any difficulty with the installation, let alone that the pipes had unauthorised doubler plates welded on. The only way to inspect the area where the fracture first manifested could only have been done using a mirror and light: an additional check unlikely to happen without any reason to suspect an issue in the exhaust manifold. And so, despite undergoing all the requisite inspections, the crack remained undetected, with additional stress every time the engine was started.

As G-ARIE had recently been flown without ill effect, it seems likely that the fracture in the exhaust pipe became critical the day of the crash, either at engine start or early in the flight. The fractured pipe leaked large amounts of exhaust gas which entered into the cockpit, disabling the pilots.

As a result of this incident, the UK Air Accidents Investigation Branch recommended that carbon monoxide detectors be required on all piston-engined aircraft. If G-ARIE had had a carbon monoxide detector fitted in the cockpit, they would have been aware of the presence of the gas before they were incapacitated and almost certainly could have returned to the airfield safely and with minimal ill effect. At the very least, said the AAIB, the Civil Aviation Authority "should vigorously promote that all such aircraft should have a current carbon monoxide detector fitted to facilitate an early warning of the presence of this gas."

Official Documentation

- Original accident report:
  *http://www.aaib.gov.uk/cms_resources.cfm?file=/
  dft_avsafety_pdf_507786.pdf*

Photography

- *G-ARIE* photographed by Ken Elliot.

WHEN ONE ENGINE ISN'T ENOUGH

A Learjet 35A. Photo by Noel Jones.

IT WAS A ROUTINE 150-hour inspection when a technician found metal chips in the oil filter of the right engine of the Learjet. The maintenance company who usually carried out repairs to the aircraft did not have the parts available and with only a maximum of twenty flight hours allowed after finding the chips, it was urgent to get the repairs done at once. On the 7th of February 2001, two pilots and the chief technician ferried the plane from its base in Rome to Nürnberg, where the right engine was repaired and certified. The Learjet was already booked for a charter flight from Rome for the 9th of February so they planned a swift return after the maintenance was done, flying direct Nürnberg to Rome on the 7th.

The Learjet 35A was a business jet with two Garrett TFE731-2-2B turbofan engines. The aircraft type was introduced in 1976 and currently holds the record for the fastest around-the-world flight. The Italian business airplane was built in 1981.

The flight prep was carried out by phone from the repair facility. It was a fine day: visibility of 10 kilometres or more and cloud bases not below 5,000 feet with moderate wind. Everything looked great.

During the pre-flight checks, the pilots noticed an unbalanced fuel distribution between the right and left-hand tip tanks. They discussed the problem and decided it wasn't an issue, as the total fuel quantities on both sides were equal. The First Officer (Pilot Not Flying) noted that his gyro instruments had failed. The chief technician took a look and confirmed that they could run the flight and replace the gyro system once back in Rome.

The Learjet taxied to runway 10 and were given clearance for departure via Nördlingen to Rome. They took off at 15:31.

Upon departing Nürnberg, the flight crew should have contacted Nürnberg Radar immediately. This is clearly marked on the plates but although the first few minutes of the flight appear to have been quiet and without problems, the crew did not change frequencies. The aircraft flew directly towards Nördlingen climbing towards their cruise altitude of FL70 (7,000 feet).

At 15:33:49, a little less than 3 minutes after take-off, the Learjet was at an altitude of 5,900 feet with an airspeed of 250 knots and had just made a right turn in line with their route. That was when the left-hand engine failed with no warning.

Witnesses on the ground said they heard the sounds of an engine running down. Neither smoke nor fire was visible.

The First Officer immediately contacted Nürnberg Tower and reported an emergency: the left engine had failed. He informed Nürnberg that they wanted to return immediately for a landing on runway 10. It was visual conditions and they had the runway in sight.

The Tower Controller acknowledged the emergency and asked the Learjet to contact Nürnberg Radar on 118.97.

This was such an incredibly wrong-headed thing to do, it makes my teeth clench. The crew had declared an emergency. It *doesn't matter* that they should have switched to Nürnberg Radar immediately after departure. They *declared an emergency.*

The correct response from the Tower Controller should have been to acknowledge the emergency (which the controller did), offer any information that might help, for example the wind information and whether the runway was clear (which the controller didn't) and then phone Nürnberg Radar to explain the situation, leaving the pilots to deal with the emergency.

The accident report refers to the request for a frequency change as *"extremely problematic"* but then explains that the controller did not know "to what extent the reported emergency had an effect on the flight characteristics of the aircraft."

This, quite frankly, was not the controller's problem. It was an emergency; he should have treated it as such. There was no conflicting traffic, the aircraft was returning to the airfield, the whole exchange was simply unnecessary. The flight crew should have refused the frequency change.

The First Officer changed frequency to Nürnberg Radar and declared an emergency. Nürnberg Radar cleared the aircraft for a visual approach to runway 10 and asked whether radar assistance was required. Upon being told that radar assistance was not required, Nürnberg Radar asked the crew to switch back to frequency 118.3 for Nürnberg Tower.

The final flight of the Learjet, from engine failure to crash, took ten minutes. These radio calls and frequency changes used up almost two minutes.

The flight crew contacted Nürnberg Tower again and received clearance for runway 10. Nürnberg Tower asked whether airport fire services should be on standby. Apparently, the crew did not understand the question immediately. As a result, Nürnberg Tower asked them to confirm again that they had declared an emergency.

None of this conversation was as important as flying the plane. Nürnberg Tower should have been taking all possible actions to give assistance to an aircraft that was in distress. Instead, it provided pointless distractions.

Despite the interruption, the flight crew had plenty of time. The airport was clearly visual and the weather was good. It should have been possible to return to the airfield without problems.

Inside the cockpit, the voice recordings show the increased strain on the pilots. They should now have followed the checklist for *engine failure—shut down in flight*. But they didn't. The Pilot in Command asked for the *descent checklist* and then the *before landing checklist* which are used under normal circumstances.

The pilots sped through the checklists, only partly completing them. The runway was in sight and they were descending normally. Up until the final approach, everything looked fine. Six miles out, the flaps were set to 8° and then to 20° and the landing gear extended. The working right-hand engine was set to idle as they came in for their landing.

However, a Learjet with only one engine doesn't handle the same way, which is why the standard checklists should not be used.

The crew never looked at the airspeed needed for an approach with an engine failure. They never looked at the flap settings. They set up the plane as if it were a normal landing.

As per the standard checklist, the crew set full flaps, 40°.

The procedure for a single engine landing includes the possibility of landing with full flaps "if the landing is ensured". In the case of an engine failure, it is safer (and more common) to come in with 20° flaps and only extend fully if you are sure that you are going to land on the runway, especially if you fear that you don't have enough runway in which to stop.

The Learjet would have required 915 metres (3,000 feet) to land that day. Nürnberg's Runway 10 is 2,700 metres (8,850 feet).

And yet, still some distance away from the threshold, they set full flaps, 40°. The airspeed immediately dropped but they hadn't reached the runway yet. At that speed, they wouldn't make it.

The pilot immediately set the right-hand engine to full power and shouted, "Flaps 20!" followed a moment later by "Do it!" With full power coming from the right, the airplane yaws to the left. They are a couple of hundred feet above the ground and about one kilometre away from the runway.

The Learjet could not reach the required airspeed with the flaps fully extended. Increasing the thrust to full power was too late and caused the plane to yaw violently. Retracting the flaps brought the slow airspeed even closer to stall speed.

And finally, the asymmetric fuel in the tip tanks meant the Learjet was even more unstable than normal.

In the small town of Buch, witnesses saw the aircraft make reeling movements as it turned left at a low height. It appeared to turn towards the runway again but then the aircraft tumbled. The witnesses said they saw the Learjet rocking from side to side with a Dutch roll motion before it completely stalled and crashed into the forest.

It's not clear whether the pilot planned to go around or was still trying to reach the runway. He might not have known himself. In those final moments, there was no time to consider decisions.

The airport fire service, which had been alerted previously, were in standby position and rushed to the forest, reaching the accident scene within minutes. The wreckage was 230 metres (750 feet) north of the threshold.

All three occupants died on impact and the aircraft was destroyed.

The investigation focused on the left engine, to find out why it had failed. They discovered "inter-granular cracking" or fractures on the high-pressure turbine disk, which caused the failure.

The engine had done 5,200 cycles, that is, 5,200 take-offs and landings, which was over the maximum prescribed . . . by a mere 157 cycles. The engine was at the end of its service life but only just. It did not seem likely to have this type of fault at that age. However, once the investigation focused on the turbine disk, they discovered all was not as it seemed. When the turbine disk was installed into the engine, the previous cycles had not been counted correctly.

Once they looked into the history of the disk, it became clear that the high-pressure turbine which had supposedly only had around 2,500 cycles had been the victim of noncompliant cycle counting. In reality the turbine had already accumulated 6,582 cycles before it had been installed into the engine of the Learjet and had *already exceeded* the allowable maximum of 5,200 cycles.

After installation, the engine and the turbine disk had completed a further 2,731 cycles. Thus, the high-pressure turbine disk had done 9,313 cycles when the engine shut down. The left engine was quite simply an accident waiting to happen.

Left Engine had stopped before the impact

Right engine had been running at high speed

Left and Right Engines after Impact.

Sadly, the accident investigation does not come to any useful conclusions.

Causes:

The accident was caused by an in-flight failure of the left power plant appr. 3 minutes after take-off and an inadequate conduct of the subsequent single-engine landing procedure so that in short final the airplane stalled and crashed from low height.

The failure of the left engine was caused by intergranular fractures of retention posts on the high-pressure turbine disk. As a result of incorrect service life recordings the maximum number of cycles had considerably been exceeded.

Safety Recommendations: None.

—From the English translation of the official report

I rarely argue with an accident investigation but this conclusion strikes me as the second greatest failure of the accident. The whole point of an investigation is to identify and understand the failures and look at how we can stop the situations arising that caused the accident.

This accident report is *extremely problematic* in that it simply waves away the problem without looking at how and why the pilots got it wrong. The ATC handling, increasing stress and using up over two minutes of pilot focus during a ten-minute flight, should in my opinion be listed as a contributing factor. The report cites that the pilots sounded stressed and followed the wrong checklists but does not then look at human factors to analyse *why*.

A single engine failing in a twin engine within view of a modern airport should be an incident, not a lethal accident.

Official Documentation

- Original accident report:
  *http://www.bfu-web.de/DE/Publikationen/
  Untersuchungsberichte/2001/Bericht_CX002-0.01.pdf?__blob=
  publicationFile*

Other References

- Accident report translated into English:
  *http://www.bfu-web.de/EN/Publications/
  Investigation%20Report/2001/Report_01_CX002-
  0_N%C3%Bcrnberg_Learjet.pdf?__blob=publicationFile*

- **Photography**
  Unattributed photographs are taken directly from the accident report.

- *Learjet 35A* photographed by Noel Jones.

TWIN TOWERS

I WONDERED WHETHER to include this tragedy at all. On the one hand, it seemed bizarre to even consider aviation incidents of 2001 and not include 9/11. On the other hand, over ten years have passed and surely everything has already been said.

In order to make up my mind, I read the 9/11 Commission Report. It was the first time I'd read the report in full. Over the years, I've thought about individual events of that terrible morning but until now, I've not been able to think about the attacks as a whole. Reading the commission report, I found myself envisioning the unfurling of the attacks minute by minute.

There is nothing new in my analysis below, simply a change in viewpoint. Rather than looking at each plane individually, I focused on the straightforward timeline of that morning and how the information spread during the initial flights.

The following timeline is extracted from *The 9/11 Commission Report: Final Report of the National Commission on Terrorist Attacks Upon the United States (Authorized Edition).*

All times are given in local time (Eastern Daylight Time).

Tuesday, September 11, 2001, dawned temperate and nearly cloudless in the eastern United States. Millions of men and women readied themselves for work. Some made their way to the Twin Towers, the signature structures of the World Trade Center complex in New York City. Others went to Arlington, Virginia, to the Pentagon. Across the Potomac

River, the United States Congress was back in session. At
the other end of Pennsylvania Avenue, people began to line
up for a White House tour. In Sarasota, Florida, President
George W. Bush went for an early morning run.

—From *The 9/11 ommission Report*

06:45 Mohamed Atta and Abdul Aziz al Omary arrive at Logan
International Airport in Boston, Massachusetts. Atta, Omary,
as well as Satam al Suqami, Wail al Shehri and Waleed al
Shehri check in for *American Airlines Flight 11*, bound for Los
Angeles with a scheduled departure of 07:45. In another ter-
minal at Logan Airport, Marwan al Shehhi, Fayez Baniham-
mad, Mohand al Shehri, Ahmed al Ghamdi and Hamza al
Ghamdi check in for *United Airlines Flight 175*, bound for Los
Angeles with a scheduled departure of 08:00.

07:03–07:39 At Newark Liberty International Airport in New
Jersey, Saeed al Ghamdi, Ahmed al Nami, Ahmad al Haznawi
and Ziad Jarra check in for *United Airlines Flight 93*, bound
for San Francisco with a scheduled departure of 08:00.

07:15 At Washington Dulles International Airport, Khalid al
Mihdar and Majed Moqed check in for *American Airlines
Flight 77*, bound for Los Angeles with a scheduled departure
of 08:10. They are joined by Hani Hanjour and the Hazmi
brothers, Nawaf and Salem.

Several of the hijackers are flagged as a risk and, as a result,
selected for extra screening of their checked bags. Two of them set
off alarms with their carry-on bags but pass a second test. Two of

the hijackers have their checked bags held until they board the aircraft. No other consequence follows the screening.

07:23–07:48 The five hijackers of United Airlines Flight 175 board the plane and take their seats in business class.

07:30 The five hijackers of American Flight 11 board the plane and take their seats in business class.

07:39–07:48 The four hijackers of United Flight 93 board the plane and take their seats in the first-class cabin.

07:40 American Airlines Flight 11 pushes back from the gate.

07:50 The five hijackers of American Airlines Flight 77 board the plane and take their seats, two in coach, three in first-class.

Nineteen men are now aboard four transcontinental flights and ready to initiate their attack. The security screening did not stop them. Although the hijackers later claim to have bombs, this is almost certainly a bluff.

07:58 United Airlines Flight 175 pushes back.

07:59 American Airlines Flight 111 departs Logan International Airport.

08:09 American Airlines Flight 77 pushes back.

08:14 United Airlines Flight 175 departs Logan International Airport.

08:14 American Airlines Flight 11 acknowledges navigational instructions from Boston ATC.

16 seconds later, ATC instructs the flight crew to climb to 35,000 feet. No response is received from the pilots.

08:19 On American Airlines Flight 11, Flight Attendant Betty Ong uses an airphone to contact the American Airlines Southeastern Reservations Office and report an emergency aboard the flight. Flight Attendant Amy Sweeney also contacted American Airlines to report and relay updates.

08:20 American Airlines Flight 77 departs Washington Dulles airport.

08:21 American Airlines Flight 11 turns off its transponder.

A few minutes later, the microphone is keyed and air traffic controllers hear the hijackers' transmissions meant for the cabin. The first transmission is not clearly understood by the controller. The second transmission is broadcast clearly and the controller realises that the plane has been hijacked: "Nobody move, everything will be okay. If you try to make any moves, you'll endanger yourself and the airplane. Just stay quiet."

The message of the first transmission is not understood until an hour later. The hijacker had said: "We have some planes. Just stay quiet, and you'll be okay. We are returning to the airport."

08:26 Flight Attendant Betty Ong reports that American Airlines Flight 11 is flying erratically. The aircraft turns south.

08:33 United Airlines Flight 175 reaches cruising altitude of 31,000 feet.

08:34 Boston Center controller receives a third unintended transmission from American Airlines Flight 11. "Nobody move please. We are going back to the airport. Don't try to make any stupid moves."

08:37 Northeast Air Defense Sector are contacted by Boston Center. This is the first notification received by the military that American 11 has been hijacked.

You can't blame them for the initial response: "Is this real-world or exercise?" It swiftly becomes clear that this is a real emergency, and Northeast Air Defense Sector order two F-15s to battle station.

08:42 United Airlines Flight 175 flight crew report a suspicious transmission overheard from another aircraft: "Ah, we heard a suspicious transmission on our departure out of Boston, ah, with someone, ah, it sounded like someone keyed the mikes and said ah everyone ah stay in your seats."

This is the last communication from United Airlines Flight 175 flight crew.

08:42 United Flight 93 departs Newark Liberty International Airport.

08:44 Contact with Flight Attendant Betty Ong on American Airlines Flight 11 is lost. Flight Attendant Amy Sweeney reports that they are in a rapid descent and flying "way too low".

08:46 Two F-15 fighters are scrambled but Northeast Air Defense Sector do not know where to send them.

08:46 American Airlines Flight 77 reaches cruising altitude of 35,000 feet.

08:46:40 American Airlines Flight 11 crashes into the North Tower of the World Trade Center.

08:47 United Airlines Flight 175 changes transponder codes twice within a minute.

The controller responsible for this flight is desperately trying to locate American Airlines Flight 11 and does not notice.

08:51 United Airlines Flight 175 deviates from its assigned altitude. The air traffic controller attempts to contact the aircraft and receives no response.

08:51 American Airlines Flight 77 transmits its last routine radio communication.

08:52 A passenger and a flight attendant on United Airlines Flight 175 make phone calls from the cabin to report the hijacking.

08:54 American Airlines Flight 77 deviates from its assigned course, turning south.

08:56 American Airlines Flight 77 transponder is turned off. Controllers attempt to contact the aircraft but do not receive a response.

Indianapolis Center reports that the aircraft has had a serious electrical or mechanical failure and possible crash.

08:58 United Airlines Flight 175 changes heading towards New York City

09:00 American Airlines Executive Vice President Gerard Arpey learns that communications have been lost with American Airlines Flight 77 and grounds all American Airlines flights in the north east.

09:00 The passenger on United Airlines Flight 175 phones again, reports that the plane is making jerky movements and passengers are throwing up.

The call is cut off.

09:03:11 United Airlines Flight 175 strikes the South Tower of the World Trade Center.

09:03 Boston Center staff analysing the hijacker transmission from American Airlines Flight 11 realise that the initial message included the phrase "we have some planes" and the scale of the attack becomes clear.

Controllers at Boston Center request that Herndon Command Center "get messages to airborne aircraft to increase security for the cockpit". There is no evidence of Herndon taking this action.

09:12 Passengers on American Airlines Flight 77 make phone calls from the rear of the cabin to report the hijacking.

09:19 United flight dispatcher begins transmitting warnings to the 16 United transcontinental flights currently in the air.

09:20 Indianapolis Center become aware of the situation in New York and realise that American Airlines Flight 77 may also have been hijacked and reports the aircraft as lost.

09:23 United Flight 93 receives a warning message from the United flight dispatcher. The pilot responds asking for confirmation.

09:38 United Flight 93 suddenly drops 700 feet. A Mayday message is broadcast with sounds of a physical struggle in the cockpit.

09:29 The autopilot on American Airlines Flight 77 is disengaged. The aircraft is at 7,000 feet and approximately 38 miles west of the Pentagon.

09:30 Northeast Air Defense Sector scramble fighters at Langley after a report of a hijacked aircraft heading for Washington DC.

However, they are told that it is American Airlines Flight 11 that is heading towards Washington, although it had already crashed into the South Tower.

The fighter jets are given an easterly heading to send them to the Baltimore area to position between a non-existent southbound American Flight 11 and Washington DC. Their flight plan did not include a distance nor the target's location.

09:32 Controllers at Dulles Terminal Radar Approach report a primary radar return, tracking eastbound at high speed.

A National Guard C-130H cargo aircraft follows the track and identifies a Boeing 757. He's found American Airlines Flight 77.

09:32 United Flight 93 announces "Ladies and Gentlemen: Here the captain, please sit down keep remaining sitting. We have a bomb on board. So, sit." The autopilot is used to turn the aircraft around and head east.

The passengers and flight crew begin phoning to report the incident and are told of the crashes into the World Trade Center.

09:34 American Airlines Flight 77 is 5 miles west-southwest of the Pentagon. The aircraft begins a 330-degree turn and descends through 2,200 feet. The hijacker advances throttles to maximum power and dives toward the Pentagon.

09:36 Boston Center reports "Latest report. Aircraft VFR [visual flight rules] six miles southeast of the White House. . . . Six, southwest. Six, southwest of the White House, deviating away."

The mission crew commander at Northeast Air Defense Sector takes control of the airspace to clear a flight path for the Langley fighters which are well out of range. "I don't care how many windows you break," he says.

09:37:46 American Airlines Flight 77 crashes into the Pentagon at approximately 530 miles per hour.

09:38 The National Guard C-130H cargo aircraft which was attempting to follow American Airlines Flight 77 reports "it looks like that aircraft crashed into the Pentagon Sir." The Langley fighters are still about 150 miles away.

09:39 A further radio transmission is received from United Flight 93: "Uh, this is the captain. Would like you all to remain seated. There is a bomb on board and are going back to the airport, and to have our demands [unintelligible]. Please remain quiet."

09:41 United Flight 93's transponder is turned off.

The point of turning off the transponders is to make the planes "disappear" from a controller's point of view. These attempts to hide the hijacked aircraft clearly added to the confusion of the morning.

09:57 The passengers of United Flight 93 assault the cockpit.

09:58 The hijacker flying United Flight 93 rolls the aircraft left and right in an attempt to knock the passengers off balance. He tells another hijacker to block the cockpit door and continues to roll the plane.

09:59 United Flight 93 is about 20 minutes flying time from Washington DC. The hijacker pitches the nose of the aircraft up and down to disrupt the assault.

10:00 The hijacker flying United Flight 93 stabilizes the aircraft and asks "Is that it? Shall we finish it off?" He receives a response from another hijacker, "No. Not yet. When they all come, we finish it off." The pilot pitches the aircraft up and down again.

Another aircraft reports to controllers that he has seen the plane "waving his wings".

10:01 United Flight 93 stabilizes again and the hijackers agree to "put it down".

10:02:23 United Flight 93 plunges and the control wheel is turned hard to the right, rolling the aircraft onto its back. It crashes into an empty field in Shanksville, Pennsylvania, travelling at approximately 580 miles per hour.

10:07 Northeast Air Defense Sector receive notification of United Flight 93's hijack.

10:08 The National Guard C-130H cargo aircraft, which had resumed its planned flight to Minnesota, reports black smoke fifteen miles south of Johnstown. It is confirmed as corresponding to the last known position for United Flight 93.

All four aircraft were successfully hijacked and were crashed on purpose. Only three reached their targets.

```
GI S6  ATTN A$IC/CIC....GROUND STOP ALL TFC DEST TO AND THRU ZNY..
TMU1113MTURSN

GI S6  ATTN A$IC/CIC....CORRECTION...GROUND STOP ALL TFC DEST TO AND
THRU ZNY...RSQ ATCSCC REQ...TMU111307

GI S6  ATTN A$IC/CIC....ANOTHER UPDATE FOR GROUND STOP.....A$
1509Z.....THE ATCSCC STATES THAT FAA WILL NOT AUTHORIZE CLEAR
NOR GIVE SERVICE TO ANY IFR/VFR/LIFEGAURD FLIGHTS.......ONLY
MILITARY ACFT ARE ALLOWED TO FLY.....PLEASE CALL FOR RLS TO 2
FOR ANY OF THESE FLIGHTS BEFORE DEPARTING THEM./.......TMU1115

GI S5  ATTN A$IC/CIC....EFF 1330Z-UFA......GROUND STOP ALL TFC ALL
DESTINATIONS......YES YOU ARE READING THIS CORRECTLY...,..EXPECT
UPDATE 1500Z.......TMU111328DH

GI S5  ATTN A$IC/CIC....EFF 1330Z-UFA....CLARIFICATION...,....GROUND
STOP ALL TFC ALL DESTINATIONS........THIS INCLUDES LOCAL FLIGHTS /
VFR / IFR / MILITARY FLIGHTS......NO ONE FLYS........EXPECT UPDATE
1500Z........TMU111328DH

GI S5  ATTN A$IC/CIC....EMERGENCY USE OF AIR AMBULANCE FLIGHTS ARE
EXEMPT FROM THE COMPREHENSIVE GROUND STOP TMU111403CR

GI S5  ATTN A$IC/CIC....EFF 11645   THERE HAS BEEN NO CHANGE FROM
EARLIER THIS MORNING ... ALL AIR TRAFFIC IS GROUNDED -- UFA  CALL
ZJX TMU IF YOU HAVE AN EMERGENCY FLIGHT .. IT MUST BE COORDINATED
THRU THE CAMMAND CENTER FOR APPROVAL   TMU111652AP
```

GROUND STOP ALL TFC ALL DESTINA-
TIONS. . . . YES YOU ARE READING THIS
CORRECTLY

Every person involved must have been so full of horror and fear as the events unravelled. I'm not ashamed to admit that after I finished putting together this timeline, I cried.

Official Documentation

- *The 9/11 Commission Report: Final Report of the National Commission on Terrorist Attacks Upon the United States*

The Commission Report is available in paperback or as an e-book.

Negative Training: When the Simulator Lies

It was the 12th of November, 2001. The dust had not yet settled in the gap in New York's skyline when American Airlines flight 587, an Airbus A300, crashed into Queens. Flight 587 was a scheduled passenger flight from New York to the Dominican Republic with 251 passengers, 7 flight attendants and 2 flight crew. The aircraft arrived at JFK at 22:31 the night before the accident. The morning flight was the first leg of a one-day round-trip for the flight crew. All times are Eastern Standard Time (local time for the flight).

06:14 The Captain checks in for the flight. The First Officer arrives 15 minutes later.

The pair had flown together 36 times before the accident. Both were excellent pilots. They got along well.

08:59:58 The ground controller clears Flight 587 to push back from the gate.

09:02:05 "Your leg, you check the rudders," says the Captain.

The First Officer was Pilot Flying. The First Officer pressed each pedal down, maxing out at 3.7 inches on the right and 3.6 inches on the left and responded, "rudders check". The full displacement on the rudder pedals is 4 inches.

09:11:08 The controller clears Japan Air Lines for take-off. The JAL flight is a heavy Boeing 747, which requires a minimum of 2 minutes or 4 nautical miles separation. The controller adds extra radar separation between the Boeing 747 and the A300 as 747s "are often slow climbers" and clears Flight 587 to taxi into position and hold, with a caution about the wake turbulence.

09:13:21 Flight 587 moves into position on the runway.

09:13:28 The controller notes that separation is established and clears Flight 587 for take-off.

09:13:35 "You happy with that [separation] distance?" asks the First Officer. The Captain is happy. "We'll be all right once we get rolling. He's supposed to be five miles by the time we're airborne, that's the idea." There's no cause for concern.

09:13:51 Flight 587 takes off. The climb-out is normal. They are separated from JAL flight 47 by at least 4.3 nautical miles horizontally and 3,800 feet vertically throughout.

09:15:36 The aircraft encounters mild wake turbulence. The First Officer responds with very aggressive movements on the control column.

09:15:41 The Captain acknowledges an instruction from the departure controller to proceed directly to their next point of reference. This is the final transmission that the controller receives from flight 587.

09:15:44 The Captain says to the First Officer, "Little wake turbulence, huh?" The First Officer responds with "Yeah" and requests 250 knots, which is the maximum speed for flight below 10,000 feet msl. At this time, the aircraft is at approx 2,300 feet msl.

09:15:51 The Airbus encounters more wake turbulence. There's slight bumpiness and the plane's left wing drops, causing a slight roll to the left. Again, the First officer responds aggressively. He moves the control wheel to the right and depresses the right rudder pedal, hard. The aircraft responds to his manoeuvre by rolling to the right. The First Officer moves the control wheel rapidly left and right, with a series of alternating full rudder inputs.

09:15:54 The First Officer, in a stressed tone, asks for max power. The aircraft is travelling at 240 knots. The Captain does not change the power setting but instead asks, "You all right?" The First Officer replies, "Yeah, I'm fine," but the strain is clear in his voice.

09:15:55 The Captain offers words of support, "Hang onto it. Hang onto it!"

09:15:58 The aircraft is travelling at 251 knots when a loud bang sounds in the cockpit. The right rear main attachment fitting has fractured. The aerodynamic load on the vertical stabiliser is extreme. The vertical stabiliser rips off under the pressure.

The vertical stabiliser, also known as the fin, is the vertical section of the tail on the Airbus A300. An aircraft cannot fly without a vertical stabiliser.

The recovery of the vertical stabiliser from
American Airlines flight 587.

09:16:00 The Cockpit Voice Recorder records a grunt and then
the First Officer cursing. A sound similar to a stall warning
chimes for 1.9 seconds.

09:16:07 The First Officer says "What the hell are we into . . .
we're stuck in it."

09:16:12 The Captain says "Get out of it, get out of it."

Both crew members still somehow believed that this was wake
turbulence. The First Officer's aggressive rudder input in response
to the perceived turbulence caused the entire upset and now had
stressed the aircraft beyond its structural limits. The plane, no
longer airworthy, began to fall out of the sky.

The cockpit voice recording ended two seconds later.

Northwest Airlines flight 1867 was lined up on runway 31L ready for departure. The Captain saw pieces falling from the A300 ahead and then watched the aircraft enter a nosedive and crash. Four homes were destroyed and six others damaged. 260 people aboard the aircraft and five on the ground were killed in the impact.

The media frenzy was immediate. In the wake of 9/11, terrorism was an obvious conclusion. What else could make a plane break apart in the sky? The initial speculation was that there must have been a bomb or some other deliberate act to destroy the aircraft.

But the Flight Data Recorder told another story. The vertical stabiliser was ripped off of the aircraft because of the stresses that the pilot had put the plane under in the course of the flight.

During both bouts of turbulence, the First Officer responded very aggressively with excessive force. When the left wing dropped, which was not in itself a cause for concern, the First Officer depressed the right rudder pedal, hard. The aircraft responded to this manoeuvre by rolling to the right, which should have been expected. The First Officer responded with a series of fast and excessive corrections, moving the control wheel rapidly left and right, with a series of alternating full rudder inputs over the next seven seconds.

The investigation was able to prove that the structural damage was not a result of a flaw in the aircraft. There was no structural fault with the fin. The composite materials were strong enough to withstand normal pressures. The design of the A300-600 vertical stabilizer exceeded certification requirements.

The "limit load" of the stabiliser is the maximum that the stabiliser is expected to bear. The ultimate load is the limit load multiplied by a safety factor of 1.5. An aircraft is expected to experience limit load only once in its lifetime and it is never expected to actually experience ultimate load.

At 240 knots, the rudder pedals on the A300-600 required 30 pounds of force to achieve full rudder deflection. The First Officer applied 140 pounds of pressure during the seven seconds before the break-up. The Captain never realised that the increasing sideslips and rolls of the aircraft were not caused by unexpected wake turbulence. However, the ongoing "turbulence" was the direct result of the First Officer's forceful left-right-left-right on the rudder pedals.

The continued rudder deflections led to increasing sideslip angles that produced extremely high aerodynamic loads on the vertical stabiliser. When it snapped, the strain was *double* the limit load, more than any structure on the aircraft can be expected to bear.

Why had the First Officer reacted with such force to the wake turbulence encounter? An encounter which was so minor, it actually required no reaction from the cockpit at all.

Investigators soon discovered it had happened before.

A flight engineer reported that in 1997, the same First Officer was flying a 727 on approach, 7 miles out at an altitude between 3,000 and 5,000 feet. They encountered wake turbulence from a 737 in front. The First Officer responded by immediately applying full power and executing a go-around. As the 727 was the larger aircraft and there was more than sufficient altitude, a go-around was a clear over reaction to the encounter. The flight engineer recalled it as one of the more memorable events in his flying career.

In a separate report, a 727 captain recalled that the aircraft encountered wake turbulence when the First Officer was flying. The captain said the encounter required only a small aileron input to roll the airplane to wings level. The First Officer responded very aggressively on the rudder pedals.

Specifically, the captain indicated that, when the airplane was at an altitude of between 1,000 and 1,500 feet, the first officer "stroked the rudder pedals 1-2-3, about that fast." The captain thought that the airplane had lost an engine and was thus focused on the engine instruments. The captain stated that he then asked the first officer what he was doing and that the first officer replied that he was "leveling the wings due to wake turbulence." The captain, who had his feet on the rudder pedals, thought that the first officer had pushed the rudder to its full stops.

The captain recalled being startled by the first officer's rudder inputs and indicated that they did not level the wings but created left and right yawing moments and heavy side loads on the airplane. He further indicated that the first officer did not need to be so aggressive because the 727 was "a very stable airplane."According to the captain, he and the first officer discussed this event later in the flight. The captain pointed out to the first officer that his use of the rudder pedals was "quite aggressive," but the first officer insisted that the American Airlines Advanced Aircraft Maneuvering Program (AAMP) directed him to use the rudder pedals in that manner.

The captain disagreed with the first officer and told him that the AAMP directed that the rudder was to be used at lower airspeeds. The captain told the first officer to review the AAMP when he returned home and to be less aggressive on the rudder pedals when they flew together.

—From the official report

The AAMP, Advanced Aircraft Maneuvering Program, is an advanced training for dealing with upsets in aircraft attitude put on by American Airlines. In 1996, a review of accidents from 1987 to 1996 showed that the leading causal factor for accidents involving large multi-engine transport-category aircraft was loss of control. There were conflicts between the manufacturers' advice and the training being offered by the airlines. The chief flight test pilots from Airbus, Boeing and McDonnell Douglas joined the working group in order to offer unified advice as to airplane handling and recovery techniques.

> Two of the areas in which the airplane manufacturers and the airlines had differing opinions were the use of rudder and the use of simulators. Regarding the use of rudder, the Airbus chief test pilot indicated that the existing upset recovery simulator training courses emphasized using rudder for roll control at low airspeeds. He stated that, although the rudder remained effective down to very low airspeeds, the airplane manufacturer test pilots were "very wary" of using rudder close to stall speed.
>
> —From the official report

American Airline's AAMP consists of classroom instruction, manuals, videotapes and simulator flight training. In 1997, shortly before the above incidents, the First Officer had attended ground school training and read the AAMP training manual.

Aircraft manufacturers were unhappy with the airplane upset recovery training being offered by the airlines, including specifically the AAMP training offered by American Airlines. They formally complained about the specific courses, including the AAMP offered by American. The chief test pilots from Airbus, Boeing and

McDonnell Douglas banded together (an unexpected alliance) to try to convince the airline training managers to de-emphasise the use of rudders in their courses. They warned the airlines that excessive rudder could cause excessive sideslip, leading the pilot to lose control of the aircraft, exactly as happened on American Airlines Flight 587 four years later.

Internally, an American Airlines A300 technical pilot wrote a letter in 1997 to express his concern that the AAMP encouraged the use of rudders as primary roll control. The letter specifically stated that the AAMP instructors were teaching pilots to use the rudder to control roll in the event of a wake turbulence encounter.

Airbus tried to convince American Airlines to change the course. The chief test pilot wrote a letter to American Airlines to state that the rudder should be used to avoid sidelip but not as the primary source of roll. He also wrote that simulators were particularly inaccurate for large sideslip angles and the pilot could draw the wrong conclusions. The vice president of Airbus also voiced his concern about the AAMP's emphasis on rudder and their simulator use for upset recovery training.

Boeing weighed in with a letter addressing the same issues and in regards to the upset training, said, "the excessive emphasis on the superior effectiveness of the rudder for roll control vis-à-vis aileron and spoilers, in high angle of attack, is a concern."

The Boeing chief test pilot said that he vehemently disagreed with the aggressive use of rudder at high AOAs because "it is extremely dangerous and unpredictable."

The McDonnell Douglas chief test pilot expressed "serious concerns and disagreement" about the rudder theories presented in the AAMP.

The American Airlines managing director of flight operations technical was quoted in an internal memo that he had "grave concerns about some flawed aerodynamic theory and flying techniques that have been presented in the AAMP." The memo also said that it was wrong and exceptionally dangerous to teach pilots to use rudder as the primary means of roll control in recoveries from high AOAs.

Nevertheless, American Airlines defended the AAMP and the rudder and continued training pilots with a combination of ground school and simulator exercises.

A closer look at the simulator training showed disconcerting similarities to Flight 587. The standard simulator exercise went something like this:

The pilot is told that he is taking off behind a heavy 747 and issued the appropriate wake turbulence warnings, which meant he should expect a wake turbulence encounter after take-off.

During climb-out, at an altitude between 2,000 and 2,500 and an airspeed of 240 knots, he experiences some light chop. The simulator inhibits the use of controls for up to ten seconds in order to ensure that the simulation will reach an excessive bank as per the training. The pilot is told to react quickly to the upset; however anything the pilot does with the control wheel and rudder pedal inputs during this stage of the exercise has little or no result.

The aircraft rolls in one direction (determined arbitrarily by the computer) and then almost immediately rolls in the opposite direction to *at least* 90°. The controls remain inhibited until the airplane reaches 50°, when yaw and roll control are phased back in. Rudder input is required as a part of the recovery technique.

The issues with this simulator training are numerous:

1. This wake turbulence scenario is totally unrealistic. There has *never* been a reported accident from a heavy transport-category airplane departing from controlled flight as the result of wake turbulence.

2.   The simulation associates wake turbulence with the risk of a
     major upset, including an uncommanded roll of 90° or more.
     An A300 is not going to go into an extreme bank angle as a
     result of wake turbulence.

3.   Inhibiting the controls at the beginning of the exercise means
     that large wheel and pedal inputs have no effect. The pilot
     could use full control wheel turns and full pedal deflection
     and the airplane would still roll to at least 50° in the opposite
     direction. This teaches the pilot that he needs to react aggres-
     sively to get any response at all. Pilots who position their con-
     trols at full deflection are rewarded in the simulation with the
     least recovery time after the controls are reinstated, even
     though full deflection was never required.

4.   The scenario, meant to teach upset recovery, actually teaches
     pilots to treat wake turbulence as a potentially catastrophic
     event, requiring an immediate and aggressive response.

The First Officer has no record of unusual rudder use before
his AAMP training in 1997. However, the AAMP manual he received
as a part of his ground training in 1997 stated directly that the use
of rudder was the most effective roll control device at high angles of
attack. (The manual was revised in 1997 as a result of
manufacturers' concerns, but the First Officer never received the
revised version.) During classroom training, pilots were instructed
that full rudder inputs could be appropriate in certain extreme
situations, despite manufacturers warnings to the contrary. It was
after the First Officer had received this training that he overreacted
to the turbulence on approach. When the First Officer defended his
heavy rudder usage on the 727 to his Captain on the second event,
he explicitly stated that the AAMP directed him to use the rudders
in that manner in a wake turbulence scenario.

Then he continued his training, including four simulator sessions. The simulation encouraged his aggressive reactions, and misrepresented the aircraft's actual response to large rudder inputs.

And then, the simulation became reality.

Flight 587 took off after a heavy 747 and they were advised of possible wake turbulence. The aircraft rolled slightly to the left. The First Officer responded with full right rudder, which in the simulator would have had little or no effect, as the controls were inhibited. In reality, the aircraft sideslipped and rolled aggressively to the right as a result of his aggressive response. But if we look at it from the First Officer's point of view, the aircraft responded with a hard roll to the right, *just like in the simulation.*

The First Officer almost certainly had no idea that the airplane's motion was caused by his overreaction, rather than the wake turbulence. And so he continued exactly as he had in the simulator, responding with an aggressive input to the left.

Except the simulation didn't end. The "turbulence" became worse. And although he'd been trained for this encounter, nothing that he did was anything like what it had been on the simulator.

American Airlines immediately blamed the design of the A300, saying that it was flawed. It was true that the A300 rudder pedals were more sensitive than any other aircraft out there. It was also clearly true that the pilots—and the instructors, it seemed—were not aware that the sensitivity of the pedals increased dramatically at higher airspeeds.

Airbus responded with a bulletin on rudder use, which stated directly: Sudden commanded full, or nearly full, opposite rudder movement against a sideslip can generate loads that exceed the limit loads and possibly the ultimate loads and can result in structural failure. The bulletin also clarified that rudders should not be used to induce roll or to counter roll when induced by turbulence.

American Airlines A300 feet standards manager argued that they had never received such limitations nor prohibited manoeuvres on rudder use before the accident. Nevertheless, it was clear that Airbus, Boeing, McDonnell Douglas and American Airline's own managing director of flight operations technical had all stated clearly, four years previously, that the training encouraged dangerous flying techniques, especially in regards to rudder usage.

The Safety Board agreed that the Rudder Control System Design in the Airbus A300-600 had much higher sensitivity that other transport-category aircraft. The variable stop design meant it became more sensitive as airspeed increased, rather than a relatively constant rudder pedal sensitivity. The use of rudder at high airspeeds is rare and this sensitivity would not have an effect on standard rudder use (for example, during a crosswind landing or engine-out). However, it did mean that relatively small pedal displacements in the cruise could lead to maximum rudder movement. At 240 knots, only 30 pounds of pressure was required to reach full rudder deflection. The flight data recorder from Flight 587 showed that the First Officer applied up to 140 pounds of pressure during the accident sequence. A less sensitive pedal would not have saved him.

The Safety Board concluded that the A300-600 was specifically susceptible to potentially hazardous pedal inputs at higher airspeeds. However, they agreed with Airbus that the situation should never have arisen:

To elevate the characteristics of the A300-600 rudder system in the hierarchy of contributing factors ignores the fact that this system had not been an issue in some 16 million hours of testing and operator experience—until the AAMP trained pilot flew it.

—From the official report

Despite this, the National Transportation Safety Board listed both as contributing factors:

The National Transportation Safety Board determines that the probable cause of this accident was the in-flight separation of the vertical stabilizer as a result of the loads beyond ultimate design that were created by the first officer's unnecessary and excessive rudder pedal inputs. Contributing to these rudder pedal inputs were characteristics of the Airbus A300-600 rudder system design and elements of the American Airlines Advanced Aircraft Maneuvering Program.

—From the official report

The order of the contributing factors is because the Board wanted more attention to be given to aircraft rudder characteristics, although two members of the board actively voted against the hierarchy as given, for fear that it diminished the role of the AAMP in the accident.

In the end, the First Officer, considered an experienced and competent pilot by his contemporaries, was flying the plane exactly as he believed he had been trained to. Negative training is a situation in which training leads to less effective performance in the operational environment than would have occurred if no training had been conducted. The Advanced Aircraft Maneuvering Program was supposed to improve his skills and make him a safer pilot. Instead, it did the opposite. If the First Officer had not taken part in the AAMP, he and his passengers might be alive today.

The strength of this accident report is that it didn't stop at the first cause, even though it was clear early on that the rudder inputs by the Pilot Flying had caused the disaster. Investigators delved further, not content with the easy answer. And in the end, they were able to show exactly how the pilot had come to this point and thus how to avoid it in future. Although the situation is tragic, this report is a triumph of aviation investigation.

Official Documentation

- Original accident report:
  http://www.ntsb.gov/doclib/reports/2004/aar0404.pdf

Other References

- Summary article:
  *http://www.rvs.uni-bielefeld.de/publications/compendium/
  incidents_and_accidents/AA587.html*

Photography

All photographs are taken directly from the accident report.

CONCLUSION

T HE STRENGTH OF ACCIDENT investigations is that they are not simply a blame-allocation exercise. One of the reasons that aviation is now so safe is because every accident is treated seriously, rather than dismissed the moment someone is found who could be held accountable.

In aviation, we take it seriously that we can learn from the mistakes of others, and accident investigations must remain strongly biased towards "stop this from happening again" rather than allocating blame. I hope that with these analyses, it's possible to see the progress towards safer aviation around the world.

This is only a small selection of accidents from around the world. I have chosen especially dramatic events which are interesting to dissect and understand, so it would be unreasonable to try to draw greater conclusions from such a small number. These flights have one factor in common: they occurred within a twelve-month window. But from this selection alone, it is clear that accidents are not simply a matter of aircraft size, hours in the cockpit or lack of modern computer aids.

The accidents and incidents of 2001 also shed light on how vigilance and understanding have made certain classes of incidents more rare: windshear, uncontrolled fire, avionics confusion, uncontained engine failure, structural failure. These accidents are not a single point of failure but an unfortunate combination of events. The sequence of events leading to the failure has become a critical part of the analysis.

Many changes have come into effect since these accident investigations took place. Airbus have changed the logic of their flight control system. American Airlines have modified their advanced pilot training. The FAA have run a promotional campaign recommending carbon monoxide detectors. And of course, we have experienced first hand the changes around the world in airport security as a direct result of the most tragic air incident in 2001. This reactive process can be frustrating: even when safety is increased, each new regulation or recommendation adds complications. Despite all this investigation and analysis, some new combination will always occur. However, this focus on the fine detail and the true causes of every accident is also the reason why flying is still the safest form of travel (six times safer than travelling by car and twice as safe as rail, according to the BBC), despite constant increase in traffic.

Why Planes Crash Case Files: 2001 is an entry-point into 21st century aviation. I hope that the analyses have offered a clear view of aviation in 2001 and the trials and tribulations of the modern pilot. If you enjoyed this book, please email me at *sylvia@planecra.sh* to let me know. You can also visit *http://planecra.sh/2001* for the references and original accident reports.

WHY PLANES CRASH

CASE FILES
2002

ACKNOWLEDGEMENTS

I **WANT TO** acknowledge Cliff Stanford again for his never-ending patience as I worked through this book, not to mention the dozen other serious distractions I encountered.

Thank you to Anatoly Belilovsky and Ken Liu for answering cultural questions, and especially to Anatoly for translation help. Any errors or simplifications are mine, but I appreciate the time both of them spent to help me to understand the underlying issues.

The cover photograph is by Greg Jensen. I'd also like to thank Oleg Belyakov, John O'Neill, Alain Durand, Torsten Maiwald, Sean Waugh, Hullie from nl, NOAA Photo Library, Ray Barber, and anynobody for making their photographs and illustrations available to me as a part of this book.

I also received great input from Dominic Hall, James Noble and Rick Fisher, who all helped this book to be accessible.

Contents for

Case Files 2002

INTRODUCTION

*W*HY *PLANES* *C*RASH: *Case Files 2002* is the second in my series on modern aviation accidents and incidents around the world. I find it fascinating to focus on the 21st century, a time when most planes don't crash. These accidents are especially interesting because they offer us a detailed view into complex systems and how humans interact with them. I've included well-known accidents from 2002 but also many that aren't very well known, from different countries and including both commercial and general aviation. My intent is to give the reader a broad cross section of the aviation issues from 2002 and over time, a view of the first decade of this millennium and what it meant for aviation.

It always sounds wrong to hope that the reader will enjoy reading about fatal crashes, but I do hope you will find each account interesting and educational in its own right.

If you'd like to know when the next book in the series is out, please leave me your email address at *http://planecra.sh/notify* and I'll be happy to mail you once it is released.

Note: Links to all references used in this book may be found at *http://planecra.sh/2002.*

DISASTER AT THE AIR SHOW

O**NE OF THE MOST** tragic accidents in recent history is hard to reach concrete conclusions about because there are no published investigation results and no final report to be read. The accident took place at Sknyliv Airport, near Lviv in the Ukraine, in July 2002. Over ten years later, the local community has still not recovered.

The airport is six kilometres (3.7 miles) from Lviv city centre. It is officially known as Lviv Danylo Halytskyi International Airport, named after Daniel Romanovych, King of Galicia and Volhynia from 1253 to 1264.

When the Soviet Union dissolved in 1991, a large number of military aircraft were left on Ukrainian territory and taken over by the Ukrainian air force. Most of the aircraft in the air force are still Soviet made and the majority are not considered airworthy. In 2014, the Ministry of Defence stated that they held 507 combat planes and 121 attack helicopters but only 15% were serviceable. The Air Force is grouped into the 5th and 14th Aviation Corps, the 35th Aviation Group and a training aviation command. 2002 was celebrated as the 60th anniversary of the Ukrainian Air Force's 14th Air Corp which was created at the start of the Second World War.

On the 27th of July, the Ukrainian Air Force hosted a grand event to commemorate the 60th anniversary of the Ukrainian Air Force's 14th Air Corp. It was a beautiful summer day and over 8,000 people attended to watch the best pilots in Ukraine put on a display: the Ukrainian Falcons.

The Ukrainian Falcons are Ukraine's aerobatic demonstration team, established in 1995. The pilots are the elite of the Ukrainian Air Force's fighter pilots and were to show off their skills on the Sukhoi Su-27.

Ukrainian Sukhoi Su-27UB taken 2011 *(Photo by Oleg Belyakov)*

The Russian twin-engine super-manoeuvrable fighter aircraft entered service in the Soviet Air Force in 1985. The two-seater Su-27 is an amazing long-range fighter aircraft and is still a favourite at air shows around the world.

> The Su-27 belongs to the same class [as] the US F-14 and F-15, but unlike the American fighters it can fly at an angle of attack of 30 degrees and can also perform the "Pugachev Cobra", an aerobatic maneuver in which the aircraft pitches the nose beyond the vertical at a rate of 70 degrees per second and after that recovers to level flight. Thanks to this maneuver, the Flanker has been the highlight of every air shows [sic] from the end of the 80s to the middle of the 90s.
>
> —From the Aviationist

However, at the Sknyliv Air Show, something went terribly wrong.

Up until that day, the air-show tragedy at Ramstein U.S. Air Force base in Germany in 1988 was considered the worst ever air show disaster, when 70 people were killed and 400 were injured after two Italian military jets collided in midair and crashed into the crowds. Since then, air shows around the world have separated crowds from the flights during aerobatic displays. As a comparison, in the UK, the minimum lateral distance between the aerobatic display line and the crowd line is based on the speed of the aircraft. There must always be at least 100 metres (328 feet) separation and, if the aircraft is flying over 300 knots indicated airspeed, the minimum distance increases to 230 metres (750 feet). Aerobatic pilots must plan their flying sequence, so that they can regain the display line without ever infringing on the separation-from-crowd area, and may not overfly the spectator enclosures or the car park.

Lt Col Vladimir Toponar and his co-pilot Yuriy Yegorov flew the two-seater Sukhoi Su-27UB fighter jet in tandem with a similar aircraft. State officials claimed that the stunt was flawed from the start, but on what basis is unclear. In fact, it is hard to understand exactly what happened that day.

There is no official English transcript of the radio transmissions that day at the airfield. The following has been translated from the Russian transcript by Anatoly Belilovsky and rendered to standard aviation terms by me. Any errors in the following text are mine.

The radio information refers to the people on the ground by name, which appears to me to include high-level military giving air traffic services and commands. I have referred to the people on the ground as *control* for this transcript. At 12:40, the discussion between the pilots and the control seemed to consist of normal exchanges.

Control: 2,000 metres, thin haze, light cumulus Grade 2 or 3. Weather is clear, 10 km visibility.

Co-Pilot: There's the weather.

Pilot: Take control for now.

Co-Pilot: Got it.

Pilot: Right turn.

Co-Pilot: Roger.

However, at 12:43 as they began their performance, the responses by the pilots made it clear that something was not right.

Pilot: Where are the spectators? [expletive]!

Co-Pilot: I don't know where they are, [expletive]!

Pilot: There, I see them!

Co-Pilot: [expletive]! Not on the right!

Pilot to Control: Executing left turn.

Co-Pilot: Should we go?

Control: Turn left, turn left!

The pilots continued their manoeuvres under stress although they were both quite clearly not happy with where the crowd line was in relation to their routine. No official information has been released regarding the official display line and its separation from the crowd line.

It is, however, clear that the required separation was not there from the beginning. The spectators were lined up along both sides of the airfield, limiting options for evasive action by the pilots.

A commercial pilot who worked at the airfield later told the Ukrainian Weekly that the air show was moved from the field's opposite end at the last minute. He also claimed that another pilot who was supposed to perform that day opted out, citing inadequate preparation.

The air show was dangerous.

The pilots infringed on whatever separation had been planned between crowd and display (if any) from the start. An aerobatic pilot viewing a video of the aircraft said that it looked as though the manoeuvre was planned to be parallel to the crowd line but instead was performed heading towards the spectators.

Nevertheless, the show went on. And at 12:45, less than a minute later, it went wrong.

Control: "Turn."

Co-Pilot: Turn out [expletive]!!!!

The SU-27 came out of a roll while the aircraft was still descending at high speed.

Control: Take the plane out of the manoeuvre!

Control (another voice): Take plane out of manoeuvre, add revs!

Control (first voice): Full power.

Cockpit warning: Angle of attack critical.

Cockpit warning: Experiencing hypercritical G-loads.

Control (second voice): Full power!

As the flight crew desperately attempted to climb, the left wing dropped and clipped a tree.

12:45: 18 Cockpit recording ends.

The aircraft hit the ground and skidded towards the apron. It struck an Il-76 transport aircraft and then cartwheeled into the crowd as the fuel exploded into a giant fireball. Sharp fragments and burning jet fuel sprayed into the crowd.

Veteran pilot Serhii Senyk remembered watching through a video camera as the Su-27 surged low above the spectators, rattling their eardrums and bodies. The plane looped into the air and prepared for another descent when it clipped its wing against a birch tree on the horizon.

"I knew that was it," Mr. Senyk said. "I dropped my camera and my first thought was my wife and son." In the next seconds, the careening plane cartwheeled and clipped four rows of barbed wire fence, dragging them across the field of spectators like a human mower before exploding into flames.

"This was covered with human meat," Mr. Senyk said, staring at the wide concrete road on the Sknyliv airfield. "It was hell." He ran to where he left his wife and child, only to see they were gone. He left the Sknyliv airfield that day with his two surviving sons.

—From the Ukrainian Weekly
Volume 75 No. 31–5 August 2007

Although the news reports at the time said that the pilots ejected early, investigators discovered that they actually ejected one second *after* the aircraft impacted. Amazingly, they survived. Seventy-seven bystanders, there to spend a summer day watching the air force show off, did not.

A further 543 were injured, with a hundred needing hospitalisation for injuries and burns. Twenty-seven children died in the collision. Thirteen children lost at least one parent, while three children lost both.

Yuri Motuziuk, was left an orphan, alive and alone on the airport tarmac, covered in ash and soot and crying after the debris and the jet fuel fireball killed his parents, an image carried by television around the world. Petro Mykhailiv lost his son, Andrii, 32, his stepdaughter, Natalia, 31, and two granddaughters, Andrianna and Natalya, aged 6 and 8. The elder Mykhailiv had a heart attack at the morgue while identifying their remains. Bohdan Onyshchak lost his

11-month-old granddaughter, Yaryna, her father, 25
year-old Oleh and another son, Yurii, 23.

—From the Ukrainian Weekly]
August 4, 2002, No. 31, Vol. LXX

Two days after the accident, the Prosecutor-General stated that
the pilots had used an illegal flight path and that Ukraine's air force
commander had been relieved of duty and detained along with two
other officers involved in the planning, calling it an issue of military
negligence.

There were many incidents when criminal negligence came
into play, when several heads of Ukraine's air force acted
criminally. . . . We believe that the pilots were given the
wrong task with violations of safety procedure."

But he went on to blame the pilots, noting "signs of criminal
offence".

"They used this vehicle incorrectly," he said, adding they
could either be detained or put under house arrest pending
the outcome of the investigation.

—From BBC News report
29 July 2002

"The Ukrainian president spoke out against the air show, saying,
"How is it possible to understand when the army, working with
insufficient funds, completing difficult work for our countrymen,
spends its money not on raising the defence capability of the state,
but on an entertainment show? I want to note that the guilty must

be punished. And just those, those with direct and full responsibility for the tragedy. Not the second-class, little men."

The secretary of National Security and Defence Council was asked to head a special investigative commission to determine the causes of the crash. At the announcement of his appointment, he told reporters that he would examine at least seven possible scenarios to determine whether pilot error or technical problems had caused the crash and that all possibilities that could exist were still under consideration, including terrorism. In the same interview, he then said, "There were several things the pilots should have done, according to procedures, which they did not." He expected to have a conclusion within two months.

The investigators announced almost immediately that the issue was that the pilots had tried to complete a risky aerobatic manoeuvre at too low an altitude. The pilot made a straight vertical descent to 200 meters above the ground before finally attempting to take the aircraft back up in a failed manoeuvre that led to the crash. They discovered that faulty maintenance had in fact left the left engine's RPM lower than it should be; however this was dismissed as not relevant to the accident. "The plane was responsive and entirely under the pilots' control."

Both pilots were accused of attempting manoeuvres that they were not experienced with, although local press said that they had performed the same manoeuvres at previous air shows, including Le Bourget. The pilots also came under fire for reacting too slowly to the automated warnings in the cockpit.

Meanwhile the pilots stated that the flight map they received did not match the actual air show layout. This appears clear by their initial confusion on the radio when they began the show but were unable to find the crowd line. The chief pilot, who was responsible for the flight, also argued that he had requested additional training flights at Sknyliv airfield so that they could practise on site, but the request was denied as too expensive.

The Ukrainian president blamed the military and dismissed the head of the Air Force; however the investigation appeared to be centred on the pilots. Initially, the spokesperson for the investigation stated that he wanted to know why no general rehearsal took place but this issue doesn't appear to have been followed up on, despite the captain's defence that he'd requested the opportunity to practise on the airfield and been denied. The Prosecutor-General said in a news conference that the crash investigation had found "circumstances testifying to criminal negligence and careless treatment of responsibilities by officials". But at that same news conference, he blamed the pilots specifically for what he hinted was a criminal offence.

The official report was completed at the end of 2002. Although the details were not publicly released, the investigation reported the cause of the crash as pilot error. A contributing factor was that the spectators were allowed too close to the air display.

The two pilots of the Soviet-era jet were arrested on various charges, including failure to properly prepare for the event with a practice drill at the Sknyliv site and for performing their stunts over the crowd, which is expressly prohibited by law. Several high-ranking Ukrainian navy generals were relieved of command as well. Minister of Defense Oleksander Shkidchenko also submitted his resignation, which President Kuchma did not accept.

—From The Ukrainian Weekly
January 12, 2003, No. 2, Vol. LXXI

In January 2003, the case was turned over to the court.

On the 24th of June, 2005, the two pilots, two senior military officials and a flight security official were jailed. The officials were blamed for failing to stop the flight in time and for failing to secure a sufficient security zone. The pilots were found guilty of failing to follow orders, negligence and violating flight rules. The pilot was sentenced to fourteen years in prison and his co-pilot was sentenced to eight. The head of flight operations received six years and his deputy head of flight operations received five. The safety director received a four-year suspended sentence and the commander of the military division was acquitted on the grounds that technical issues did not cause the crash.

In addition to the jail sentences, the pilot was fined 7.2 million hryvnia ($1.42 million; €1.18 million) and the co-pilot 2.5 million hryvnia.

The court awarded the equivalent of $200,000 US to be paid to the families of the victims who died and a lesser compensation for those who were injured.

Most relatives weren't even aware of how the court determined the damages, and they complained the awards were relatively meager.

"Ten thousand hryvni—is that money? It's not even $2,000 (U.S.)," said Irene Reshetilova, whose grandson, a 4-year-old American citizen named Nikita Bastrakov, suffered psychological damage during the Sknyliv tragedy.

"(Relatives of) those who died received either 35,000 or 200,000 hrv ($7,000 or $40,000)," Ms. Reshetilova said. "We don't understand their grading system."

Her grandson has sleep and speech disorders that need medical attention, for which the compensation has been inadequate, she said.

"The child was lying on dead bodies," Ms. Reshetilova said. "He saw heads. It affected his mental development. I had an entirely healthy child."

—From the Ukrainian Weekly
July 3, 2005, No. 27, Vol. LXXIII

The chief pilot denied responsibility for the deaths and immediately announced his plans for appeal, arguing that the crash was the result of technical problems and a faulty flight plan. The three judges and the prosecutor were all employees of the Ministry of Defence. The chief pilot claimed that the verdict was based on the government investigation which was targeted with creating a scapegoat.

"I'm accused of an error in flying technique and that I lost control of the flight," he said. "The former was not proved. There are documents saying that there was no violation in the maneuver. The latter could be proved by an objective review. But it was held illegally and examined by people interested in my imprisonment.

—From the Ukrainian Weekly
July 3, 2005, No. 27, Vol. LXXIII

In 2008, the Supreme Court of Ukraine rejected an appeal to challenge the not-guilty verdict for four ex-generals of the Air Force.

The appeal argued that they were involved in the organisation of the air show and therefore culpable.

According to the Zakhidna Informatsiyna Korporatsiya, the head of flight operations, was pardoned after serving two years. His deputy was released after three years, for exemplary behaviour. The safety director with the suspended sentence still works in the air force. The co-pilot had his sentence reduced to three and a half years and was released in 2008.

In 2012, the chief pilot was still serving time in a Kyiv Oblast penal colony, where he did farming work to pay off his 7.2-million-hryvnia fine.

He was released at the end of 2013 after serving eight years, under the conditions that he report in once a month. He is banned from driving any kind of vehicle, including a bicycle. He commutes to work on roller-blades. He has also begun development on a full fighter simulator, in an effort to help Ukrainian pilots with the endemic lack of proper training in the Air Force. The Ministry of Defence believes that only 10% of the Air Force pilots are currently competent for combat flight.

In a Ukrainian interview at the end of his prison term, the chief pilot repeated that he was not to blame.

> From the mission briefing it is obvious that flight area parameters we were given significantly exceeded the safe margin of separation from spectators. What happened is the fault of organisers. Planes must not fly over spectators. During the show, I had to make several advanced manoeuvres in a few minutes. During the half-barrel, I noticed decreased thrust of both engines and the airspeed fell. But the cause remains unknown! Ground control ordered us to continue the flight. During the last manoeuvre—an oblique loop with a turn—the plane became

uncontrollable. During the trial they said it was caused by pilot error due to inexperience. I have 27 years in the cockpit with 2000 hours flying time. I was a member of the Ukrainian Falcons . . . To the last I struggled to lift the plane, [but] copilot Yury Egorov hit the catapult and we two ejected with our seats.

—"I carry no guilt; I've simply been made the scapegoat"
from *Facts* (Ukrainian Website) 20 September 2013
(translated by Anatoly Belilovsky)

The Sknyliv crash remains the worst air-show disaster of all time.

References

- BBC NEWS | World | Europe | Ukraine shell-shocked by air disaster—
  http://news.bbc.co.uk/1/hi/world/europe/2161661.stm

- BBC NEWS | World | Europe | Pilots blamed for Ukraine air disaster—
  http://news.bbc.co.uk/1/hi/world/europe/2159332.stm

- Владимир Топонарь: «За мной вины нет. Меня просто сделали козлом отпущения»—Газета «ФАКТЫ и комментарии»—
  http://fakty.ua/170017-vladimir-toponar-za-mnoj-viny-net -menya-prosto-sdelali-kozlom-otpucsheniya

- The Ukranian Weekly:
  http://www.ukrweekly.com/

- The Aviationist: Spitfire vs Bf 109 and F-14 vs Su-27: the difference is always the pilot—
  http://theaviationist.com/2013/05/31/ spit-vs-bf109-dogfighters/

- Ukraine Puts Mothballed Mig-29 Fighter Jets Back in Service / Sputnik International—
  http://sputniknews.com/military/20140404/ 189043839.html

Photography

- Ukrainian Sukhoi Su 27 by Oleg Belyakov
  *http://www.airliners.net/search/photo.search?
  photographersearch=Oleg%20V.%20Belyakov&
  distinct_entry=true*

SUICIDE BY PLANE

In the US, a student may not fly solo until their 16th birthday but training flights, where the instructor is the pilot-in-command, are possible. What better way to celebrate your 16th birthday than with your first solo flight!

The student pilot checked in at the school. He'd done 19 hours in the aircraft already and, that day, he was planning to work on traffic patterns. His flight instructor was just finishing up a previous lesson. He told the student to go ahead and do the pre-flight checks on the training aircraft and handed him the keys. The plane was a two-year-old Cessna 172R, a four-seater single engine aircraft commonly used for flight instruction.

This attracted some attention after the event, but it is absolutely standard. I remember that as a student pilot I was amazed and awed that I was given the full responsibility of verifying that the aircraft was airworthy. I was just a student, surely someone should be checking my work? But no, it is important that pilots understand from an early time that this responsibility belongs to the pilot and no one else. After a few weeks, it became commonplace.

Also, this student was trusted by the flying school. The FAA said that he often helped out by washing and fuelling aircraft as needed. Denying him access to the aircraft would not have made sense, especially as once he was 16, he would be expected to fly it on his own as a part of his licensing progress.

A lineman fuelling another aircraft saw the student walk to the Cessna with what he believes were the books for the aircraft. He recognised him as one of the students. He finished fuelling the aircraft and as he drove to his parking position, he saw the student remove the tie-downs, so presumed that the student must have previously completed his pre-flight checks. He parked the fuel truck about 50 feet (15 metres) from the Cessna.

As he got out of the fuel truck, he heard the aircraft engine turn over unsuccessfully. He walked towards the Cessna and was near the wing tip when the engine started running. The student applied power and started rolling forwards, most certainly not standard procedure. The aircraft turned left towards Taxiway A without making a call to Ground Control. It did not stop at the hold short line but entered runway 35R without permission and took off immediately.

The departure time was noted as 16:51.

The tower controllers were alarmed and immediately called out to the student pilot on frequency and also on the emergency frequency 121.5 MHz. They received no response. The Cessna climbed out and turned right towards the southeast. They notified Tampa approach and McDill Air Force Base.

16:52:40 Saint Petersburg Tower: I don't know if you can see him, a mile to our southeast is primary target, southeast bound. Do you show that on your radar, a primary target to our southeast?

16:52:48 Tampa West Satellite: I see, ah, I see something down there.

16:52:40 Saint Petersburg Tower: Okay, that's a Cessna departed here unauthorized. We don't know what he's doing, he just took off.

A local Coast Guard helicopter had just taken off when they heard that a Cessna had departed the airfield and was travelling towards the Air Force base.

The student had not spoken to anyone. The helicopter offered to help and were asked to try to verify the Cessna's intentions. The Cessna continued southeast and climbed to 3,700 feet as the helicopter set off in pursuit.

The Cessna entered McDill Air Force Base's restricted airspace and descended towards the tower. It flew past, in front of and below the tower windows, and then pulled up again. He then overflew two KC-135 tankers, passing less than a hundred feet above them. Northeast of the Air Force base, he turned crosswind as if attempting to return. The Coast Guard helicopter caught up to him.

They were now 14 miles (22 kilometres) from St. Petersburg-Clearwater International and the Cessna was heading northeast, towards downtown Tampa. The Coast Guard Helicopter flew alongside the Cessna at about 400–500 feet (120–150 metres) away. As they were only five miles (eight kilometres) from Peter O. Knight Airport, the crew gestured through the open side door that he should route there and land the aircraft.

The student pilot made eye contact and gestured back but the helicopter crew had no idea what the gesture meant, if anything. The Cessna did not deviate from its course. There wasn't much else they could do.

They called Tampa.

View of downtown St. Petersburg Florida from
Spa Beach Park by John O'Neill. Buildings
from left to right, Progress Energy Plaza (For-
merly Bank of America Tower), Florencia
Condos, The Ovation, Wells Fargo.

17:02:46 Coast Guard helicopter: Yes sir, we're currently in the
vicinity of Tampa General [unintelligible] chase to a single
Cessna [call sign] November Two Three Seven One November.
Been advised he took off from Saint Pete. It's a fifteen-year-
old student, took off with unauthorised clearance. We're
trying to give him hand signals to maybe get him to land at
Peter O Knight, however he doesn't seem to be responding
and, uh, we're just, we may impede on your airspace here,
sir.

Two F-15 combat jets were scrambled from Miami to intercept the aircraft but they arrived too late.

The Cessna continued northeast, now only 300 feet above downtown Tampa. At 17:03, it flew directly into the 28th floor of the 42-story Bank of America building.

The wings sheared off as the aircraft collided into the building. A woman was working on the floor where the plane struck. "Suddenly you're looking out into the open air, the blue sky, 28 floors up."

Air traffic control worked together to stop departures in the area, an attempt to clear the skies as much as possible while they worked out what was going on.

The student was dead on impact. Although the plane leaked fuel, there was no fire. No one else was hurt. When they opened the cockpit, they found a 2-page scrawled suicide note on his person.

I have prepared this statement in regards to the acts I am about to commit. First of all, Osama bin Laden is absolutely justified in the terror he has caused on 9-11. He has brought a mighty nation to its knees! God blesses him and the others who helped make September 11th happen. The U.S. will have to face the consequences for its horrific actions against the Palestinian people and Iraqis by its allegiance with the monstrous Israelis—who want nothing short of world domination! You will pay—God help you—and I will make you pay! There will be more coming! Al Qaeda and other organizations have met with me several times to discuss the option of me joining. I didn't. This is an operation done by me only. I had no other help, although, I am acting on their behalf.

Investigators found no evidence that he was connected to any terrorist groups at all.

I don't know why this is the bit that made me wince but when I read the analysis of the wreckage I realised: the boy had his seatbelt on.

The post-mortem confirmed that the pilot was not under the influence of alcohol or drugs. The cause of death was listed as "Lacerations of brain fractures of skull due to blunt impact to head." The manner of death was listed as suicide.

> The National Transportation Safety Board determined the probable cause(s) of this accident to be:
>
> The pilot's unauthorized use of an aircraft for the purpose of committing suicide."
>
> —From the official report

In the 20 years previous to this accident, 140 aircraft were stolen and then crashed. Of those, two others were determined to be suicides. A further 18 suicides took place in non-stolen aircraft: that is, the pilots either used their own aircraft or rented an aircraft. 2002 seems marked by these violent death-by-aircraft incidents but the question of what, if anything, can be done to save these pilots and their aircraft remains unanswered. It is certainly clear that airport security is not the critical factor.

Official Documentation

- Original accident report:
  *http://www.ntsb.gov/_layouts/ntsb.aviation/brief2.aspx?
  ev_id=20020110X00053&ntsbno=ATL02FA032&akey=1*

Other References

- Scan of the suicide note:
  *http://www.thesmokinggun.com/documents/crime/
  teen-pilots-suicide-note*

- ATC transcript at PIE and WSAT:
  *http://www.sptimes.com/2002/04/22/Worldandnation/
  transcript.shtml*

Photography

- View of downtown St. Petersburg by John O'Neill:
  *http://commons.wikimedia.org/wiki/File:Downtown_St._
  Petersburg_Florida_from_Spa_Beach_Park.JPG*

I HAVE CONTROL
AIR CHINA FLIGHT 129

CONTROLLED FLIGHT INTO TERRAIN (CFIT):
When seemingly competent pilots fly an aircraft into the ground.

Boeing's 2000 Statistical Summary of Commercial Jet Airplane accidents showed that out of the total of 7,282 fatalities, over 30% were caused by accidents classed as CFIT. Controlled Flight into Terrain can be relied upon to lead to many casualties and severe aircraft damage.

The majority of CFITs take place during take-off and landing. We know that accidents occur as a chain of events; there is rarely a single simple cause. This is why a stabilised approach is so critical: when coming into land, the aircraft configuration and approach path *must* be right, or else the approach should be broken off. Pilots are often tempted to continue; after all, nothing is seriously wrong. A bit of good flying will rescue the situation and land without mishap. It's only when we look at the statistics, and how critical accidents so often contain these minor issues: lack of a briefing, the crew in a rush to land and the approach outside of the specified range for speed or descent speed, that the picture becomes clear. An unstabilised approach, one where speed, descent rate or flight path are even just a little outside of normal limits, becomes clearly recognisable as a precursor for death and destruction.

On the 15th of April in 2002 at twenty past eleven, a Boeing 767-200 crashed into the side of a mountain. This is its story.

Air China Flight 129 was a scheduled passenger service from Beijing, China to Busan, Korea. Busan is served by Gimhae International Airport in Gangseo-gu. There were 155 passengers, eight flight attendants, and three flight crew on the plane.

The captain graduated from the Civil Aviation Flying University of China in 1994 and joined Air China. He had completed his captain upgrade training and was certified for Command in November, 2001. At the time of the accident, he had accumulated 6,497 hours of flight time, of which 6,287 hours were on the Boeing 767.

He was originally scheduled for a flight from Beijing to Moscow on the 12th of April but changed his schedule in order to take the National Airman English Test Level II. He arrived at Beijing the day before the flight where he met with the rest of the flight crew.

The first officer entered the Air Force Academy in 1989 and joined Air China in 1993. His first flight on the B767-200 was in February of 2002 and the accident flight in April was his third flight as first officer. He had accumulated 5,295 hours of flight time, 1,215 hours of which were in Boeing 767s.

The second officer graduated from the Civil Aviation Flying University of China in 1997 and soon thereafter was hired by Air China. He had accumulated 1,775 hours of flight time, 1,079 of which were on the Boeing 767.

All three flight crew passed the routine physical examination at Beijing and received the pertinent paperwork for their flight the following day.

At 08:37 Beijing local time 15 April 2002, Air China Flight 129 departed Beijing airport for Gimhae Airport.

It was just over three hours later when the flight crew began to prepare for their approach into Gimhae. All further times are given in Korean Standard Time, which was the local time at Gimhae Airport where the accident occurred.

At 10:50, the flight crew picked up the local weather and airport information time-stamped as Oscar (each subsequent update is called by the subsequent item in the ICAO spelling alphabet) using the automatic terminal information service (ATIS).

Gimhae international airport information Oscar, time at zero one two eight UTC, weather wind two three zero at six knots, visibility two miles rain fog, sky condition three octa five hundred, six octa one thousand, eight octa two thousand five hundred temperature one six, dew point one three, altimeter three zero zero zero, active runway three six left, advisory runway three six right or one eight left will be used as taxiway and parallel taxiway will be closed. Advise you have information Oscar.

—Weather Information 15 April on the
Automatic Terminal Service

10:50:17 Second Officer: "I can't hear it clearly."

10:50:25 First Officer: "I can't hear it clearly at all."

The ATIS information means the airport was suffering with rain and fog, with scattered low clouds, broken clouds at one thousand feet and fully overcast at 2,500 feet. The active runway was 36 (heading due north). Due to the bad sound quality, it's possible that the flight crew did not clearly understand the weather conditions that day. Certainly, the captain later seemed surprised that it was raining at the airport. They discussed the runway information and the first officer, who was pilot flying, conducted an approach briefing for the Instrument Landing System (ILS) approach to runway 36L.

During their discussion, the ATIS recording updated from information Oscar to information Papa.

The captain and the first officer had previously flown into Gimhae on runway 36 and the crew was experienced with ILS approaches. However, the second officer seemed concerned.

11:01:02 Second Officer: "I will do communicating, others keep listening, I came to Busan not too often."

This is an important statement: he was clearly asking the crew for help, by asking them to listen in on his radio calls. This attempt at crew coordination is an example of Crew Resource Management (CRM), which is a major focus of modern aviation research.

> "Crew coordination is the advantage of teamwork over a collection of highly skilled individuals. Its prominent benefits are:
>
> - an increase in safety by redundancy to detect and remedy individual errors; and
>
> - an increase in efficiency by organized use of all existing resources, which improves the in-flight management."
>
> —ICAO Doc 9683

In stressful conditions, there is a high risk that crew coordination will break down, which is why there is such emphasis on teamwork and efficient resource management at all stages of flight.

However, no one responded to the second officer's request for help. He handled all radio communications with Air Traffic Control (ATC) from that stage on.

11:06:53 First contact with Gimhae approach.

The approach controller instructed the aircraft to take heading 190 and descend to six thousand feet. At this stage, they were about 32 nautical miles northwest of Gimhae radar. They confirmed they had information Papa from the ATIS and were told to expect a straight-in approach to runway 36.

Air China Boeing 767-2J6/ER *(Photo by Alain Durand at Beijing)*

However, at this point, the wind began to turn.

The approach controller's Automatic Meteorological Observation System (AMOS) display showed signs of a tailwind along runway

36L. This meant that inbound aircraft would be landing with the wind coming from behind them, which is a problem.

The approach controller contacted Air China 129 to ask their approach category.

An aircraft will get clearance for an instrument approach procedure. The aircraft category is based on the aircraft's stall speed when configured for landing. A small single engine aircraft is usually category A. Airline jets are commonly category C and large jets are typically category D.

It's standard practice for the air traffic controller to ask the aircraft's category. The approach category tells the air traffic controller the aircraft's final approach speed (Vref). This way, he knows whether it is safe to issue approach clearance based on current weather conditions.

The Boeing 767 is an odd aircraft because the approach category varies by model and by configuration, so it can be either category C or Category D. The landing speed varies by just a few knots but it is just enough to change its category.

In accordance with the ICAO standard, the definition of aircraft category is based on 1.3 times stall speed in the landing configuration at maximum certificated landing mass.

Category "C"—Indicated air speed is 224 km/hour (121 knots) or more but less than 261 km/hour (141 knots)

Category "D"—Indicated air speed is 261 km/hour (141 knots) or more but less than 307 km/hour (166 knots)

—From the English translation of the official report

In a standard landing configuration for a straight-in approach, the B767-200 has a final approach speed of 137 knots, which means it is classified as approach category C as in Charlie.

11:08:50 Gimhae approach controller: Air China 129, request approach category

11:08:55 Second officer: Please say again.

11:08:57 Approach controller: Air China 129, request approaching category.

11:09:01 The first officer tells the second officer, "Approach category Charlie".

11:09:02 Second Officer: What?

11:09:06 Second officer: Charlie, Air China 129.

11:09:10 Approach controller: Air China 129, roger copy, this time active runway change one eight right, wind 210 at 17 knots, expect circling approach one eight right.

Now, here's where it gets messy. At this point, the ATIS information was updated to information Quebec, notifying all aircraft of the change in runway direction and that a circling approach to runway 18 is required. The ATIS also announced that the airport was now closed to *all aircraft in approach category D*.

The reason the circle to land approach is limited by category is because a tight turning radius is needed in order to execute the circling approach. Aircraft in category C are able to circle within a radius of 1.7 nautical miles from the centre of the threshold of runway 18. Aircraft in category D will circle with a radius of 2.3 nautical miles. It's all about the turning circle.

A *circle-to-land approach* is a non-precision approach, which requires the flight crew to have the airfield in sight at all times. At Gimhae, an aircraft in approach category D would have to fly much higher to avoid the high terrain north and east of the airfield. To remain clear of terrain, the category D aircraft would not be able to descend below 1,100 feet.

On this day, the airfield was covered with low cloud. The circle-to-land approach was not available for approach category D because it was impossible for an aircraft to both avoid the mountains and keep the airfield in sight. Only aircraft able to maintain a tight turning circle would be able to keep clear of the rising terrain.

The other important note is that the circle-to-land approach requires a slightly different configuration of the aircraft: the flaps are set to 20 degrees instead of 30 degrees. As a result, the stall speed is higher, which means the VRef is higher.

In the B767-200 with flaps 20, the indicated airspeed would be around 145 knots, placing it into approach category D.

So the crew were in an odd situation where their B767-200 aircraft was category C for the straight-in approach; however, now that the wind had changed and runway 18 had a circle-to-land approach, the B767-200 was a category D.

And because of the bad weather, the airfield had just closed to category D traffic.

But no one knew. The controller did not specify the circle-to-land approach until *after* he'd confirmed the approach category. None of the crew commented on the change of runway, nor that the circling approach might change the approach category. The controller did not mention that the ATIS information had been updated, nor did he ever mention that the airport was now closed to approach category D.

Even if the controller had clarified the situation, it might not have made a difference. As a part of the investigation, they discovered that neither the air traffic controllers nor the captain knew that the approach category is defined by indicated airspeed. I have to admit, it's the first time I've heard of an aircraft changing approach category based on the type of approach, rather than simply by aircraft type. Nevertheless, I would expect the crew in charge of the Boeing 767-200 to know this fact about their own aircraft.

In any event, the controller asked the question one more time.

11:09:29 Approach controller: Air China 129, confirm your category is Charlie or Delta?

11:09:35 Captain (in cockpit): Charlie.

11:09:36 Second Officer: Charlie, Air China 129, Charlie.

11:09:39 Approach controller: Air China 198, roger.

At this stage, they needed to reconfigure for the new approach for runway 18R. The first officer read out that the Minimum Decision Altitude (MDA) was seven hundred feet, but other than that, no approach briefing to confirm the navigation details of the approach was done.

The flight crew had prepared for a straight-in instrument approach to runway 36L. Now everything had changed. They needed to fly a completely different, non-precision approach which they had not prepared for. None of the flight crew had ever flown this approach at Gimhae before.

Taken somewhat unawares, the flight crew discussed the change in plans but did not do a full approach briefing. Specifically, there was no mention of crew coordination nor of urgent issues which should be watched for. The aircraft was not reconfigured for the circling approach. Standard call-outs were skipped. Everything started happening way too fast.

11:12:27 Captain: We won't enlarge the traffic pattern, the mountain is all over that side.

> The captain testified that his plan for the circling approach was to visually identify the runway on the final approach course to 36L, then turn 45° left to the heading of 315°, fly for 20 seconds and turn right onto the downwind leg parallel with the runway direction (heading 360°), then after passing abeam the north end of the runway, time 20 seconds outbound for the base and final turns to landing.
>
> —From the English translation of the official report

11:12:27 Captain: It's raining. We didn't receive any information on rain?

The captain's surprise at the weather is the first clear sign of mental overload and lack of crew coordination. The ATIS recording clearly stated to expect rain and fog. Neither the first officer nor the second officer corrected him.

11:14:47 Captain: I'll take off my sunglasses, let my sight adjust to the outside, the visibility is not so good.

The aircraft descended to 2,600 feet and turned left heading 090.

11:16:33 Approach controller: Air China 129, turn left heading 030, cleared for ILS DME [distance measuring equipment] runway 36 left, then circle to runway 18 right, report field in sight.

He was asking the flight crew to turn left and follow an instrument approach to 36, as per their original flight plan. Then they should execute the circle for the approach to runway 18-R. He further asked them to let him know as soon as they had the runway in sight through the clouds and fog.

The second officer should have repeated the key information in the clearance to confirm that the flight crew understood. Instead he mumbled his way through a partial read-back, "Turn left heading 030, cleared [unintelligible] approach 18 right, Air China 129."

The captain corrected him, saying "circle to land." The first officer repeated the clearance in the cockpit for him: "Cleared for ILS approach 36 left, and then circle to land 18 right, report runway in sight." The second officer snapped, "OK, OK, I understand, circle to land 18 right, turn left 030."

At this point the flight crew were still flying a precision approach on the Instrument Landing System (ILS). They were to get the runway in sight before starting the circling approach, and they were to keep visual contact with the runway throughout. If they lost sight of the airport, the pilot was *required* to break off the approach.

Flight 129 initiated the circling approach using the minima for category "C" circling approach, with a Minimum Descent Altitude (MDA) of 700 feet and minimum visibility of 3.2 km.

According to the captain's testimony, he had no experience with the circling approach at Gimhae airport, and the circling approach training on B767 aircraft used only Beijing airport. Since Gimhae airport was not classified as a special airport requiring an additional training, the captain was probably unaware of the danger posed by terrain in the vicinity of the circling approach area north of the runway during the circling approach.

—From the English translation of the official report

11:17:30 Captain: Do we have to maintain this altitude?

The first officer replied. "Do not maintain, continue down to 700 feet." Then he added, "Too strong wind, gear down?"

Two seconds later, the landing gear was extended. The captain acknowledged gear down and asked for flaps set to 20, which is standard for the circling approach and part of the configuration which put the B767-200 into approach category D. The aircraft was now flying faster and with a wider turning circle than the circling approach allows for in low visibility.

11:18:39 The captain confirmed that he had the runway in sight.

Two minutes later, the second officer reported the runway in sight. At this point the aircraft altitude was 952 feet, airspeed 158 knots and ground speed 187 knots.

11:18:44 Approach controller: Air China 129, contact tower one eighteen point one, circle west.

Second Officer: Circle, circle, 18 right, Air China 129.

At no point did the approach controller comment on the partial read-backs or do anything to verify that his instructions were understood. When listening to the recordings, the Chinese officials felt that the request to contact the tower was unclear. At any rate, none of the flight crew said anything about contacting the Tower.

The first officer stated, "I have control," disconnected the autopilot and flew manually.

The aircraft descended to 700 feet

11:18:55 Captain: OK, maintain 700 feet, watching the altitude.

Earlier that day, an inbound pilot reported the cloud base at 500 feet. A pilot who landed after the accident reported the cloud base at 600–700 feet. But no one on the flight deck of Flight 129 mentioned the clouds at all.

The Boeing 767 was at 672 feet, airspeed 158 knots with a left bank heading of 16.7°. The maximum speed for a category C aircraft is 140 knots.

The aircraft should have made a standard 45° turn to the left to enter downwind, so that they would be travelling alongside the runway (with a flight track parallel to it) at a set distance away from it.

Instead, the first officer made a shallow turn (somewhere between 5° and 19°). The captain did not correct the bank angle nor mention the width of the pattern nor discuss a time check. As a result of the shallow turn, the speed and the wind, the circling approach was already off track.

The tower controller had not heard from Flight 129 at all. He had the aircraft briefly in sight at the midpoint of the downwind leg and called out to them twice, with no response. He then contacted the approach controller on a direct line to ask him to talk to Flight 129 again and ask them to change to the tower frequency.

11:19:17 Captain: "20 seconds," and then, "Keep watching the runway."

Twenty seconds referred to the time check for the second turn into the base leg.

Having flown parallel to the runway, the pilots must watch for the runway end on their right. When the plane is lined up with the end of the runway (abeam), the timer starts. At the end of the twenty seconds, the aircraft needs to turn right, into the base leg.

Based on simulator data, Flight 129 would have overshot the final approach course based on their current flight pattern. They were flying so close to the runway, it would have been difficult for the crew to confirm the runway visually during the turn. Their indicated airspeed was 158 knots as they passed abeam, with a groundspeed of 177 knots.

The correct decision would have been to break off the approach and start over. Yet no one on the flight deck said a thing.

11:19:52 The approach controller repeated his earlier request: "Air China 129, contact tower, one eighteen one." This time, the second officer attempts a read-back: "Contact tower one two one . . . one one eight decimal one, good day, Air China 129."

11:20:00 Three things happened at once:

- The captain asked, "Can you see abeam end of runway?" and the first officer replied, "Abeam runway end."

- The primary local controller called on the emergency frequency, "This is Gimhae tower on guard, Air China 129, if you hear me, contact one one eight point one."

- The aircraft passed abeam the far end of the runway downwind. The twenty-second count down began at 11:20:02

11:20:13 First Officer: The wind is too strong; it is very difficult to fly.

At the same time, the second officer finally reported on tower frequency 118.1. This transaction should have happened at the beginning of the pattern. In this critical stage of flight, the crew's workload was high and the radio contact was adding to the stress.

11:20:15 Thirteen seconds into the twenty-second countdown, the captain announced, "Turning base," apparently directing the first officer to start the turn.

11:20:17 Fifteen seconds in, the captain said, "I have control" and took over as pilot flying.

Critical for this stage of the pattern are: correct indicated airspeed and altitude, continuous visual contact with the airfield and a timely base turn.

11:20:22 Twenty seconds have elapsed. The aircraft had not yet initiated the base turn. In fact, the flight data recorder showed a slight heading change to the left, which was probably the captain trying to widen the pattern from the bad downwind turn.

11:20:24 First Officer: "Turn quickly, not too late!"

11:20:25 The tower controllers issued the landing clearance but mentioned that they don't have the aircraft in sight. This clearance should have been given well before the base turn in order to spread the workload.

11:20:33 The distracting instructions from the controllers got worse: the initial controller accidentally cleared Flight 129 to runway 36L and the secondary controller then corrected this clearance to runway 18R.

In the Civil Aviation Administration of China (CAAC) response to the investigation, the Chinese investigators stated:

> According to the regulations specified in Chapter 4 Paragraph 8 "Precautions for Radio Communication", ROK Air Force textbook Air Traffic Control Management (5–345): "When aircraft is in the final approach, touchdown, landing run, missed approach and initial takeoff ascending phase, it is the time that needs a pilot to concentrate his mind. Therefore, the controller should minimize all the communications as much as possible, provided they are not necessary control instructions. However, it should be ready to issue the information that has affected on safety of aircraft, such as to confirm or notify the airport conditions."
>
> After issuing the landing clearance, the tower controller had not issued any direct safety alert to CA 129, and on the contrary, four times communications irrelevant to the safety alert were made with the flight crew, which distracted the crew's attention. **If the controller had thought it was necessary to communicate with the flight crew, he would have cautioned the crew to watch carefully the mountainous terrain, or to issue a direct safety alert.**
>
> —From the English translation of the official report

The captain should have focused on the base turn and then asked the controllers to repeat the clearance afterwards. But he paused to listen to the instructions and he did not initiate the turn.

11:20:37 The captain disconnected the autopilot and finally began the delayed base turn. His bank angle was 5–15 degrees, rather than the standard 25 degrees. Not until 11:20:42, *forty seconds* after the time check started, did the aircraft finally pass through 360 degrees to the south.

Flight 129 entered the base turn 1.1 nautical miles outside of the protection area for category "C". The aircraft was at the minimum descent altitude (MDA) for category "C" in order to clear terrain, flying at 700 feet above mean sea level.

During the second half of the base turn, Flight 129 entered into cloud. They had no visibility of the runway or the ground.

> Since the base turn was flown manually, the captain would have had to consign much of his attention to the attitude indicator and aircraft control, in addition to keeping external references and the runway in sight, which would have placed him under twofold workload. Therefore, it would have been difficult for him to become aware of the situation outside the aircraft.
>
> That may explain why he did not call the first officer for the completion of the landing checklist after the flaps were set to 30°, thereafter, with the second officer's incorrect reply to the tower transmission being left uncorrected, and why he did not later remember the contents of the exchanges with the tower.
>
> —From the English translation of the official report

11:20:41 The secondary controller saw Flight 129 fly into the cloud and asked, "Can you landing?"

The tower controller knew there was high terrain near the base turn area and must have been worried that the aircraft couldn't keep the runway in sight as a part of the circling approach. He wanted to know if the flight crew intended to continue their approach to land. His phrasing is non-standard and difficult to understand.

At the same time, the *Minimum Safe Altitude Warning* (MSAW) displayed on the radar display. However, Gimhae ATC was used to false MSAW alerts because of a limitation of the settings. No one in the tower paid any attention to the warning that the aircraft was dangerously low. They were completely focused on the non-standard pattern for the circle-to-land approach.

The approach controller used the intercom to ask the tower controller, "Does it seem to go around?"

He did not receive a response and he did not follow-up. Neither did he ask the flight crew what they were doing.

At the same time, the second officer replied to the tower controller, "Roger, QFE three thousand, Air China 129."

This was not a sensible response to the question asking whether they could land safely. Although it has to be said, *any* answer other than, "No, we're going around" was the wrong one.

The tower controller tried to clarify by asking, "Air China 129, say again your intention," but there was no response.

11:20:54 First Officer: Pay attention to the altitude.

11:20:57 Captain: Assist me to find the runway.

11:20:59 First Officer: It's getting difficult to fly, pay attention to the altitude.

This exchange was probably as they flew into the cloud and lost all visibility.

The controllers knew that Flight 129 was executing a turn near mountainous terrain and should have been in sight but wasn't. If they'd looked at the tower radar, they would have seen that Flight 129 was outside of the protection area. They would have spotted the Minimum Safe Altitude Warning (MSAW) visual alert several times. It would have been clear that the aircraft was perilously close to the mountains. Instead, they continued to search for the aircraft out the window.

In the event an MSAW is generated in respect of a controlled flight, the following action shall be taken without delay: a) if the aircraft is being provided with radar vectors, the aircraft shall be instructed to climb immediately to the applicable safe level and, if necessary to avoid terrain, be given a new radar heading; b) in other cases, the flight crew shall immediately be advised that a minimum safe altitude warning has been generated and be instructed to check the level of the aircraft.

—ICAO Document 4444, Para.15.6.4.2

Even without having seen the MSAW, they should have immediately issued a warning about the mountains or at least made it clear that Flight 129 was near high ground. All of the air traffic controllers on duty were totally focused on Flight 129 and yet they failed to offer clear advice or help; instead they distracted the flight crew with questions.

Having said that, the circle-to-land procedure at Gimhae is a non-precision approach which *requires* the flight crew to maintain visual contact with the runway and its environment. I suspect that part of the problem was that the controllers were convinced that the aircraft would break off its approach as it was now clearly in cloud.

They simply couldn't believe that an approach so badly wrong might continue.

11:21:05 Tower controller: Say position now.

The second officer started to reply with, "Air China 129, on base." The first officer interrupted his call, saying "Turn on final." The second officer resumed his call with "Turning on final, QFE three thousand, Air China 129."

At the same time, the captain asked the first officer if he could see the runway. "No, I cannot see out," replied the first officer.

In the investigation, the Gimhae tower duty chief said that the runway lights, approach lights and circling guiding lights for runway 18R were on at the time of the accident. The captain stated that although he saw the runway while on the downwind leg, he did not see any lights.

At the risk of repeating the obvious, the first officer should have reported losing sight of the runway the instant it happened. He should have stated that there was a problem the moment the aircraft flew into cloud. He should have called for a go around as soon as they deviated from the normal approach path.

The investigation team ran reconstructions of the event, using the same pattern, and found that breaking off the approach just six seconds before the impact would have cleared the mountain.

Only at the last minute, with no visual reference and well outside of the circle to land pattern, does the first officer do the right thing.

11:21:12 First Officer: Must go around.

If the captain had immediately responded, they still *might* have missed Mt Dotdae, which was directly in their flight path, hidden by the cloud.

But he didn't. The captain said that he planned to initiate a go-around after finishing the turn to final so that they were travelling in the direction of the runway and away from the mountains. So he continued the shallow turn.

He suddenly saw terrain in front of them through a gap in the clouds. The first officer shouted, "Pull up! Pull up!" That was the last thing the captain remembered.

The tower controller said, "Clear to land 18 right, Air China 129."

The flight data recorder logged that the captain did pull back on the controls but it was much too late.

11:21:17 The Cockpit Voice Recorder recorded the sound of the ground impact at 704 feet and then went dead.

The Boeing crashed into Mt Dotdae at an elevation of 204 metres above mean sea level (MSL), 4.6 kilometres from the runway threshold, completely outside of the protection area for both category "C" *and* category "D".

All items inside the aircraft fell down, seats were thrust forward, and all lights went out, making it dark inside the aircraft, except for light streaming in through the broken fuselage. There was fire erupting throughout the cabin, filling it with heavy smoke and making it difficult to breathe, and people were screaming. Most of the passengers briefly lost consciousness during impact, with feet and legs of some passengers stuck under the seats in front of them.

—From the English translation of the official report

A flight attendant came to with his body crushed underneath the wreckage. He crawled out of the cabin and shouted "Go, go," to passengers to get out of range of the burning aircraft, while someone helped to drag him away.

The captain has no memory of how he escaped from the cockpit.

Passengers crawled through gaps in the broken fuselage. Explosions sounded and there were pillars of fire and smoke shooting up from the exploding aircraft.

Time was of the essence.

11:21:17 The tower controller called on frequency to confirm the position of the aircraft. He called five times, with no response. A few minutes later, he switched to the emergency frequency and called for Flight 129 another ten times.

The crash was only 4.6 km from the threshold but the Tower controllers could not see it.

11:22 A local resident phoned the Gimhae fire department to say that he heard a loud explosion after seeing a plane fly by at low altitude. The first rescue team was dispatched.

This was the first notification for emergency services.

11:25 The tower controller used the tower hotline to inform Gimhae Air Force Base Operations of a lost communication situation. He then contacted the Gimhae Airport Flight Information Office. He did not state that this was an emergency or make it clear that an aircraft may have just crashed.

11:31 Two passengers who escaped the burning aircraft used their mobile phones to report the crash to the fire station.

11:40 Gimhae Air Force Base Operations contacted the fire department.

11:42 The tower controller contacted Incheon ACC to ask if they'd heard from the missing aircraft.

He clearly could not believe that Flight 129 was gone. Twenty minutes after losing contact, he still had not reported the crash and still had not declared an emergency. If he had looked at the flight's last known position on the radar, he would have been able to report the location and time of crash immediately.

11:43 The captain from the first rescue team requested helicopter rescue support.

11:43 The Gimhae Fire Station emergency situation room informed the Gimhae police station of the crash.

11:45 The tower controller used the crash-phone and bell in accordance with the emergency notification situation, almost 25 minutes after losing contact with Flight 129. If civilians hadn't contacted emergency services, this would have been their first notification.

11:58 The first rescue team arrived at the scene. They reported that it was raining and that the top half of the mountain was covered in thick fog.

When the rescue team from the Gimhae fire station arrived on the accident site through a trail behind the Dongwon [apartment building] located in Ginae-Dong, Gimhae, the fuselage was engulfed in flames, and there were continual explosions from the front of the fuselage, with pillars of fire rising. It was raining at the accident site, with the visibility of about 10 m due to a dense fog. They heard survivors' screaming for help from a distance, but they were not able to see them because the hill was thickly wooded, so they searched for survivors by clearing the forest.

—From the English translation of the official report

They are on the scene only because the local resident made a timely report of the accident. A total of 1,009 rescue workers and firefighters went to the scene.

The aircraft was completely destroyed. 8,000 square meters of forest was damaged on Mt Dotdae, including twelve gravesites.

12:12 The rescue teams from the Gimhae police station arrived on the scene.

The combat police unit #2502 received a mobilization instruction from the Gyeongnam Provincial Police Agency, and arrived on the accident scene from about 12:25, and began the rescue work. The total number of the police mobilized from the Gimhae police station, combat police unit #2502, surrounding area police stations and standing police units was approximately 2,000 on the day of the accident.

The Navy's third fleet command learned of the accident through the YTN broadcast about 12:00, arrived on the accident scene from about 14:00 on, and carried out the rescue work. The total number mobilized from the Navy's third fleet command was 226 on the day of the accident.

—From the English translation of the official report

Flight 129 carried three flight crew, eight flight attendants and 155 passengers.

The teams rescued 39 people. In the days after the accident, two of the rescued died as a result of their injuries. The captain, two flight attendants and 34 passengers survived the crash.

The crash site in the forest of Mt Dotdae

The Korean Aviation Accident Investigation Board (KAIB) concluded their 168-page report with the following probable causes.

---

1   The flight crew of flight 129 performed the circling approach, not being aware of the weather minima of wide-body aircraft (B767-200) for landing, and in the approach briefing, did not include the missed approach, etc., among the items specified in Air China's operations and training manuals.

2   The flight crew exercised poor crew resource management and lost situational awareness during the circling approach to runway 18R, which led them to fly outside of the circling approach area, delaying the base turn, contrary to the captain's intention to make a timely base turn.

3   The flight crew did not execute a missed approach when they lost sight of the runway during the circling approach to runway 18R, which led them to strike high terrain (mountain) near the airport.

4   When the first officer advised the captain to execute a missed approach about 5 seconds before impact, the captain did not react, nor did the first officer initiate the missed approach himself.

—From the English translation of the official report

Drafts of the report were sent to China (state of aircraft registry and operator) and the United States (state of design and manufacture of the aircraft) requesting comments. The comments submitted by the US National Transportation Safety Board (NTSB) were accepted and the report was revised to take them into account.

The comments submitted by the Civil Aviation Administration of China (CAAC) were not all accepted. Despite multiple technical meetings, the KAIB and the CAAC could not reach agreement. Thus, the final comments by the CAAC were added as an appendix to the official report.

The CAAC report agrees that the flight crew response and training were lacking. However, their argument focuses on the ATC failures and how they contributed to the workload on the aircraft, which can be clearly seen on the timeline. They also bring up the question of whether the runway and circling approach lights were actually on (the system was reset shortly after the accident so it is not possible to know for sure). They also argue that although Gimhae is classed as a "special airport class A" within Korean Flight Safety Regulations (which means that special training is required for captains who fly into the airport), this classification was not publicly available nor were the CAAC nor Air China notified. Certainly, Air China did not list Gimhae airport as a special airport, and no special training or flight experienced was required for Chinese pilots flying into Gimhae.

The focus of the report leads to a different combination for the causal factors of the accident.

3.2 Probable Causes

[The] Chinese investigation team believes that possible causes of the accident might be:

At the time of accident, weather condition was poor with low cloud, precipitation and low visibility. There was strong tailwind on the downwind leg and the mountainous area north of the airport was covered by cloud. The flight crew mishandled in performing the circling approach to runway 18R. The flight crew did not make the base leg turn at the proper time, thus led the aircraft to fly outside the circling approach protection area. The flight crew didn't execute miss approach when they lost the sight of the runway during the visual maneuvering of the circling approach.

When MSAW warning appeared on the radar display, the controller failed to provide safety warning to the flight crew; unintelligible frequency transfer instruction and frequent communication with the flight crew had an impact on the flight crew's operation of base turn and final approach.

—From the English translation of the CAAC report

The core issue here is whether the failure of the air traffic controllers was a causal factor or a contributing factor. It is obvious that there were issues with the air traffic control support and their use of available resources. It is clearly critical that the safety recommendations from the report include a hard look at Gimhae Air Traffic Control procedures and training.

When all the safety nets fail, the tragic outcome causes a lot of pointed fingers. Why did it fall to pieces, step by step?

The crash was Air China's first fatal one since its establishment 47 years ago. Air China has no record of any accidents prior to Flight 129.

The key here comes down to communication between Air Traffic Control and the pilot. However, it seems clear that the flight crew was not communicating properly among themselves, let alone ATC. The flight crew failed to switch to tower frequency when they were cleared for the circling approach. They also misunderstood and responded incorrectly to other ATC communications.

I would argue that other than approving the approach, there was nothing the air traffic controllers did that led the aircraft towards the mountain. I'm not surprised that the KAIB argued against this revision. However, the frustration of the CAAC is easily understood in the context of 2002 and the sudden focus on aviation in the Far East, which had previously been considered extremely safe.

Official Documentation

- Original accident report:
  http://dlps.nanet.go.kr/SearchDetailView.do?cn=
  MONO1200511924

Other References

- Accident report translated into English:
  http://web.archive.org/web/20061017200424/
  152.99.129.24/eng/board/view.jsp?id=4

Photography

- Unattributed photographs are taken directly from the accident
  report.

- B-2552 photographed by Alain Durand
  http://cdn-www.airliners.net/aviation-photos/photos/8/4/
  9/0669948.jpg

Exploding Passenger

In the West, we talk about 9/11 as the tragedy that changed aviation security forever. However, in China, the tragic accident where the public feel that everything changed happened half a year later on the 7th of May 2002. The events of that day, now simply referred to as 5.7, opened everyone's eyes to how a single man could deliberately use an aircraft with tragic consequences. That same incident changed airport security forever.

The stunned public struggled to understand this tragedy, which happened just twenty two days after the Air China Flight 129 crash at Gimhae. The exact details of the accident were never released. For this analysis, I've had to rely on the popular press—an ironic position for me to be in: so many of my articles have been written in order to *correct* media presentation and now I have to rely on it.

On the 7th of May, 2002, China Northern Airlines Flight 6136 crashed into the bay near Dalian Zhoushuizi International Airport.

The airline situation in China can be a bit confusing. China Northern Airlines was one of the six airline corporations formed after the Civil Aviation Administration of China (CAAC) airline operations were divided in 1987. Each airline division was named after the region of China where it had its hub. The CAAC remained in place as a government agency and no longer provided any commercial flight service (it's now a part of the Ministry of Transport). China Northern Airlines has since merged with China Southern Airlines.

China Northern Airlines McDonnell Douglas
MD-82 *(Photo by Torsten Maiwald)*

The airline had their headquarters at Dongta Airport in Shenyang. Their total fleet consisted of eight Airbus A300s, six Airbus A321s, 27 McDonnell-Douglas MD-80 series and 13 McDonnell-Douglas MD-90 series. The majority of the fleet was transferred to China Southern Airlines when the airlines merged in 2003. Two were sold to other airlines and two were written off.

China Northern Airlines had been involved in an incident just one month earlier, where a man attempted to hijack one of their MD-82 aircraft on a domestic night flight from Dalian to Yangji via Shenyang. Nine minutes after takeoff, a male passenger grabbed a cabin-crew member and threatened her with a knife. He demanded that the flight divert to South Korea. In-flight security personnel and passengers quickly managed to overpower him. The flight landed safely at Shenyang, where the aircraft was surrounded by a hundred armed police who stormed the aircraft and arrested the man. The flight continued to Yangji and arrived just two hours after schedule.

China Northern Airlines flight 6136 was a scheduled domestic flight from Beijing Capital International Airport to Dalian Zhoushuizi International Airport. Dalian is the southernmost city of Northeast China, at the tip of the Liaodong peninsula.

The aircraft was a McDonnell Douglas MD-82: a twin-engine medium range commercial jet airliner. The airline had 27 McDonnell-Douglas MD-80 series purchased between 1988 and 1995 (one was written off in 1993). The accident aircraft, registration B-2138, was delivered to China Northern Airlines in 1991 and had logged 26,000 flight hours. It was one of 35 MD-80 series jets which had been assembled from kits in Shanghai.

The 7th of May was the end of the Labour Day Golden Week, one of three week-long holidays celebrated in China at that time. Millions of domestic travellers had toured the country and many airlines laid on extra flights. The majority of the passengers on flight 6137 were Dalian residents travelling back to work after their break.

The aircraft departed Beijing at 20:37 local time with one hundred and three passengers on board. The initial flight proceeded normally with an expected arrival at Dalian at 21:40.

The aircraft was approaching its destination when it first became clear that something was wrong. At 21:20 local time, the captain contacted Dalian requesting an emergency landing, reporting a fire in the cabin. The weather was clear and there was no report of any aircraft failure before the emergency call reporting the fire.

Four minutes later, the aircraft lost contact and disappeared from all radar. One hundred and three passengers and nine crew members were lost.

The first clue as to what happened was a report from a boat fishing in the bay near Dalian. He reported that "a plane with fire and smoke crashed into the sea, broken in two parts". Search and rescue teams were notified at 21:40 and over 30 vessels were immediately mobilised to the crash site in the bay, 20 km (12 miles) east of Dalian airport.

Rescue teams discovered a food trolley, burned black and broken in half, floating among the wreckage along with signs of an intense on-board fire.

It took a week to find the cockpit voice recorder. The flight data recorder was also recovered a few hours later. The recordings didn't explain what had happened, only that there was no warning and no record of a mechanical failure that could have contributed to such a rapid crash.

A fire in an aircraft is one of the most dangerous situations that a flight crew can encounter and, once a fire has become established, it's almost impossible to extinguish. In 2002, the UK CAA analysed data from aircraft fires and found on average that the flight crew had just under twenty minutes from the first indication there is a fire on board to the situation becoming "unsurvivable".

Aircraft fires usually start as an electrical fire or as an engine fire. However, the data confirmed that neither of these was the culprit. The voice data showed that the crew were immediately aware of the rear cabin fire and their emergency response was immediate and methodical. However, the quick burning fire was burning too fiercely. They never had a chance to extinguish the flames before the aircraft crashed into the bay.

No official accident report has been released to the public. The final report was completed at the end of 2002 and the conclusions made in the report were passed on to the Xinhua News Agency, who published them on the 8th of December, 2002. Only summary information was reported, without any investigative details. Officials stated that as the investigation showed that a crime had been committed, the details should not be released or published, in order to prevent people with ulterior motives learning insider information. As a result, only the conclusions were published. Similar decisions have been made in the US and UK where terrorist activity has been suspected.

Xinhua Headline

头条新闻

北航大连 "5·7" 空难原因查清：乘客纵火

(2002-12-07 09:45:06　稿件来源：新华网)

长达4米的飞机残骸上 "中国北方航空公司" 的标志清晰可见。（资料照片）

Xinhua published the conclusions made as a
part of the official investigation *(From Xinhua
News Agency)*

Nevertheless, it is somewhat frustrating to try to make sense of the accident, as we are reliant on the news reports on the time. Air China Flight 129's controlled flight into terrain was still in the headlines and the media reports were often scaremongering or inflammatory. Airline travel suddenly seemed a dangerous venture with two Chinese passenger planes lost in less than a month.

Forensic results on the passengers showed that most of the passengers died from carbon monoxide inhalation and were dead before the aircraft broke apart. Investigators analysed the deformation of the remnants to better understand the pattern of the fire. They knew they were not dealing with an "ordinary" fire because of the speed with which it spread. They found no signs of burning or explosion in any of the engines. The flight data recorder did not show any malfunction that would point to an electrical fire. There was no evidence of a galley fire in the ovens.

Although most of the aircraft was destroyed in the fire, the speed of the conflagration itself left evidence on the wreckage to show that the fire began in the rear cabin, which matched the flight crew report to ATC shortly before the crash.

The single position in the aircraft that showed the most burn damage, which investigators believed must be the origin of the fire, was a passenger seat near the middle of the aircraft. The passenger was a Chinese man named Zhang Pilin who had been on a business trip that day, leaving behind his wife and seven-year-old son.

The investigation had discovered where the fire had started but not how or why. Their attention turned to the passenger who held the seat. Zhang Pilin lived in Dalian with his wife and son. He had worked for a foreign trade company but resigned in 2001 to start his own decorating business, buying a house by the sea as his first renovation project. He had over a dozen employees in May 2002 and, although there were debts, there don't appear to be any debts out of the ordinary that he would have struggled to pay off.

That day, Pilin had flown from Dalian to Beijing, although his friends and family knew of no reason why he needed to be in Beijing. An internal report released to the press confirmed that he had bought two air insurance policies in Dalian before departure and then another five air insurance policies in Beijing.

Video surveillance showed that he spent several hours at Beijing airport, smoking cigarettes in the waiting hall.

His wife, who has claimed his innocence throughout, did not know that he was flying to Beijing and was unable to give any reason why he needed to go there that day.

Meanwhile, forensic testing was done on and around Pilin's seat to try to understand how the fire had started. Investigators soon had their answer when they discovered traces of gasoline.

Aircraft are manufactured from fire-resistant materials; however, gasoline makes for an immediate conflagration. In a horrific twist that even Pilin was unlikely to have planned, Pilin's seat was directly over the bus bar which led to the cockpit. This is a strip which allows for very high currents to be distributed along the aircraft. It seems likely that the explosive ignition of the gasoline fire damaged the cable bus. The flight crew had only two minutes to react to the fire, which almost immediately caused an aircraft command system failure. Within seconds of the fire raging in the cabin crew of the aircraft, the flight crew completely lost control of the aircraft. Within minutes it had crashed into the sea.

The newspapers reported that several water bottles filled with gasoline were found in Pilin's apartment but this was not mentioned in the Xinhua reporting of the official investigation results. The reported investigation conclusion did confirm that Pilin was on board with a few bottles of liquid which was believed to be the gasoline used to start the conflagration.

It seems odd now to think of him simply boarding the aircraft with a few bottles of gasoline but, at that time, passengers were allowed to carry two bottles of liquor on board with them. Airport security was focused on metal detectors to ensure that weapons were not taken on board.

It was four years later when British police uncovered a terrorist plot to detonate liquid explosives on board seven passenger aircraft travelling from the UK to the US. That plot led to security changes for carry-on items and the now generally accepted restrictions to the amount of liquids which passengers can take on board. Liquids and gels were not yet controlled as carry-on items.

However, there was never any published explanation of Pilin's motive. There were the inevitable media stories of Zhang as a suicidally depressed man with huge debts and/or a terminal illness, but none of these were confirmed by the government investigators. Public opinion on the case was strongly divided as a result of this, with conspiracy theories finding an easy foothold in the press and on the Internet. However, the government held fast that the evidence shown in the official report was itself a handbook to crime and that the details must remain confidential.

The insurance companies did not pay out on any of the policies purchased by Pilin.

As a result of this tragic event, which became known as "5.7", airport security was increased in airports in China and Hong Kong. Passengers were limited in taking liquids into the cabin, a security measure that wasn't adopted by the US and Europe until 2006. Screening methods directly after the accident included insisting that the passengers take a drink from any liquids they wished to carry on board.

In a bizarre twist, ten years after the crash, the British tabloid press accused two members of the Communist Party of having blown up the aircraft to kill the wife of a rival politician. However, the same articles also claimed that the crime was a mystery because the black box was never discovered, whereas government officials at the time made it quite clear that both the CVR and the FDR data had been recovered and were analysed as a part of the investigation.

There was a lot of skepticism in the Chinese media after the investigation results were published. Pilin did not appear to have any motive for suicide, let alone mass murder. He was married with a young son and lived a comfortable lifestyle running his own business. His wife told the press that he had phoned her from Beijing and promised her that he would talk to her when he returned.

That was the last she ever heard from her husband. To this day, she is sure that he died an innocent man.

Official Documentation

- Original accident report:
  http://www.fomento.gob.es/NR/rdonlyres/
  92DDBB9A-E936-42FC-A353-A2C7F39CE860/22834/
  2001_006_A2.pdf

Other References

- Xinhua News Agency: " '5-7' Crash Reasons Identified: Passenger Arson"
  http://news.xinhuanet.com/newscenter/2002-12/
  07/content_652361.htm

- UK CAA Paper 2002/01: A Benefit Analysis for Enhanced Protection from Fires in Hidden Areas on Transport Aircraft—
  http://www.skybrary.aero/bookshelf/books/210.pdf

- Zhang Pilin | Murderpedia, the encyclopedia of murderers—
  http://murderpedia.org/male.P/p/pilin-zhang.htm

Photography

- China Northern Airlines MD-82 taken by Torsten Maiwald:
  http://www.airliners.net/photo/China-Northern-Airlines/
  McDonnell-Douglas-MD-82/0220937/L

OUT OF THE FRYING PAN

W<small>HEN WE TALK</small> about Human Factors as a causative category, we mean an airworthy aircraft involved in an accident caused by decisions taken by people.

We distinguish between pilot error which is weather related and pilot error which is caused by or which leads to mechanical issues. In addition, we have another pool of human factor errors which can be caused by air traffic controllers, weather reporters and even operations staff at the home airport. All of these can lead to disruptions which threaten safe flight.

We usually categorise accidents based on which type of human factors came into play. In the incident of Crossair Flight 850, in which a Saab 2000 was written off, the correct category appears to be "all of the above".

The Bundesstelle für Flugunfalluntersuchung (the German Federal Bureau of Aircraft Accident Investigation, also known as BFU) released a detailed report on Crossair Flight 850 in both German and English. The sequence of events makes for a remarkable read, where just about every person involved could have reacted better. It is a textbook example of "Swiss cheese" theory: all the holes lining up and culminating in disaster, in this case leading to the wheels being ripped off of a Saab 2000 in a small airfield in Germany in visual conditions (with clear sight of the ground).. Every individual issue was minor. As they converge we can see how each action limited the options available to the flight crew.

On the 10th of July, a Saab 2000 and her crew were assigned at short notice to cover a scheduled Basel to Hamburg flight, which had been originally scheduled to be flown in an Embraer 145.

The flight crew had weather reports (METARs, TAFs, wind charts) valid to 18:00 UTC which showed that they could expect some thunderstorms en-route. They took on an additional 570 kg of fuel in case they had to wait out a thunderstorm over Hamburg, which they knew from experience could close the airfield for 20 to 30 minutes. There was no reason to expect any unusual or extreme weather based on the information the crew received. They felt perfectly well prepared for the flight.

However, a SIGMET (Significant Meteorological Information) was issued at 15:00 UTC for the Bremen region, including the flight's destination: a line of thunderstorms advancing northeast and extending up to flight level 380. The flight crew were involved in pre-flight preparation and never saw the SIGMET. They also had no idea about the additional warnings of thunderstorms for the area to the east of Bremen.

The flight departed at 16:09 UTC, over an hour after the Bremen SIGMET was released.

(Note: the accident report uses local time for the flight, which I have converted to UTC for consistency. All times in this document are given in UTC. The crew and ATC spoke to each other in English; the spoken transcripts have not been translated.)

Issue Number One: The Operational Control Centre did not notify the crew of extreme weather warnings in the destination area.

The final report concluded that if the flight crew had been alerted, these SIGMETs would have made it clear that the area did not have a few isolated thunderstorm cells, but a thunderstorm front of considerable proportions. This knowledge would have influenced the decisions made by the crew during the flight.

The SIGMET was issued at 15:00 and the aircraft did not depart until 16:09, plenty of time for the Operational Control Centre to pass updated weather information to the flight crew. However, no one did.

16:09 Crossair Flight 850 departed Basel.

17:36 The flight was cleared to descend to 3,000 feet for an instrument approach into Hamburg runway 23.

17:38 As a result of severe turbulence, the flight crew aborted the approach into Hamburg at 3,300 above sea level.

17:41 The flight entered a holding pattern to see if the weather cleared so they could land at Hamburg rather than divert.

17:49 The crew requested a diversion to Hannover, their second alternate.

While in the holding pattern, the crew had time to consider their next decision. The accident report offers a list of options:

- Another approach to Hamburg

- Approach to one of the standard alternate airports

- Consult the Flight Management System data base for another suitable alternate airport (NAV-Display)

- Contact operations and request support

- Contact air traffic control with a request for suitable alternatives

The flight crew almost immediately decided against a further approach into Hamburg. They contacted ATC to ask about their planned diversion airfield, Bremen. It was also beset with thunderstorms and although the storms were passing, it would involve the flight attempting to penetrate the front. They decided instead to fly to their second alternate, Hannover.

Issue Number Two: Whilst in the holding pattern, the crew had ample opportunity to get a full picture of the surrounding area. They did not ask ATC about other airfields in range nor did they request updated information about the weather in the area. In fact, at that point Lübeck was immediately below them and free from storms, while Hannover was already behind the cold front. However, the crew blindly followed their flight plan.

> If there could be no landing at the original declared destination, a diversion to a predetermined alternate airport is a standard operating procedure. Because Bremen was behind the weather front and the crew was not prepared to penetrate the front or fly around the frontal area, the decision to divert to the second alternate—Hannover, which by that time was also behind the cold front—is not understandable. This shows the BFU that the list and sequence of alternates was followed diligently instead of trying to get an idea of other options and possibilities.
>
> —From the English translation of the official report

The investigators discovered that the pilots had not had any training in decision-making skills. Although the report does not cite this as a cause they clearly believed it was a contributing factor to the initial failure to gather more information.

17:52 Crossair Flight 850 left the holding pattern and proceeded

towards Hannover. The flight encountered further thunderstorms and the crew realised they couldn't fly around the
storm cell to reach Hannover.

18:13 The crew aborted the flight to Hannover and requested a
diversion to Berlin-Tegel, which showed on their weather
radar as clear of the storms.

18:15 They listened to the Berlin-Tegel Automatic Terminal Information Service. The recording said that the local weather was
CAVOK (Ceiling And Visibility OK) with NOSIG (NO SIGnificant change expected).

Issue Number Three: The recorded weather information at
Berlin-Tegel was incorrect. The approaching weather was already
recognisable when the report was assembled. A NOSIG is a specific
forecast that the weather situation will remain unchanged for the
next two hours. The ATIS was not updated as the storm front
approached. Now the flight crew have not only insufficient
information but also incorrect information.

In the 30-minute time period between the two routine weather
reports, weather conditions had deteriorated rapidly. These weather
conditions were the direct result of the approaching cold front and
did not happen unexpectedly.

18:17 Crossair Flight 850 established contact with ATC at Berlin.

18:18 Crew received a low-fuel warning and requested a priority
approach, explaining that they only had fuel remaining for 40
minutes. They were given instructions for runway 08.

18:20 Berlin-Tegel weather was updated with TEMPO, including
warnings of thunder showers. No one informed the flight
crew.

18:26 A SPECI (a SPECIal unscheduled report) was released as the line of thunderstorms reached Berlin. No one informed the flight crew.

18:28 The turbulence was so strong by now that Crossair Flight 850 was forced to abort their approach. They requested further airport options in the area. Berlin ATC recommended Eberswalde-Finow, which was 27 nautical miles (50 km) away.

The low-fuel situation meant that the flight was treated as an emergency and would be given priority at all airports. However, Eberswalde-Finow was also hit by the thunderstorms.

18:32 The crew looked at nearby airfields on their onboard Flight Management System and changed their heading towards Neubrandenburg, 46 nautical miles away.

18:34 Berlin ATC informed the flight crew that there was a thunderstorm over Neubrandenburg. However, the weather was reported clear east of Berlin. ATC recommended changing heading towards Werneuchen, 20 NM away.

Werneuchen was not in the Flight Management System and so the crew did not have a chart for the airfield. However, they were running out of options.

Because of the changing weather and the necessity to alter track several times, the crew found themselves in a situation where, instead of a routine diversion to an airport, the shortage of fuel and the weather situation made a precautionary landing necessary at any airfield with a

> suitable runway. Although it was still unlikely that an engine
> would stop very soon because of lack of fuel, there was hardly
> any other alternative. The crew therefore accepted an airfield
> that was totally unknown to them, Werneuchen Special
> Airfield.
>
> —From the English translation of the official report

Crossair Flight 850 changed heading. Meanwhile, ATC contacted the chairman at the flying club. Werneuchen was a former military aerodrome which has been used by civil aircraft since 1990. The original length of runway 08/26 was 2,400 m x 80 m. The chairman took the call on his mobile phone and warned ATC that the western end of runway 08 included a displaced threshold.

The western end of the runway had an earthen wall built up on it. Werneuchen had been given permission to build this wall, no more than four metres (13 feet) high, in order to keep the runway from being used for illegal car races. There was also a 70 cm (just over 2 feet) clay wall which ran along the entire width of the runway. The usable runway at Werneuchen is 1,500 metres.

Issue Number Four: Somehow, there was a major communication breakdown regarding the displaced threshold. The chairman definitely brought it up. However, the ATC supervisor was under the impression that there were *two* runways at Werneuchen. He told the controller, ". . . he should not take the short runway, there is an earth wall after five hundred metres." The controller had the aerodrome chart but it made no reference to the displaced threshold.

The controller passed the runway data to the crew and relayed the message from his supervisor.

> The contents of the message were incomprehensible for the
> flight crew without having the possibility of checking or
> interpreting the approach and runway plates. The choice of
> the word "should", would normally be understood by the
> crew as a recommendation, and was therefore not perceived
> as a warning. The message contained none of the key
> vocabulary with which the crew would have been familiar,
> such as closed portion, obstacle, blocked, displaced threshold.
>
> —From the English translation of the official report

18:39 Werneuchen: "And there is an earthen wall, so he should
pay attention, that he does not attend er does not land on
this five hundred meter strip—he should land on the one
thousand five hundred metre strip"

18:39 ATC Supervisor: "Yes good, he'll do that anyway"

18:39 ATC controller to Crew: "We just eh been informed that you
should use the easterly part of the runway eh so eh in you eh
you are not before landing before the threshold of zero
eight—genau."

The flight crew was flying to an airfield that neither of them had
ever been to before, without charts to reference it, and without any
clear warning of the displaced threshold or the correct length of the
runway. The weather was clear so they could at least have a good
look before they landed.

Issue Number Five: The runway markings were no longer clear.
The military runway markings were still clearly visible, as you can
see from the Google maps image of the airfield. The crosses painted

on the disused area had eroded. Their visual check would not have made it clear that any part of the runway was closed, even on direct approach.

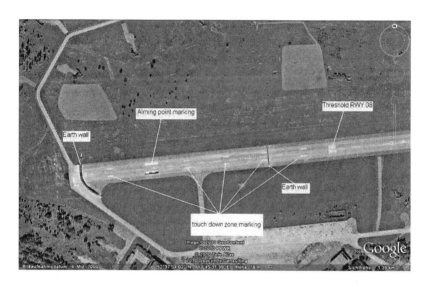

Aerial view of the aerodrome west end as seen
in 2000

Clear marking of flight operation areas, in particular runways, is an essential safety mechanism for the prevention of accidents. A runway must be clearly visible for pilots in the air, and distinguishable from other flight operation areas. The markings at Werneuchen Special Airfield did not meet the requirements or recommendations of ICAO Annex 14, or the national regulations then in force.

—From the English translation of the official report

18:40 Crew: "Ja we're just abeam the threshold zero-eight now making a left hand eh downwind if you agree for zero-eight."

Issue Number Six: The crew had never been to this airfield and did not have a chart or any information other than what had been passed on by ATC. Standard procedure is to overfly the runway and get a good look at it. However, the weather was deteriorating and they were low on fuel. The pilots never discussed overflying the runway but instead proceeded directly to land. At this point, visibility was good and they had clear sight of the airfield. Although the runway markings were not clear, the earthen walls would have been apparent if the crew had flown along the runway for a visual check.

And now the stars were all in alignment for the wipeout of the

---

At 20:40 the crew reported Werneuchen in sight and lined up for an approach to Runway 08. They did not have the frequency for the Airfield and continued to speak to Maastricht Upper Airspace Control. The crew approached runway 08 directly without radio communication with the airfield and—due to the weather and shortage of fuel— without first inspecting the runway from the air.

—From the English translation of the official report

Saab 2000.

20:41 Final approach of Crossair Flight 850 into Werneuchen Runway 08.

The first officer was the pilot flying. He asked, "Touch down where?"

The captain responded, "Wherever you like, my friend."

They descended through 500 feet above ground level. The captain said, "It's longer than . . . It's longer than . . . longer than Bern, hä."

Bern is 1,510 metres—the same length as was actually available in Werneuchen. But the crew had not realised that there was a displaced threshold. They were reacting to the original military runway (2,400 m × 80 m) rather than the 1,500 metres (5,000 feet) of usable runway. It was not until immediately before the collision that the crew could see the earthen wall across the runway.

The west side of the 70 cm high earthen wall
with impact mark of the nose wheel

20:42 The Saab 2000 touched down and collided into the earthen wall. All three landing gear legs broke off. The aircraft slid 350 metres and then came to a halt. The crew opened the doors and the flight attendants evacuated the passengers. Only one minor injury was sustained.

21:00 The thunderstorms passed over the airfield with wind gusts up to 52 knots.

The BFU cite the following direct causes of the accident:

Immediate Causes:

The extent and intensity of the thunderstorm frontal system, plus the speed of change in the weather system.

Insufficient use of available resources when making decisions in flight (pro-active).

The loss of alternative landing options, coupled with increasing time pressure (reactive).

Aircraft touched down outside operational area of an airfield.

Earth wall was not detected, followed by collision with the same.

Systematic Causes:

Insufficient information with respect to weather situation and development, both prior to and during the flight.

Insufficient information about Werneuchen Special Airfield due to inadequate chart illustration, plus absence of and misunderstood communications.

Insufficient signs and markings of operational and non-operational airport areas.

No safety recommendations were made.

—From the English translation of the official report

From the first moment, when the SIGMETs were not passed onto the crew, the options began to reduce. The crew took on an additional 570 kg of fuel to deal with delays, enough for approximately 45 minutes additional flight. At Werneuchen, the Saab 2000 had 420 kg of fuel remaining in its tanks. In the end, a series of questionable choices and bad information meant that the flight crew felt pressured to land in a rush on an airstrip for which they had no details.

The Saab 2000 was a write-off, and although weather (especially thunderstorms) is frequently a problem for pilots, the loss of the plane in this instance was solely an accumulation of human factors.

Until this point, the ATC Supervisor was under the impression that the chairman of the flying club was on site at Werneuchen. It was only after ATC lost contact with the plane that he realised the error. He hung up to call the fire brigade and then phoned the Werneuchen number again to ask if maybe the chairman would drive out to the airfield to see what happened. "No, it would take me an hour and a half to get there," said the chairman. "There is only just one [person], he is seventy-eight or eighty years old but is very mobile. But he could drive out; should I ask him to do so?"

Official Documentation

- Original accident report:
  http://www.bfu-web.de/DE/Publikationen/
  Untersuchungsberichte/2002/
  Bericht_02_AX002_Saab2000_Werneuchen.html

Other References

- Accident report translated into English:
  http://www.bfu-web.de/EN/Publications/
  *Investigation%20Report/2002/Report_02_AX002_*
  Saab2000_Werneuchen.pdf?__blob=publicationFile

Photography

- All photographs are taken directly from the accident report.

FLYING INTO THE HEART OF THE STORM

EVERYONE HAS HEARD of brave Captain Sullenberger, who landed on the Hudson River in 2009 after bird strikes caused both of his engines to flame out and fail.

Not so well known is a similar event just seven years earlier, when Garuda Indonesia flight 421 ditched into the Bengawan Solo River in Central Java. Both engines flamed out as the aircraft was descending through 19,000 feet.

Garuda Indonesia flight 421 was a Boeing 737-3Q8 flying the scheduled domestic route from Mataram Airport in Ampenan to Yogyakarta. The aircraft was configured with 104 passenger seats: 22 in business class and 82 in economy class. On the domestic flight that day there were 54 passengers and six crew. The captain was very experienced with over 14,000 flight hours, over five thousand of them on the Boeing 737. The first officer had over seven thousand hours. There were four cabin-crew working the flight.

The day started out normally enough. It is a 625-kilometre (390-mile) flight from Ampenan to Yogyakarta. Ampenan is on Indonesia Central Time (UTC+8) and Yogyakarta is on Indonesian Western Time (UTC+7). For the purposes of this article, all times are given in UTC in line with the accident report.

Garuda Indonesia Boeing 737-300 *(Photo by Hullie from nl)*

08:32 The flight departed Ampenan airport in visual conditions.

08:46 National Oceanic and Atmospheric Administration (NOAA) weather satellite image shows a supercell of cumulonimbus clouds that may have topped out as high as 63,000 feet.

Cumulonimbus clouds are dense towering cloud formations signalling thunderstorms and atmospheric instability. They are the largest of all clouds and can produce torrential rain and flash flooding. They can develop into supercells, thunderstorms characterised by a deep, persistently rotating updraft and associated with violent weather. Supercells are the least common classification of thunderstorms and have the potential to be the most severe.

Super cell thunderstorm *(Photo by Sean Waugh
and shared courtesy of the NOAA Photo Library)*

09:00 The flight was uneventful until the aircraft reached the
Yogyakarta area. The captain clearly became aware of the
thunderstorms as, around this time, he requested a route
change in order to avoid the weather.

09:08 Flight 421 descended from the cruising altitude of 31,000
feet to 28,000 feet to avoid eastbound traffic. At this stage,
the aircraft target on the Yogyakarta Approach radar system
was normal, showing as westbound and on track. A further
descent from 28,000 to 19,000 feet was cleared by ATC.

The flight crew prepared to enter turbulence by decreasing the
speed to *VRA*: the Turbulence Penetration Airspeed as defined for
their aircraft.

All airspeeds are referred to as V-speeds. This comes from the French word *Vitesse* which means speed or rate. The VSO is the slowest; this is the stalling speed of an aircraft configured for landing. VNO, marked as a green arc on an airspeed indicator, is the normal operating range. VNE is "Never Exceed" and is the maximum speed that the aircraft would ever be operated in smooth air. The VRA is the airspeed for in "Rough Air". The VRA is pre-calculated by the manufacturer as the speed least likely to risk structural damage to the aircraft.

Flying too fast into turbulence increases the danger of "g-loads" and structural failures. Flying too slow increases the danger of stalling. VRA is slower than the cruise settings but not so slow as to allow turbulence to generate a stall.

If the wing hits a severe updraft, the angle of attack over the wing will increase and the wing will stall. Bringing the aircraft closer to stall speed reduces the vertical load of the wind shear on the wing itself as the lift on the wing reduces. If the aircraft hits a downdraft, the slower speed will prevent the aircraft exceeding the maximum speed for normal operations.

So, the flight crew set their speed to VRA, which, for the Boeing 737, is 280 knots. They turned on the seatbelt light, which cued the cabin crew to ensure that the passengers had buckled up. The engine ignitions were set to flight mode, a setting used in heavy precipitation to allow for in-flight engine starts. They turned the anti-ice on and requested a descent to FL 190 (19,000 feet) from Bali Air Traffic Control, which was approved.

09:13 The descent continued. The aircraft entered the clouds at 23,000 feet. The flight crew saw red cells on their radar screen indicating cumulonimbus cells, with green and yellow areas to the left and right of their intended flight path. The selected range on the equipment was set to 40 and 80 nautical miles.

They swiftly encountered severe turbulence. Rain and hail clattered against the aircraft. The crew began to look for a detour. The captain felt that a left turn would give them the most favourable route, flying through a gap between two cell targets. The first officer suggested flying to the right; however, that meant flying into military airspace as well as towards the high ground of the Merapi mountain.

It was probable that the flight path of the aircraft during weather detour when flying into the gap went toward radar shadow cause by an excessive amount of active weather cells in that area. The clearer area was in side the Military Restricted Area, which could be entered in certain situations by obtaining permission which should be established between the relevant authorities.

—From the official report

The captain decided it was safer to fly left. As they watched the radar screen, his proposed routing turned solid red. The gap which the captain had hoped to use to get past the cumulonimbus cells closed before their eyes. They'd flown right into the storm.

09:20 Up until now, controllers following the flight on Yogyakarta's radar thought it looked normal and stable. But then the aircraft suddenly turned southwest as the aircraft was passing through 18,500 feet. The aircraft was in "severe cumulonimbus cloud formations" with turbulence and heavy rain and hail.

The cockpit voice recording includes the sound of rain hitting the fuselage. The rain and hail is so torrential, it is almost impossible to hear the conversation in the cockpit. After the event, investigators tried to filter out the sound using a frequency separator but the frequency of the noise was the same as the frequency of the voices so we do not know what was said.

That's when the engines died. They flamed out: the flame in the combustion chamber goes out and the engine fails.

09:22 ATC expected to hear that the aircraft had reached the next waypoint but Garuda Indonesia flight 421 failed to report in. Semarang Approach called the aircraft twice but there was no response. They contacted Yogyakarta Approach to check the radar target on Yogyakarta's Secondary Surveillance Radar. The radar read-back showed the aircraft descending at a ground speed of 390 knots.
The aircraft was hurtling towards the ground.

The flight crew attempted to relight the engines following the Emergency Checklist for *Loss of Thrust on Both Engines*. The procedure failed; the engines did not relight. Although the checklist stated that they should wait three minutes between attempts, it was only one minute later when they tried again. The engines did not relight. The aircraft was still in the heavy rain and hail—the same environment which had caused the engines to fail in the first place. The flight crew's attempts likely just introduced more water into the engine core.

09:24 Radar showed the speed increase to 410 knots at which point the radar target faded out and disappeared.

The cockpit recordings showed that the aircraft was in heavy precipitation, a mix of rain and hail. The recording was entered into the sound database of the UK Air Accidents Investigation Branch (AAIB) who confirmed that the rain was the heaviest ever recorded on a cockpit recorder, a record previously held by the Doha crash in 1979.

09:32 The Primary Surveillance Radar showed Garuda Indonesia flight 421 as moving fast in an unstable flight path before it disappeared off the radar completely. A few seconds later it reappeared but then at 09:33 it disappeared again. That was the last radar target of the flight.

As if the situation wasn't horrific enough, during the flight crew's second attempt to relight the engine, the aircraft lost all power. The flight crew couldn't know it at the time but investigators discovered that there was a fault in the newest cell of the battery: the level of electrolyte in that cell was much lower than the others.

> One of the cells of the battery had been found to have lower electrolyte level to the point causing an insufficient current storage. It caused a high resistance and resulted [in] the voltage of the battery dropped, and will therefore account for the reported failure of the battery. **The loss of the battery liquid was due to spewing effect** (i.e. convective movement of electrolyte out of the cell).
>
> The spewing was caused by high temperature and overcharging. The reason why the high temperature and overcharging could occur was the absence of high temperature sensor on the battery which functions is to stop

> charging when the battery temperature is too high. The detachment of the temperature sensor was due to corrosion of the sensor mounting.
>
> —From the official report

This meant that the battery was unable to maintain sufficient power during the second relight and failed completely.

Two seconds before the cockpit voice recorder stopped functioning, the Ground Proximity Warning Sensor (GPWS) sounded in the cockpit. They weren't yet that close to terrain: the sensor was reacting to the heavy precipitation. The rain was so heavy that the GPWS thought they were flying into a mountain.

At 8,000 feet, the aircraft descended into visual conditions. With no engines and no electronics, the crew's only choice was to try to land the plane. The captain saw the Bengawan Solo River and decided that it was the safest place to ditch.

They navigated the stricken aircraft down into the river between two iron bridges which were approximately 2 kilometres apart. The Boeing 737 came to a halt facing upstream with the nose up and pointing slightly to the right. The Bengawan Solo River was approximately 75 metres wide and ranged from one to five metres deep at the landing site. The belly submerged into the river with the wings largely intact.

The rough landing damaged the right-hand cargo door, and the nose landing gear and right-hand main landing gear were ripped right off, later found some 50 metres (150 feet) away. The seats came off of their fittings and the floor on the aisle of business class second row collapsed. The left-hand aft lavatory and lower part of the aft galley were ripped off of the aircraft. The crash landing tore a large hole in the floor at the aft cabin section.

There was one fatality: a cabin-crew member was discovered in the river, somehow dragged out of the aft jump seat of the aircraft by the impact. Her neck, arms, right femur and left lower leg were all broken. All her toes were missing.

The flight crew kicked open the cockpit door to get to the cabin. They worked with the cabin crew to evacuate the passengers. A fisherman helped to carry the injured passengers to the riverbank. The captain also phoned ATC on his mobile phone to inform them of the crash.

09:40 Within minutes of the crash landing, Yogyakarta Approach was notified that an aircraft had crashed near Serenan village.

Amazingly, despite losing both engines and all electronics, the flight crew had successfully force-landed the Boeing 737 on the Bengawan Solo River.

"There was thick smog outside and suddenly we felt turbulence. I couldn't see a thing but after the emergency door was opened I saw water," a passenger told local television reporters. A young mother told the daily newspaper that she had to lift her seven-month-old baby up in the air when water started to flood the plane.

Another cabin-crew member, also in an aft jump seat, was found severely wounded on the river. All other occupants of the aircraft were safely evacuated to the riverbank. Local villagers helped the evacuation and offered shelter to the passengers and their belongings in an empty house near the river. A few hours later, the rescue team, local police, the air force and airport staff arrived on site.

Members of the cabin crew and passengers reported that they had no idea they were crash landing in the river.

Most passengers did not suspect an emergency when the impact occurred, and most were wearing their seatbelts. Some passengers have said that they thought it was a very rough landing. Only after the cabin crew scrambled to the exits and screamed "Emergency! Emergency, please evacuate the aircraft" did they realize. Some realized when seeing a vast pool of water out of their windows when the aircraft stopped.

—From the official report

There are five causes of engine flameout:

- environment

- engine capability

- operating procedure

- fuel

- commanded shutdown

Commanded shutdown could be ruled out by the Flight Data Recorder, and fuel issues by the aircraft still having fuel in the tanks at the time of impact and the fuel samples showing that the fuel met the quality standard. Operating procedures were ruled out based on the information on the Flight Data Recorder and flight crew interviews. Both engines flamed out at the same time, although they were not the same age and they had different maintenance histories, which means that engine capability was an unlikely culprit. No abnormal conditions were found in the engine controlling system nor the hardware.

The engines had all proper modifications concerning water/hail protection which meant that the engines were able to sustain the hail ingestion in line with the FAA requirement: 10 grams per cubic metre from 10,000 to 15,000 feet altitude.

The investigators tried multiple methods to determine the density of the hail which was encountered by Garuda Indonesia flight 421, including the Ground Proximity Warning Sensor's trigger point and the sound of rain and hail recorded from the cockpit. Based on these tests, they believe that the aircraft encountered hail/water content as high as 18 grams of hail per cubic metre of air. This is the equivalent of flying through 10,000 ice cubes per second.

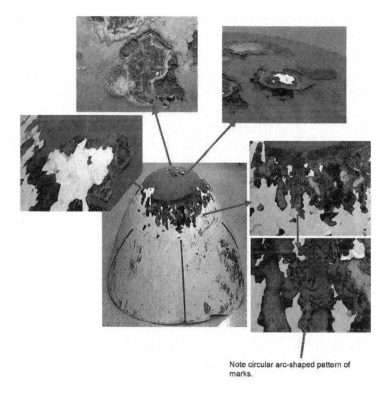

Note circular arc-shaped pattern of marks.

Detail of damage on the nose radome

> Environment, in this case the presence of hail, exceeding the certification standard, was the most probable cause since according to flight crew's interview, the aircraft encountered severe weather at the time. The modified engine is known to have a large water ingestion limit and has been proven to withstand hail concentrations in excess of the required certification standard. Presence of hail, however, still becomes a threat to the engine if the hail density is in excess of the required hail certification standard.
>
> —From the official report

Investigators found three other instances of weather-induced flameout on the Boeing 737s using the same engines. In every case, the aircraft was descending with low idle power and the flight crew were trying to dodge adverse weather condition.

> The NTSC determines that the probable causes of the accident were the combination of
>
> 1) The aircraft had entered severe hail and rain during weather avoidance which subsequently caused both engines flame out;
>
> 2) Two attempts of engine-relight failed because the aircraft was still in the precipitation beyond the engines' certified capabilities; and
>
> 3) During the second attempt relight, the aircraft suffered run-out electrical power.
>
> —From the official report

Avoidance becomes key but once they'd headed into the thick of the thunderstorm cells, there was no getting out. The situation was horrendous but landing that aircraft at all is absolutely a testament to the skill and concentration of the flight crew that day. Aircraft with a lot less wrong with them have not turned out so well.

Official Documentation

- Original accident report: "Final Indonesia NTSC Report GA421 B737 PK-GWA Solo"— *http://www.dephub.go.id/knkt/ntsc_aviation/baru/Final%20Report%20PK-GWA_release%20GA%20Solo.pdf*

Photography

- Unattributed photographs are taken directly from the accident report.

- Garuda 737-300 by Hullie from nl: *https://en.wikipedia.org/wiki/File:_737-300.JPG*

- Super cell thunderstorm photograph taken by Sean Waugh and shared courtesy of the NOAA Photo Library *https://www.flickr.com/photos/51647007@N08/5033797028/*

NUMBER ONE ON FINAL FOR MOORABBIN

AIRCRAFT FLYING AT an airfield follow a circuit, also known as a pattern. This is a standard path flown by aircraft around the airport in order to enable pilots to find each other, as each knows the route that the others will fly.

The evening of the 29th of July was busy at Moorabbin airport in Victoria, Australia. Six aircraft were in the circuit when a tragic accident showed just how easy it is to lose track of your position in the circuit.

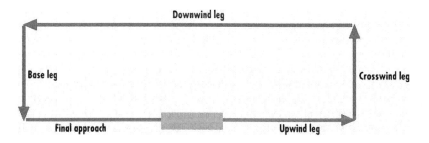

A normal circuit pattern

A circuit is generally left-hand, which means that the turns are all performed to the left, which increases the visibility for the pilot in the left seat. For multiple aircraft flying repeated circuits for training, separation is provided by the fact that each aircraft has a different take-off time. Newly arriving aircraft join the circuit in the downwind leg, taking care to fit in with existing traffic. However, most pilots know the frustration of being in a circuit behind a slower aircraft or in front of a faster one, which can cause confusion when trying to keep everyone in order.

After 18:00, Moorabbin airport is no longer under the jurisdiction of air traffic control in order to save costs. Instead, the airport becomes a Mandatory Broadcast Zone (MBZ). Within the MBZ pilots are required to fly visually in order to see and avoid the other aircraft and to carry a serviceable radio. The radio is a requirement because the pilots must announce their position at specific points. Specifically, they must make a mandatory broadcast when

- Entering the MBZ (whether inbound, transiting or joining the circuit)

- Commencing taxi for take-off

- Entering the runway

- Taking off

These mandatory broadcasts are meant to alert every pilot in the MBZ as to what the other pilots are doing.

The hours of MBZ operation were increased at Moorabbin in 1998 in order to save costs by reducing the number of controllers employed at the tower; however, even prior to the increase, the airport did not offer an air traffic control service after dark.

That night, the left-hand circuit was in use for runway 17L under the rules of the MBZ. The weather was clear and the visibility good. The runway lights were on and six aircraft were in the MBZ. A normal circuit pattern at Moorabbin is flown at 1,000 feet above ground level.

> The pilot of an aircraft would normally reach a height of at least 500 ft AGL on the upwind leg of the circuit, before commencing the turn onto the crosswind leg. While on the crosswind leg, the pilot would normally continue to climb the aircraft to the MBZ circuit height of 1,000 ft AGL. On late downwind and just prior to turning onto the base leg, the pilot prepares for the descent to the landing threshold. The pilot would normally aim to configure the aircraft for a rate of descent such that the turn on to the final approach would be completed no lower than 500 ft AGL.
>
> —From the official report

At Moorabbin, it was customary, although not required, to make a broadcast when entering the base leg of a circuit. When flying a circuit, especially if training and flying multiple circuits, it can get difficult to keep track of the location of all the other aircraft in the area and often impossible to see them visually (as some will be behind you at any given point).

All six of the pilots in command of aircraft in the MBZ held their commercial pilot's licence or higher: although there were student pilots in the circuit, they were all highly qualified pilots in their own right, studying for higher licences.

The two aircraft in the collision were VH-EUH and VH-CNW, both Cessna 172s operated by the flying training school at Moorabbin.

VH-EUH was a 172 built in 1998 flown by a student pilot who held his commercial pilot licence and had 178 hours flying experience (although only 2.5 hours in the Cessna 172). This was his first night VFR (Visual Flight Rules) flight and he was flying with an instructor from the flight school. The instructor had over a thousand hours flying time.

VH-CNW was 172R built in 2000, also flown by a student pilot who held her commercial pilot licence. She had 236 hours flying experience, with 8.8 hours on type. She was working towards her Air Transport Pilot Licence, and just that morning she'd completed the systems examination towards which she'd been studying long periods over the previous days. After her exam, she'd done a 48-minute solo aerobatic flight. She reported feeling fatigued before the accident flight; however, the investigation stated that there were no indications of personal, physiological or medical issues that might have influenced her performance that evening.

As is common in small airfields, there are no recordings at Moorabbin airport when running under the MBZ procedures; however the other pilots in the circuits all had the same recollection of the radio calls made.

Both aircraft were reported as operating normally and within weight and balance limits. They were both flown that day at similar speeds. Under normal conditions, the difference in take-off times would have kept them naturally spaced apart in the circuit so no risk of conflict would occur.

Both pilots made all the relevant mandatory broadcasts as well as the common discretionary broadcast that they were established on the base leg.

Based on radar information, we can see that the two aircraft flew very different circuits that evening. There is a lot of fluctuation in the circuit and both VH-EUH and VH-CNW flew circuits which were within the range of normal for Moorabbin. A two-and-a-half-hour snapshot of the radar data at Moorabbin for the 29th of July shows the variety of circuits flown that afternoon, along with VH-CNW in red and VH-EUH in blue super-imposed.

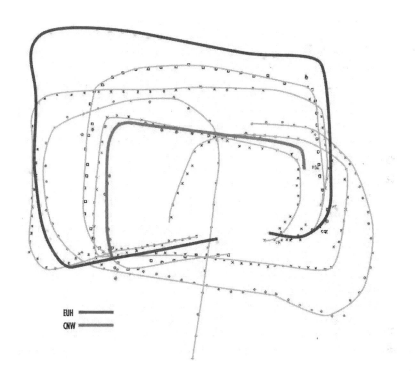

Radar plot of aircraft in the Moorabbin circuit
between 1830 and 1845 on 29 July 2002

The pilot doing his night rating with an instructor was in
VH-EUH and the figure shows that the circuit pattern they flew that
day was very wide. This was described by the Chief Pilot of the flying
school as the normal circuit size flown by their instructors.

The pilot doing her ATPL was flying solo in VH-CNW and she
flew a much tighter circuit pattern, although it was still within the
range of dimensions being flown by other pilots at Moorabbin that
same day and at the same time. VH-CNW's circuit before the
accident had a downwind leg one nautical mile abeam of the runway
and the crosswind and base legs were 2.2 nautical miles apart. She'd
previously flown at Bankstown airport and when investigators.

looked at the radar plot there, they discovered that over a two hour period, the average circuit had a downwind leg one nautical mile abeam of the runway and the crosswind and base legs were 2.2 nautical miles apart. In other words, the pilot of VH-CNW flew circuits of an acceptable dimension for Moorabbin and damn near perfect for Bankstown where she'd done most of her night training.

The larger circuit as flown by VH-EUH would have taken about 7 minutes to complete. The shorter circuit flown by VH-CNW would have taken about four and a half minutes to complete. This difference in circuit distance for two aircraft flying at the same speed sounds like a schoolbook maths problem. In the end, it put them both on final approach at the same time.

The VH-EUH crew broadcasted that they were on the base leg and continued on their larger circuit. At this point, VH-EUH would have been visible to the aircraft behind, VH-CNW.

The aircraft began flying almost as if in formation: VH-EUH was turning onto final approach as VH-CNW turned onto base. VH-CNW would have lost visibility of VH-EUH during the turn from the downwind leg onto the base leg. At this point, VH-CNW was higher and to the left, so obscured from the two pilots in the aircraft ahead. Not to mention that both student pilots would have spent a significant time looking inside the aircraft during the night flight, especially in the turns.

The pilots flying VH-EUH were established on long final when they heard VH-CNW broadcast that she was established on base. They likely assumed that she was one leg of the circuit pattern behind them, which meant that she would turn onto final shortly before they landed. Likewise, the pilot on VH-CNW probably heard the call when VH-EUH turned on final but presumed they were far enough in front of her to be clear of the runway by the time she turned on final.

A third aircraft, also a Cessna 172, was on final approach, ahead of VH-EUH and abeam VH-CNW for a touch-and-go landing. This aircraft at that moment would be considered number one to land, with the aircraft behind it on final approach as number two.

VH-EUH continued its final approach. The pilot of VH-CNW turned onto final approach, so in a normal circuit situation, it would be behind VH-EUH and have the aircraft in sight. The third aircraft touched the runway and was airborne again and upwind for another circuit. A fourth aircraft was on the runway and had commenced a take-off roll.

However, when VH-CNW turned onto final approach, the aircraft was directly above VH-EUH. This means that neither aircraft had visibility of the other during this critical moment of flight. None of the pilots seemed aware that two aircraft were now established on short final and both considered themselves number one to land after the departing aircraft on the runway. VH-CNW had a higher rate of descent as they aimed for the same touchdown point.

It's easy to envision the scenario: there was a lot to pay attention to and plenty to see without looking in the wrong direction for an aircraft that you didn't know was there. The pilot of VH-CNW has no idea that the aircraft she heard call final is now invisible below her and the pilots of VH-EUH presume that the aircraft who called final is behind, not on top of them.

The pilot of a Cessna 152 on the base leg of the circuit, however, saw the two aircraft and made a general broadcast that two aircraft were on final.

The pilots on VH-EUH saw the runway with no one before them, they were obviously clear to land. VH-CNW could also see the runway and could not see VH-EUH directly below.

VH-CNW responded to the call that two aircraft were on final with a calm position report to state that she was on late final, establishing her belief that she was clear to land.

They were both still in flight just above the runway threshold when they collided. The two aircraft became entangled and smashed onto the runway. They burst into flames while the aircraft, still entangled, slid down the runway. Both aircraft were consumed by fire. The student pilot and his instructor were able to escape from the burning Cessna. The pilot in VH-CNW survived the collision and impact with the ground but could not break free of the fuselage and died in the fire.

> Ground marks and wreckage after the initial impact point on the runway confirmed that the aircraft hit the ground with the lower aircraft, EUH, banked to the right. The wheel rim of the right main landing gear failed at the initial impact point, and the right main landing gear leg also failed as the two aircraft slid along the runway. The right wing strut separated from EUH during the ground slide, and the right wing separated from the fuselage at the leading edge before the aircraft came to rest. The left main landing gear of the upper aircraft, CNW, was observed by the instructor pilot to penetrate the rear window of EUH. The impact damage was consistent with that observation.
>
> —From the official report

Moorabbin airport does not have a rescue or fire fighting service. The Metropolitan Fire Brigade were on the scene and fighting the fire in 7 minutes and 46 seconds after receiving multiple emergency calls. The aircraft were both already heavily fire-damaged by the time they arrived. Investigators could not determine why the pilot of VH-CNW could not evacuate her aircraft and save herself.

There's no mention in the report of what the other aircraft in the circuit did at this point, but having seen the wreckage and flames on the runway, it would be obvious to them that they needed to divert to another airfield. As all of the pilots were qualified, this wouldn't have caused much confusion and I'm guessing that they flew to Melbourne airport to the north, where they left their aircraft for the flying school to pick up when Moorabbin reopened. Unfortunately, the gouges in the runway required the airport to remain closed for repairs to the runway surface after the runway was cleared of wreckage.

The investigation focused on the issues with see-and-avoid. As can be seen with this case, none of the pilots involved comprehended that they were on a collision course based on the broadcasts, even though additional discretionary broadcasts were made in an attempt to increase situational awareness for everyone in the circuit. If a pilot is alerted to the fact that an aircraft is nearby and given useful location reference, then he is likely to find it by searching the appropriate area. A visual scan's effectiveness is based on the amount of traffic information provided and on how conspicuous the target is.

Eye movements in a visual scan occur in a sequence of rapid jerks (saccades) and brief rest periods (fixations). Human eyes can make about three fixations per second but the more complex the scene, the more time each fixation takes. The brain *only* assimilates information during the fixations. If the saccades are too large, then that leaves large areas of unsearched space between the fixation posts.

As a result, the investigators came to the conclusion that the pilot of VH-CNW could have been actively scanning for aircraft during the turn from downwind onto the base leg and from the base leg onto the final approach and yet still not have seen the other aircraft in the darkness, because of the physiological limitations of the human eye.

In more specific guidance material, the FAA *Advisory Circular 90-48C* (Pilots' Role in Collision Avoidance) recommended that pilots use a series of short, regularly spaced eye movements not exceeding 10 degrees, with each area being observed for at least 1 second to enable better detection. **A problem with such a method is that it would take 54 fixations to scan an area 180 degrees wide and 30 degrees vertical.**

—From the official report

In addition, night flight requires more attention to the instruments and looking inside the aircraft than a daytime flight might. With six aircraft in the circuit, it was all too easy for a pilot to see the wrong aircraft and convince herself that she'd found the aircraft she was looking for.

The key issues highlighted by the accident report were:

- Circuit procedures—the operational and safety consequences of different sized circuits that may have led to misperceptions about the location of other aircraft in that circuit in the absence of a visual sighting;

- Human factors—the human tendency to accept information that supports a pilot's situation assessment, rather than critically re-evaluate the information on which that situation assessment was based;

- Airspace management—the evaluation of risks associated with the reduction in the Moorabbin airport air traffic control tower hours of operation.

The investigation specified three factors to the accident. The different-sized circuits, as mentioned above, was clearly a significant factor, although the report is quick to point out that rigid adherence to a standard circuit size could also be problematic. That none of the pilots involved ever saw the other accident aircraft, which would have allowed them to avoid the collision, was clearly a limitation of the see-and-avoid system, although again, there is no clear solution as to how to improve the situation or even why this does not occur more often.

Finally, the report listed as a factor that the broadcasts made by the pilots didn't help their situational awareness. For this third issue, the flying school at Moorabbin made an immediate change to their training. Students were already trained to make the (discretionary) call to state that the aircraft is established on the base leg, but now they are taught to include the aircraft's position in the landing sequence.

That night at Moorabbin, an aircraft was on short final for a touch-and-go when VH-CNW turned base with VH-EUH on final. If VH-CNW had called number two to land at that point, then VH-EUH would have been alerted both that there was an aircraft which they had not taken into account, as well as the fact that the other aircraft did not know that they were there on final and next to land. This simple bit of information can remove presumptions in the circuit and may well help avoid such tragic accidents in the future.

Official Documentation

- Original accident report:
  *http://www.atsb.gov.au/publications/investigation_reports/20
  02/aair/
  aair200203449.aspx*

Photography

- All photographs are taken directly from the accident report.

How to Break a Passenger Plane

ON THE 25TH OF MAY in 2002, a Boeing 747-200 flying over the Taiwan Straight disappeared.

China Airlines is the largest airline in Taiwan (Republic of China), initially created after the Chinese civil war to provide charter flights for the local population. Scheduled flights were begun in the 1960s with the first international route offered to Saigon, followed by Tokyo and then-British-controlled Hong Kong.

When Japan opened an international airport at Narita, they kept Air China as the only international operator from the now-domestic Haneda airport. This was solely to keep the air carriers from the People's Republic of China and Taiwan from crossing paths.

Interestingly, Hong Kong didn't see this as an issue and the air carriers crossed paths hourly at the then-British airport. In 1995, the Taiwanese China Airlines replaced the national flag with a plum blossom as their logo, in part to reduce tensions with the People's Republic of China.

The China Airlines service from Taipei to Hong Kong continued after control of Hong Kong was transferred to the People's Republic of China in 1997. The ninety-minute route was immensely popular and although the traffic consisted of just two airlines (Taiwan's China Airlines and Hong Kong-based Cathay Pacific Airways), they ran 13–17 round trip flights per day. Taiwan to Hong Kong became the busiest air corridor in the world and, as of 2013, although the number of passengers had dropped from 5.5 million to 4.9 million, it was still the busiest international air route.

China Airline's poor reputation in the 1990's led to an overhaul of maintenance and operational procedures, which, along with their pilot training program, successfully turned the company's safety record around. Eventually, the People's Republic of China and Taiwan were able to negotiate an agreement regarding the political "airline war" and in 2008, China Airlines began to operate regularly scheduled flights across the Taiwan Strait into mainland China.

In the midst of all this, a Boeing 747-200 flying at 35,000 feet over the Taiwan Strait terrifyingly vanished from radar.

China Airlines flight CI611 was a scheduled passenger flight flying the popular route from Chiang Kai-Shek International Airport in Tapei, Taiwan to Check Lap Kok International Airport in Hong Kong. Flight CI611 departed Chiang Kai-Shek International Airport at 15:07 with two pilots, one flight engineer, sixteen cabin crew and two hundred and six passengers. The departure and climb were uneventful.

The aircraft was a Boeing 747-200 passenger jet.

The Taiwanese flight crew were not new to the job. The captain was an experienced pilot with 10,148 flight hours. He had a good relationship with his family and he was well respected by his colleagues. His first officer had 10,173 flight hours and was the pilot flying for the flight. He was on a scheduled day off but was called for the flight early that morning. The flight engineer, with 19,117 flight hours, was the most experienced in the team, having joined China Airlines in 1977. He liked to exercise and had recently stopped smoking.

Together, they were an experienced crew. That helped them not one bit on their flight from Taipei to Hong Kong.

But I'm getting ahead of myself. At the time, there was very little information.

15:16:24 The controller at the Taipei Area Control Center
   instructed Flight CI611 to continue its climb to Flight Level
   350 (35,000 feet) and maintain that altitude.

15:16:31 Flight CI611 flight crew acknowledged the transmission.

15:28:03 Taipei Area Control lost radar contact with Flight CI611.

18:00 Two and a half hours later, search and rescue helicopters
   discovered the floating wreckage of the aircraft, 23 nautical
   miles northeast of Makung, Penghu Islands.

Recovery of the cockpit by the salvage crew

The salvage crew worked through a typhoon to try to recover
the wreckage as quickly as possible. They soon had enough evidence
to show that the aircraft had broken up at 35,000 feet and the pieces

had tumbled into the Taiwan Strait. The investigation crew had one core piece of information: for the aircraft to disappear off of radar so quickly, the aircraft almost certainly experienced an in-flight break-up.

The investigation examined the following scenarios:

- Midair collision

- Engine failure/separation

- Weather/natural phenomena

- Explosive device

- Fuel tank explosion

- Cargo door opening

- Cabin overpressure

- Hazardous cargo/dangerous goods

- Structural failure

Some of these were easily dismissed: there was no other aircraft in the area and the wreckage discovered was all attributable to the Boeing 747. There were no reported weather phenomena that day by any other aircraft on the route. The investigators went over the wreckage of the aircraft, searching for physical clues. When they inspected the pieces known as *Item 640* and *Item 630*, they finally found the clues that they were looking for.

Wreckage Item 630

Fatigue cracks were found on wreckage Item 640. There was a cumulative length of approximately 25.4 inches, including a 15.1-inch fatigue crack and other smaller fatigue cracks aft and forward extending from hole +14 to hole 51. The fatigue crack pattern shows an increasing growth rate through thickness and propagating inward. This can be attributed to the cracks growing from many origins on the skin surface at the scratch locations.

—From the English translation of the official report

Investigators were sure that they were looking at pre-existing fatigue cracks and not damaged caused by the accident. When they inspected the piece in the laboratory, they discovered a fatigue crack pattern with increasing thickness as it propagated inward: the cracks growing from scratches found on the skin. These scratches had sanding marks where someone had attempted to blend them out. Investigators also found fretting damage where rivets held the skin and doubler. They concluded that the fretting damage was most likely caused by the cracks being pushed open and closed during pressure cycles. Every time an aircraft is pressurised during flight, it undergoes a "pressure cycle". The fuselage is stressed every cycle and over time, cracks can develop around the fastener locations. Maintenance programs are meant to catch this evidence of metal fatigue and replace the affected portions of the skin before there is any risk of failure. But in this case, something went wrong.

Items 630 and 640 had been covered with doublers: a piece of sheet metal used to strengthen and stiffen the aircraft skin, which is placed over the skin of the fuselage in order to strengthen that section of the plane. The cracks were discovered underneath the doublers, out of sight. The investigators had discovered hidden metal fatigue and multiple site damage (MSD).

MSD is one of the two sources of Widespread-Fatigue-Damage (WFD), it is characterized by the simultaneous presence of cracks at multiple structural details that are of sufficient size and density that the structure will no longer meet its damage tolerance requirement and could catastrophically fail.

Almost all of the fatigue crack was located underneath the doubler and would not have been detectable from the exterior of the aircraft.

Further, because the cracking initiated from the external surface of the fuselage skin and propagated inward, the damage also would not have been visually detectable from inside the aircraft until the crack had propagated all the way through the fuselage skin.

—From the English translation of the official report

They could estimate that it would have taken somewhere between 2,400 and 11,000 pressure cycles for the cracks to break through to the interior of the fuselage skin. But they had no information when the cracking had begun.

The investigation began to focus on the history of the aircraft.

Two years before, Boeing had introduced a Repair Assessment Program, focusing on pressurised skin inspections for specific repair conditions. The skin, constructed from sheets of aluminium alloy, is connected with lap joints (along the length of the aircraft) and butt joints (around the cross-section of the fuselage). At the lap joints, each sheet overlaps the adjacent sheet. The butt joint has its name because the skin sheets butt up against one another but don't overlap. The integrity of the fuselage is determined by the number of pressure cycles: an aircraft that does multiple short hops every day will be more at risk of fatigue than one that does three long-haul flights each week, even though their time in the air is the same.

The accident aircraft was due for a repair examination process once it had accumulated 22,000 pressure cycles. In May 2001 the Boeing 747 had accumulated 20,400 pressure cycles, with an average of 900 cycles per year over the last three years. Thus, the aircraft had about 40 months before it needed to go through the required repair examination process. They planned to conduct the repair assessment in November 2002, including what is marked as the "number-16 doubler".

One pair of doublers had been installed as a result of a tail strike in 1980. The maintenance team checked the records and found they did not have much information about the repair. As a result, they attempted to document the current state of doublers so that they could estimate how much time would be required to complete the repair assessment in November 2002. As a part of this documentation, they took photographs underneath the aircraft showing the region of the badly documented repairs from various angles.

These photographs confirmed what investigators already feared. There was staining at the edges of the repair work: evidence of hidden skin damage beneath the doublers.

They had found the missing link: a tail strike incident almost twenty years before.

On the 7th of February in 1980, the Boeing 747 landed hard at Hong Kong, striking its tail against the runway. The bottom skin of the fuselage scraped along the runway, causing abrasion damage. The aircraft was ferried back to Taiwan unpressurised the same day for temporary repairs. The temporary repair was completed overnight. The Boeing Field Service Representative and the China Airlines chief engineer agreed that the damaged skin needed to be replaced and that the permanent repair should be conducted per the Boeing Structure Repair Manual.

The logbook then shows that the aircraft was grounded for "fuselage repair" from the 23rd to the 26th of May. There are no details regarding the repair other than that it was completed as per the Boeing Structure Repair Manual.

This isn't unreasonable. There is no requirement to keep detailed records when it comes to minor repairs. Also, the repair took place before the operations and maintenance overhaul that China Airlines conducted in the 1990s.

Under modern regulations, China Airlines would not be able to categorise the tail-strike as a minor repair. Records for a major repair must be kept for two years after the aircraft is destroyed or withdrawn from service. However, at the time China Airlines maintenance did not consider this to be a major repair and did not keep the paperwork. The investigation had to rely on the recollections of retired staff to recreate the detail of the repair.

The Boeing Field Service Representative remembered the aircraft. He said that he had read the engineering memorandum, which stated that the permanent repair would be a skin panel replacement as per the Structure Repair Manual. He said that according to the Structure Repair Manual, China Airlines maintenance staff should cut out the damaged skin, add filler and place a doubler to completely cover the damaged area. For this repair, the doubler must oversize the filler by at least three rows of rivets.

However, he never saw the final repair and had no idea if this is what they'd done. He said that China Airlines did not have the responsibility to report to him regarding the repair operation.

China Airlines procedure was clear: there was no reason to inform Boeing or the Field Service Representative as it was only a minor repair and it was easy to follow the Structure Repair Manual procedure.

The Boeing Structure Repair Manual allows for scratches in damaged skin to be blended out if they are within allowable limits. However, if the damage is too severe, then the damaged area must be replaced or repaired. Either the old skin must be replaced with new skin or the damaged skin must be cut off and a doubler applied. It is not acceptable in such a case to apply the doubler over the damaged skin.

When investigators examined the scratches on item 640, they found that the scratches, after the blending, were about 13.5% of the skin thickness (0.0096 inch) and the length of the scratches on the damaged skin was over 20 inches. They also found scratches passing directly through fastener locations. This damage from the tail strike was beyond the allowable limit as specified by the Structure Repair Manual.

The damaged skin should have been cut off before the doubler was applied or the skin should have been replaced.

A minor repair does not have to be reported to the CAA. Boeing stated they received no report of the work, which they would have argued as a major repair and requiring removal of the damaged skin. There are no detailed maintenance records for the repairs; however, even without documentation, it is clear how they repaired the abrasions simply by examining the wreckage:

> Instead . . . a doubler was installed over the scratched skin. In addition, the external doubler did not effectively cover the entire damaged area as scratches were found at and outside the outer row of fasteners securing the doubler. When the doubler was installed with some scratches outside the rivets, there was no protection against the propagation of a concealed crack in the area between the rivets and the perimeter of the doubler.
>
> —From the English translation of the official report

The China Airlines chief structural engineer still remembers that repair. In order to follow the Structure Repair Manual, they were going to have to cut out the skin in the damaged area and apply a large reinforcement doubler. Because the cutout area was so large, he believed that they would have difficulty in following the Structure Repair Manual procedure. So they didn't.

Instead, they applied the reinforcement doubler directly onto the damaged skin. He said that he did inform the Boeing Field Service Representative that they'd run into problems with the repair but he never received a response.

He decided that this meant that Boeing agreed with the repair method he had applied.

Boeing have no record of the repair and the Boeing Field Service Representative insists that he never received any such information from China Airlines. As China Airlines did not keep any paperwork pertaining to the repair, it is impossible to know whether the communication happened. It seems likely that the Field Service Representative never knew about the haphazard fix, as I'd hope that he would have responded urgently regarding the critical nature of the repairs.

The one thing that is absolutely clear is that the repairs did not follow the Structure Repair Manual. China Airlines procedures at the time had issues with quality control and the "minor" repair was approved. As a result, the damaged skin was hidden from sight. Almost all of the fatigue crack was located under a doubler with only small blended out scratches visible at the edges. The crack would not be visible from the inside of the aircraft until it had propagated all the way through the fuselage skin. From that date onward, there was no standard means of checking the durability of the damaged skin hidden behind the doubler. The crack pattern was not detected in any of the structural inspections.

It is impossible to know now how bad the damage was before the flight but based on the fretting marks and deformed cladding, investigators believe that there was a continuous crack of at least 180 cm (71 inches) hidden by the doubler. That's 1.8 metres or 5'11", the size of a tall man.

And with that, the fate of Flight CI611 was sealed.

As the aircraft climbed to 35,000 feet, the pressure upon the growing crack became too great and the skin separated. The aircraft rapidly lost pressure and the cabin temperature dropped to below freezing within seconds. The fracture progressed upwards, severing the power wiring. Pieces of the aircraft began to peel off. The tail came away and all four engines snapped off almost simultaneously.

It happened quickly. The passengers and crew probably never knew what happened.

An interim safety bulletin was released during the investigation. At the Boeing 2003 Structures conference in Amsterdam, at least four other carriers reported scratching beneath repair doublers. A lack of understanding about aircraft skin scratching and ageing commercial fleets had become a disaster waiting to happen.

Official Documentation

- Original accident report:
  http://www.webcitation.org/6NvDtiaIm

Other References

- Accident report translated into English:
  http://www.asc.gov.tw/main_en/docaccident.aspx?
  uid=342&pid=296&acd_no=116

- Routes News—10 busiest international air routes and who's
  flying them—
  http://www.routes-news.com/more-features/
  15-more-features/2792-10-busiest-international-air-routes
  -and-who-s-flying-them

Photography

- All photographs are taken directly from the accident report.

L-39 Ejected on the Ground

T HE **Aero L-39 Albatros** is a high-performance two-seat (tandem) military jet trainer. It was manufactured by Aero Vodochodly for the Czechoslovak Air Force and became the most popular jet trainer in the world. *Warbird Alley* call it the most popular jet warbird on the US market.

The L-39 is a single-engine advanced trainer used by many of the world's air forces, and as such it has many of the design features and handling characteristics as the high-performance fighters that its students will one day fly. The cockpits are fully pressurized, heated and air-conditioned. Each of the tandem cockpits is equipped with enough flight controls, flight instruments, engine gauges, and system status indicators to allow either pilot to safely operate the airplane. As with most military jet trainers, the back seat was designed for instructors and, like many modern trainers, there is limited or no access to certain controls and switches in the rear "pit." In the L-39, these items include environmental controls, fuel pump switches, and the normal electrical controls. Also, the rear seat occupant cannot monitor the Exhaust Gas Temperature (EGT) simultaneously with the front-seater. In actual practice, none of these factors is a problem. There are duplicates of the really important controls in the back (and who really needs all that stuff, anyway?)

The back seater does, however, have a few unique items to himself: a fiendish array of levers and switches which allow him to fail the front-seater's instruments at will—a holdover from the airplane's days as a military trainer.

—From *Warbird Alley*: L-39 Albatros Pilot Report

This single engine aircraft has been used for basic and advanced pilot training as well as combat missions as a light, ground-attack aircraft. Most Western aircraft have had the ejection seats pinned and deactivated but in this particular model, the ejection system was still active.

G-BZVL Aero L-39C Albatros at North Weald
taken a month before the accident by Ray
Barber

G-BZVL was active in the Soviet Air Force from 1977 until 1995, when it was placed in storage. When the Soviet Air Force was dismantled, many of the member states sold their surplus jets to the civilian market. G-BZVL was purchased by an Estonian company in 2000 and allocated an aerobatic certificate of airworthiness. It was bought by a private owner in April 2001 and moved to the UK seven months later.

In 2002 the aircraft was based at North Weald and used for training. In April of that year, a student pilot began a conversion course to the L-39 aircraft. On the 2nd of June, the student had 195 flight hours, of which most were on light, single-engined piston aircraft. He had received two days of ground briefings on the aircraft and completed 18 flights over 11 hours on the L-39. The day before, he passed a verbal test on his knowledge of the aircraft and its escape systems.

The instructor had 142 hours on type but 4,300 hours in total, including 1,300 hours as an instructor on the Hawk aircraft, a similar tandem seat training aircraft, while he was in the Royal Air Force. He was assessed by the Chief Pilot in December 2001 as "extremely competent".

That day, the student pilot and the instructor were doing navigation and general handling exercises finishing with a refuelling stop at Duxford Airfield in Cambridgeshire, 40 km (25 miles) to the north.

Duxford Airfield was first opened in 1918 and is currently owned and operated by the Imperial War Museum. The site is the location for many exhibitions and the Imperial War Museum's collection of warbird aircraft. It is also a popular location for general aviation in vintage aeroplanes. (Actually, I almost had the chance to fly a Tiger Moth at Duxford! But that's another story.) It seems a particularly apt end to a training flight in the L-39.

The paved runway at Duxford is 1,503 metres (almost 5,000 feet) long. The full landing distance is 1,353 metres. Runway 06 has a slight down slope, and at the end of the runway is a 90 metre (300 feet) Runway End Safety Area followed by an earthen bank which separates the runway from the M11 motorway. In 1997, an ME 109 aircraft had attempted to carry out a forced landing on runway 06 but realised he had insufficient runway left. He lifted off again, crossed the motorway and landed in a field on the other side. This was the only recorded incident at Duxford involving the M11 in almost 30 years.

The L-39 departed North Weald with the student in the front seat and the instructor in the rear, as is standard for this aircraft. The flight was uneventful and they joined the circuit at Duxford for runway 06.

Air Traffic Control asked the L-39 to fly a slightly extended downwind leg which gave time for another aircraft to clear the adjacent grass runway.

The student did this and then turned towards the runway and onto final approach. His instructor said that the student's approach was satisfactory although he noticed the aircraft was a little fast.

The L-39 flight manual says that the pilot should reduce speed to 230 km/hr (124 knots or 142 mph) for the approach and then reduce speed to 200 km/hr (108 knots or 124 mph) as the aircraft passes the runway threshold. The aircraft then touches down at about 180 km/hr (97 knots or 112 mph).

The student had been briefed that on final, his airspeed should be at about 200 km/hr (108 knots or 124 mph) but in the final stages of the approach the instructor noticed that the aircraft airspeed was reducing through 218 km/hr (118 knots or 135 mph). At the landing flare, the moment just before touchdown, the airspeed was 210 km/hr (113 knots or 130 mph); fast but within limits. The instructor described the landing as "soft", as in a gentle touchdown, and said that the aircraft drifted slightly to the left which he attributed to the crosswind.

The aircraft touched down about 150–200 metres along the runway, which is the normal touchdown point for this type of aircraft. With normal braking, the aircraft would need about 600 metres and from the point of touchdown, there were about 1,200 metres left on the runway.

However, the student didn't brake. The instructor called out to "load the nose wheel and start braking". The L-39 has a microswitch on the nose-wheel shock absorber; until the weight on the wheel operates the switch, the braking is inhibited.

The student pushed the control column further forward but there was still no braking action. The instructor told the student again to brake and then took control of the aircraft and applied the brake lever. Nothing happened. He attempted to brake a number of times but it had no affect.

A video of the aircraft on the runway showed that all three wheels were on the ground and the aircraft attitude was normal. The aircraft was travelling with a groundspeed of approximately 80 knots (148 km/hr or 90 mph).

By now, the end of the runway was fast approaching. The instructor, aware of the earthen embankment at the far end, decided to steer the aircraft to the right into straight and level fields instead.

As he attempted to turn, though, the rudder stopped responding.

ATC saw the aircraft turning off the runway and asked if there was a problem. The student responded: "BRAKE FAILURE!" The aircraft was now running through a field of light crops and towards the M11 motorway.

The instructor decided that the best option would be to retract the undercarriage. He couldn't do this from the rear seat as the mechanism had been wire locked to prevent the landing gear being operated from the back. He asked the student to use the undercarriage retraction level in the front. However, the landing gear cannot be retracted if there is weight on the nose wheel, in the same way that the braking is inhibited if there isn't. The landing gear can only be retracted when the nose landing gear is off the ground.

The instructor never applied the emergency brake and he never told the student to do so. Both seats had access to the emergency brake lever on the left console. Pulling the lever bypasses the anti-skid system and applies braking to both wheels.

The instructor also could have shut down the engine but he never did and he never asked the student to do so.

The aircraft was going 20 knots (40 km/hr or 25 mph) when it reached the airfield boundary. It rumbled past the earthen embankment and through a wooden fence. Then it then rolled down 4½ metres (15 feet) onto the motorway.

The L-39 slid across the lanes and struck the central crash barrier, coming to rest on the other side of the motorway. The engine was still running. The leading edges of both wings and tip tanks were severely damaged. The instructor was in his seat and uninjured.

However, at the moment when the aircraft broke through the wooden fence and rolled down to the motorway, the front ejection seat fired. The instructor had not told the student *not* to eject, but this was standard; the risk is too high that the other pilot will only hear the word "eject" and act upon it. He had been trained on the ejection seat and demonstrated a good understanding of the system and yet he decided to initiate the ejection below the minimum safe speed. As they broke through the fence, he must have realised they were going to run into the motorway and decided that it was safer to eject.

By this time, the aircraft's speed was well below the minimum for safe ejection on the ground. The ejection takes a few seconds to deploy and when the seat ejected, the aircraft was running downhill towards the motorway. As a result, when student pilot was ejected from the aircraft, he followed a low, forward parabolic trajectory and the seat couldn't achieve its normal height.

The main parachute had no time to deploy. The front seat, parachute and pilot's helmet were found in a field to the east. The main parachute had been pulled from the pack but had not inflated. The student was killed immediately when he impacted the ground.

The systems on the aircraft itself did not show any immediate issues and testing at Farnborough similarly failed to find any issues with the brake hydraulics and the anti-skid system. The emergency braking system was also working as expected although it was confirmed that neither lever had been pulled on the date of the accident. Investigators noted that the Hawk aircraft, which was the similar aircraft that the instructor had flown and trained pilots on in the RAF, did not have an emergency brake system, which could explain why the instructor never thought to try the lever. Raising the landing gear is an accepted response in a situation where a Hawk has left the runway and the terrain is hazardous.

The correct procedure following the loss of normal braking is to use the emergency brakes and this emergency procedure is clearly stated in the Flight Manual. The instructor pilot did not use the emergency brake lever nor did he instruct the student pilot to do so. Instead he applied right rudder to deliberately steer the aircraft off the paved surface towards open ground. When the aircraft was running across the adjacent field, towards the M11, the instructor asked the student to raise the landing gear. In these actions it appears that the instructor may have reverted to the procedures required when flying the Hawk aircraft, which were more deeply ingrained in him than the L-39 procedures.

—From the official report

Investigators never discovered any reason why the brakes on the aircraft did not work. One likely reason was that the microswitch on the nose landing gear had jammed, which meant that the braking was inhibited despite the nose wheel being firmly on the ground. No fault was found with the microswitch after the incident but, as the nose gear had been involved with an impact with the perimeter fence, the central reservation barrier and the road, it's possible that one of these impacts unjammed the microswitch. Two other instances of brake failure of the L-39 in the UK were discovered. In both instances, the issue was caused by a malfunction of the nose landing-gear microswitch.

The landing gear selector in the front cockpit was found in the DOWN position, which implies that the student never attempted to raise the landing gear. Although the instruction was wrong for the aircraft, it could have stopped the plane. If the brake failure had been caused by a malfunctioning microswitch on the nose wheel, the same fault would have allowed for the landing gear to be retracted despite the nose wheel being on the ground, which would have stopped the aircraft.

The simple answer, however, is that the student pilot or the instructor (or both!) should have used the emergency brakes. The Civil Aviation Authority concluded with a safety recommendation that L-39 Albatros operators should include the use of the emergency wheel brakes in training and in normal operation of the aircraft in order to train pilots to instinctively reach for the emergency brake lever in a sudden emergency on the ground.

Official Documentation

- Original Accident Report:
  http://www.aaib.gov.uk/cms_resources/
  dft_avsafety_pdf_022817.pdf

Other References

- Warbird Alley: L-39 Albatros Pilot Report—
  http://www.warbirdalley.com//pr.htm

Photography

- G-BZVL Aero L-39C Albatros at North Weald taken by Ray
  Barber
  https://www.flickr.com/photos/97531768@N05/
  9401109324/

RIGHT BEFORE THEIR EYES

O**N THE 26**TH **OF JULY** in 2002, at 05:37 Eastern Daylight Time, a FedEx Boeing 727 crashed during landing at Tallahassee, Florida. Federal Express flight 1478 was on the visual approach for runway 9. There were three experienced flight crew on board: captain, first officer and flight engineer. All three pilots had good reputations as competent pilots at the airline. So how did they manage to miss the runway at Tallahassee?

The crew met at Memphis for the late night flight.

The captain held an Airline Transport Pilot certificate and had flown 13,000–14,000 flight hours. FedEx records showed he had 2,754 hours on type with 861 hours as 727 pilot-in-command. His medical certificate was valid and contained the limitation that he must wear corrective lenses.

He arrived in Memphis two days before the accident, flying in on FedEx flight 1380 arriving 23:53. He reached home shortly after midnight and did not sleep well. The family dog's health was deteriorating, and the captain slept on the sofa so that he could look after the dog during the night. It was a couple of hours before he got to sleep and then he was interrupted three times to care for the dog. He got up at 07:30 and kept busy. He went to bed about 21:30, again sleeping downstairs and getting up several times during the night to care for his dog. He woke about 07:30 the next morning and described his sleep quality as "marginal, not really good."

He checked his schedule that evening and saw that he was flying to Tallahassee in the early hours. He went to sleep about 21:00

that night and rose again shortly past midnight on the 26th of July. He drove to Memphis Airport, saying that he was relieved that he'd slept pretty well and didn't feel fatigued.

The first officer held an Airline Transport Pilot certificate and had flown 7,500–8,500 flight hours. His medical certificate was valid and had no restrictions or limitations but did specify that the holder had defective colour vision.

The first officer was unhappy with his schedule, because it "reversed day and night sleeping on consecutive days". He was off duty two nights before the accident and went to bed around 21:00 to get up early the next morning for his scheduled flight to Winnipeg. He departed Memphis at about 03:56 and arrived at Winnipeg at 06:45. He slept for 5–6 hours at a hotel there before reporting for duty again at 18:18. He departed Winnipeg at 19:02 and flew to Grand Forks, North Dakota, arriving around half an hour later. He departed Grand Forks at 20:57 and arrived back in Memphis at 23:00.

After he landed in Memphis, he was notified that he was scheduled to work flight 1478 to Tallahassee, departing in about four hours. He checked that the flight wouldn't exceed his flight and duty limits and accepted the assignment, although he told investigators later that he'd planned to file a grievance regarding the unexpected assignment.

He slept for about an hour and a half in a private sleep room at Memphis and then met the captain to prepare for the flight. He thought he'd slept well but said he didn't recall feeling alert. His friend commented that the first officer "looked tired, like everyone else at 03:30". The captain commented that the first officer "seemed tired, but maybe it was just his personality; he seemed not as communicative, not as alert. He may have been preoccupied."

The flight engineer held an Airline Transport Pilot certificate and had flown about 2,600 total flight hours. His medical certificate was valid and had no restrictions or limitations.

The flight engineer worked the day before, flying into Ottawa and sleeping at a hotel there. He flew from Ottawa to Memphis for his scheduled flight to Tallahassee, arriving at midnight. He relaxed in a recliner 30–60 minutes. He began preparing for flight 1478 at about 01:35.

This was the first time that the three men had flown together. The captain and the flight engineer had flown together once previously, although they did not remember each other.

The aircraft was a Boeing 727, registration N497FE. Federal Express had bought the aircraft from Delta Airlines in 1990. At the time of the accident, FedEx operated 128 Boeing 727s.

Federal Express flight 1478 was a scheduled cargo flight from Memphis, Tennessee to Tallahassee, Florida. The dispatch documents showed that the aircraft's weight and balance were within limits and there was plenty of fuel for the flight.

The schedule departure time was 03:12 local time in Memphis but the flight didn't actually get away until over an hour later. An adjustment to the cargo pallet caused the delay and the aircraft departure was pushed back to around 04:24.

The climb and cruise were routine and the flight to Tallahassee was uneventful. Conditions were clear. The plan was for the crew to stay in Tallahassee for about 17 hours, heading back to Memphis that night around 23:15.

Tallahassee Regional Airport (TLH) is four miles southwest of the city, at an elevation of 81 feet above mean sea level. The air traffic control tower closes each night at 23:00 and reopens at 06:00. There are two perpendicular runways. Runway 18/36 is 6,076 feet long and 150 feet wide and is located along the west side of the field.

Runway 9/27 is 8,000 feet long and 150 feet wide and is located along the south side of the field.

Both runways 36 and 27 have approaches using an instrument landing system (ILS). This is a ground-based system that provides precision guidance to the landing aircraft. It means that the aircraft can land in low visibility. Runways 9 and 18 have visual approaches, which means that the flight crew must be able to see the runway clearly during the approach in order to land safely. West of the airport is national forest property and densely wooded.

That night, runway 18/36 was closed for construction. The official notification, called a notice to airman (NOTAM), was issued 19 July, a week before the flight.

At 05:11, the flight engineer received the Tallahassee weather information. He relayed the details to the captain. The first officer asked which runway they would use at Tallahassee.

05:12:23 Flight Engineer: The weather is, winds are one two zero at five, visibility nine, one hundred scattered, and several other layers temperature and dew point are both two two, altimeter three zero one zero.

05:12:35 Captain: All right . . . sounds good.

05:12:39 Flight Engineer: What runway you think you gonna try for?

05:12:41 Captain: Two Seven.

05:12:42 Flight Engineer: Two Seven?

05:12:43 Captain: Yeah.

05:12:46 Captain: And what'd you say the winds were again, one sixty at nine?

05:12:48 Flight Engineer: One one two zero at five.

05:12:50 Captain: Two oh, yeah, two seven, yeah [unintelligble].

05:13:21 First Officer: Twenty Four.

05:13:22 Captain: Roger.

05:14:04 Second Officer (Radio): Tallahassee good morning. FedEx Fourteen seventy eight, approximately twenty-five, thirty minutes out. Aircraft is up, lookin' for a parkin' spot and the power.

Runway 27 has an instrument approach. The only other runway, Runway 9, only has a non-precision visual approach.

Meanwhile, the first officer asks his captain to click seven times in order to activate the pilot-controlled lighting.

The pilot-controlled lighting comes into effect when the Tallahassee air traffic control tower is closed. The runway, taxiway and approach lighting systems can be activated by a pilot keying the microphone with the radio tuned to the airport's common traffic advisory frequency.

Three clicks results in low intensity, five clicks results in medium intensity and seven times results in high intensity lighting.

The CVR recording revealed that the captain made several small errors during the accident flight that suggest he may not have been fully alert. These errors included

incorrect readback of the radio frequency, incorrect repetition of weather information, incorrectly addressing Jacksonville Center as Atlanta Center (twice), and repeatedly clicking the microphone button five and six times to activate the airport lighting (rather than the

> seven times requested by the first officer).
>
> These errors were not consistent with other pilots' statements regarding the captain's performance on previous flights, which described his competence, use of standard FedEx procedures and callouts, good judgment, upbeat nature, and good CRM skills. Further, there was no evidence of previous deficient performance in the captain's training or operational history.
>
> —From the official report

The flight engineer briefed the flight crew regarding parking at Tallahassee and advised them that FedEx considered TLH to be a moderate controlled-flight-into-terrain (CFIT) risk. Controlled flight into terrain is "an event where a mechanically normal functioning airplane is inadvertently flown into the ground, water, or an obstacle". The airport was considered to have a more-than-normal risk to flight crew of crashing the aircraft on approach. The point of notifying pilots of the risk is to ask them to take special care when approaching these airports.

The wind was calm, the visibility was good. This was a perfectly normal visual approach to runway 27 at Tallahassee. But then, about ten minutes from touchdown, they changed their minds, deciding to land on runway 9 instead.

05:19:38 First Officer: You wanna land on nine if we see it?

05:19:42 Captain: Uhhhhhhhh.

05:19:46 First Officer: We got a PAPI on nine, too.

05:19:48 Captain: Yeah, maybe dat . . . it just . . . be a longer taxi
   for us but . . . way we're comin' in probably two seven be
   about as easy as any of 'em.

05:19:58 First Officer: Okay.

There was no real advantage to landing on runway 9. The
runway did not have an instrument landing system, although it was
equipped with high intensity runway lights, centreline lights and a
four-box PAPI light system on the left side of the runway 9. The PAPI
light system provides guidance relative to the 3° glidepath to the
runway's touchdown zone. The airport lights, taxiway lights and
PAPI remain on for 15 minutes once activated.

The flight crew started and completed the in-range checklist.
The Cockpit Voice Recorder recorded a sound similar to the
microphone being keyed six times over 1.3 seconds.

The air traffic controller advised the flight crew to expect a
visual approach into TLH and to report when they had the airport
in sight.

05:24:23 Captain: (let's see) runway nine [unintelligible] runway
   PAPI on the left side.

05:24:29 Captain: I don't know, you wanna try for nine?

05:24:32 First Officer: We're pointed in the right direction, I don't
   know, like you said (it) . . . kinda a long [expletive] taxi back.

05:24:37 Captain: Yeah, that'd be all right.

05:24:44 First Officer: I always thought you were supposed to
   land with the prevailing wind.

05:24:48 First Officer: At an uncontrolled . . . [sound similar to cough]

05:24:49 Captain: Well at five knots it really uh ya know [unintelligible] the only [unintelligible] the only advantage you have, landing to the west you have the glides—I mean to the west you have the glideslope . . . which you don't have to the east.

The rambling conversation never really justifies a change in runway. If they do wish to land on runway 9, though, they need to have the airfield in sight.

05:26:41 Captain: You familiar with the airport here at Tallahassee?

05:26:44 First Officer: No, I'm not.

05:26:45 Captain: See the downtown area right there straight ahead?

05:26:47 First Officer: Yeah.

05:26:48 Captain: Then if you go it looks like, just about south southwest there's a little group of lights down there.

05:26:53 First Officer: Ok.

05:26:54 Captain: There's a—you can see the beacon here in just a second, right in that group of lights right—

05:26:57 First Officer: Yeah I was just tryin'—

05:26:58 Captain: —there ya go.

05:26:58 First Officer: —to see the beacon's right in the middle of the field, right?

05:27:00 Captain: Yeah, um-hmm . . . right there.

The flight engineer advised the ground staff at Tallahassee that they were five minutes out. He then followed company procedure by bringing up the approach checklist.

05:28:24 Flight Engineer: You want the approach checklist, seeing we're pretty much on our own, er?

05:28:26 First Officer: We ever decide if we're goin' nine or two seven?

05:28:28 Captain: Yeah, we can do nine if you want to.

05:28:30 First Officer: Okay runway nine, visual runway nine PAPI on the left hand side . . . approach check.

05:28:35 Flight Engineer: Briefing?

05:28:36 Captain: Complete for runway nine.

There was no benefit to landing on runway 9; runway 27 had an ILS for a precision approach and actually was more convenient, not less, for taxiing to the Fed Ex ramp.

05:29:53 Captain: Ehh you wanna call the field?

05:29:55 First Officer: Yeah, I don't see the runway yet, but I got the beacon.

The captain's question is whether the first officer is ready to contact Tallahassee to report that they had the runway in sight. The first officer agreed, saying that he couldn't see the runway yet, but he could see the beacon. That's not actually good enough but it's a reasonable expectation that the runway will become visible shortly.

05:30:03 Flight Engineer: Is it pilot-controlled lighting?

05:30:04 Captain: Yeah.

05:30:05 Jacksonville ATC: FedEx fourteen seventy-eight cleared visual approach into Tallahassee, are you showing the uh NOTAM Tallahassee runway one eight three six is closed?

05:30:13 Captain (Radio): No sir but uh, we're gonna use uh runway nine.

05:30:17 Jacksonville ATC: All right you're cleared for the visual approach and report your down time this frequency. If unable to, Gainesville radio, change to advisory approved.

05:30:56 First Officer: Okay, I think I got a runway now.

05:30:58 Captain: All right.

The first officer seems not very confident of his situation as he adds nervously, "I hope I'm looking in the right spot here."

05:31:04 Captain: Runway should be just kinda [unintelligible] that beacon there yeah, right . . . the other side of the beacon.

05:31:07 First Officer: On the other side the beacon, right?

05:33:05 First Officer: Oh yeah, I was lookin' at the wrong light.

There's a power plant located a few miles north of Tallahassee airport which has a slow, white strobe light. Another FedEx captain told investigators that the power plant light is in the line of the sight for pilots arriving from the northwest and is often visible before the rotating beacon. The Tallahassee rotating beacon is a green light, not white, but the captain told investigators that it can be very hard to distinguish as green.

The flight crew appeared to be fixated, as they continued to insist on using runway 9 after they'd had difficulty spotting it when there was a serviceable instrument approach available to them.

05:34:11 Captain: I guess the lights came on, if not I'll click 'em again here . . . when we get a little closer.

The CVR records the sound of five clicks and the captain says, "There we go."

The airport lighting activation log showed that the lights were activated about 05:34:26. All lights were on and set to medium intensity within five seconds. At no point does the captain ever click seven times, the correct number of clicks for high intensity lighting.

The PAPI lighting system on the left side of the approach end of runway 9 was activated along with the lights, automatically using its night-time settings of 20% intensity. The PAPI consisted of four identical light boxes mounted on a line perpendicular to the runway centre-line.

If the approaching aircraft is on the correct glidepath, the crew will see the two left-side light boxes show as white lights and the two right-side light boxes show as red lights. If the aircraft is too low, more red lights are visible and if the aircraft is too high, more white lights are visible.

The aircraft turned for the final approach, lining up for runway nine. The aircraft was 2.5 nautical miles from the airport. At this stage, the PAPI was displaying one white light and three red lights to the cockpit.

05:36:20 First Officer: Ehh sorry 'bout that—

05:36:20 Ground Proximity Warning System: One thousand.

05:36:21 First Officer: I was lining up on that paper mill.

05:36:22 Captain: Oh that's all right—

05:36:22 First Officer: —or something.

05:36:23 Captain: that's all right no problem

The PAPI display shifted to four red lights. The approach was much too low. No one noticed.

As the airplane descended through 500 feet agl [above ground level] at 1,248 fpm, 152 knots, and with engines operating at about 1.17 EPR, the captain announced that the approach was "stable." The Safety Board notes that, although the airplane's airspeed was within the target range, the airplane did not meet FedEx's criteria for a stabilized approach because its rate of descent was greater than FedEx's recommended 1,000 fpm, the engines' power settings were less than the expected 1.3 to 1.45 EPR, and its glidepath was low as indicated by the PAPI light guidance. According to FedEx procedures at the time of the accident, if a visual approach was not stabilized when the airplane descended through 500 feet agl, the pilots were to perform a go-around. The Safety Board concludes that the accident approach was not stabilized as the airplane descended through 500 feet agl and that the pilots should have detected this and performed a go-around.

—From the official report

05:36:49 First Officer: (I'm) gonna have to stay just a little bit higher, (or) I'm gonna lose the end of the runway.

05:36:59 Captain (Radio): FedEx uh fourteen seventy-eight short final runway nine, Tallahassee.

05:37:09 Captain: It's startin' to disappear in there a little bit, isn't it.

05:37:12 Captain: Think we'll be alright yeah.

The runway "starting to disappear" is a symptom of being too low and seems to be the first indication the flight crew had that their approach was wrong. The descent rate decreased but the aircraft was still significantly below the proper glidepath. The engine power began to increase as the first officer tried to arrest his descent.

05:37:14 Ground Proximity Warning Service: One hundred.

05:37:17 Cockpit Area Microphone: [sound of clunk]

The first officer increased the power again and then again, rapidly. He's way too low and now he knows it.

05:37:19 Ground Proximity Warning Service: fifty, forty

05:37:20 Cockpit Area Microphone: [sound of crunch]

05:37:21 Ground Proximity Warning Service: thirty

05:37:22 Cockpit Area Microphone: [sound of crunch]

05:37:22 Ground Proximity Warning Service: bank angle, bank angle

05:37:23 Cockpit Area Microphone: [sound of crunching and loud squeal begins, and continues to end of recording]

05:37:26 Cockpit Area Microphone: End of Recording

The aircraft collided with the trees in a slightly nose-up attitude with the right wing low. It then impacted the ground about 500 metres (1,500 feet) west-southwest of the runway. The aircraft burst into flames but the three flight-crew members were able to get out through the captain's-side sliding cockpit window before the fire reached them. It was just over an hour before sunrise.

The wreckage path extended over 2,000 feet. A swathe of broken trees led to the edge of the wooded area and pieces of the right wing were found in the woods. The aircraft hit the ground about 170 feet from open terrain. The ground scars increase in width from about 29 feet to 120 feet. The last 800 feet show evidence of fire. Some farm vehicles and a fence were also damaged. The aircraft was destroyed.

But how could it be that *none* of the three crew members realised that the airplane was below the glidepath until much too late?

The primary cause of accidents like this, where there's no mechanical fault or outside issue to cause confusion, is fatigue. Specifically, a common symptom of fatigue in aviators is this readiness to continue an approach despite ever-increasing signs that the approach is dangerous and needs to be broken off.

Both the first officer and the captain made small errors throughout the flight that were clear signs of fatigue. Also, the accident occurred around 05:37 local time, which was 04:37 in the flight crew's home time zone: the early morning hours are associated with degraded alertness and performance.

There's also a question of Cockpit Resource Management. Each individual member of the crew was considered competent by his peers. However, the crew had not flown together before; were they working as a team?

There was no evidence to suggest that the deficient crew coordination was a characteristic pattern of performance for these three crewmembers (a review of company records and interviews with other pilots generated positive and complimentary descriptions about their abilities). Yet, the captain and flight engineer failed to recognize the solid red PAPI display (although there was no evidence that either had deficient color vision) and take action to correct the low approach. This failure might partially be the result of their accomplishment of tasks that required their attention inside the cockpit, such as those involved in completing the landing checklist. However, it would be normal and expected for both the captain and flight engineer to monitor the runway environment at other times during the final landing sequence, and it is difficult to understand why no one reacted to the visually salient PAPI information.

—From the official report

Part of the problem seems to have been the conditions at the airfield, which had been highlighted as a risk for controlled flight into terrain in the Fed Ex manual. The airfield itself encouraged an illusion known as the black-hole approach.

A black hole approach, also called the featureless terrain illusion, happens on dark nights when there's no stars/moonlight and no view of the horizon: everything around you is unilluminated when you are approaching over water or unlit terrain. As a result, there's nothing visible below between your position and the runway, leading to a visual black hole. The danger arises from pilots relying too much on their own vision because the illusion can cause the runway to appear to be tilted and sloping. The result is that the pilot believes he is higher than he is and descends aggressively in response to his spatial confusion of the aircraft's position in relation to the runway. Boeing conducted a study using flight simulators which showed that in a visual approach in black hole conditions, Boeing instructor pilots (who had more than 10,000 hours each) generally flew excessively low approaches and crashed short of the runway.

In order to avoid this illusion, the pilot must contrast his own visual information with the data given by the instruments and, in this case, the PAPI.

Extensive testing showed that the PAPI was acting normally and that, for the approach as flown, all four PAPI lights would have displayed to the flight crew as red. At least one of the flight crew should have been watching the PAPI and all of the crew members felt that they *had* been watching it.

> During postaccident interviews, all three pilots reported observing red and white lights on the PAPI display, consistent with normal PAPI operation. Although the flight engineer and captain reported seeing a pink PAPI signal on one of the four PAPI lights at some time during the approach, they also reported seeing red and/or white lights (which would have provided appropriate glidepath guidance) at the same time.
>
> —From the official report

The pink signal can appear when the airplane is moving through the glidepath, so transiting the narrow zone between the red and white PAPI signals, or in some instances as a result of condensation. Investigators found no evidence of contamination or condensation on the lights and concluded that the airport lighting systems were not a factor in the accident.

All three of the flight crew said that they flew a normal approach until the last few seconds. The captain told investigators that his last recollection was of a white red PAPI indication and that it got a bit bumpy. "Everything visually looked normal, based on the runway, and that's why I was somewhat shocked when I felt the thumping."

As pilot monitoring, he had no idea that anything was wrong until it was too late.

However, from the start his decision-making and monitoring during the approach was not what it should have been. He'd planned and briefed a landing on runway 27, which had an Instrument Landing System and was convenient for access to the FedEx ramp. He seemed oddly indifferent to the idea of choosing a runway, and never pointed out that there was no benefit at all to landing on runway 9. When the first officer began to reconsider, instead of taking a decision as the commander of the flight, he told him that it didn't matter. Compared to the captain's normal performance, the report declares that his decision-making skills were degraded. In the final stages of the flight, he declared the approach stable as the aircraft descended through 500 feet, even though the descent rate was excessive and the engine power settings reduced. It was an unstabilised approach and he should have called for a go-around. And finally he barely even noticed the PAPI lights, which displayed four reds for most of the final approach.

The flight engineer said that when he first saw the runway, the PAPI displayed a white, a pink and two red lights. During the approach, he was scanning his instruments and looking outside for other air traffic. Everything looked and felt normal until he started to feel like they were in turbulence. He looked out the front windshield and found that the aircraft was in a slight right-wing-low attitude and he realised they were going to hit something.

The first officer was convinced that the approach was normal and that when he looked at the PAPI lights, they were two white, two red, meaning that the aircraft was on the glidepath. He remembers turning onto final and adding a touch of power and then nothing more. "I have no memory of the remainder of the flight . . . I don't know where the rest of the flight went."

None of the flight crew saw the four red lights on the PAPI during the approach. Extensive testing of the lighting system showed that there was no sign of any fault or any reason why the display might have been misleading. But there was another reason why the first officer, who was flying a visual approach and would have been looking out throughout, didn't see the PAPI warning.

The first officer had been in the Navy for 16 years and during that time had thirteen eye examinations that included a colour vision screen. The test in question was the Farnsworth Lantern (FALANT), which is meant to identify (and exclude) people with significant red-green colour-vision deficiency who would not be able to distinguish aviation signal lights correctly.

The first officer passed it 10 times with a documented score of 9/9, twice with no documented score and once with the remark "passed by history". However in 1995 when he was evaluated for an FAA medical certificate, the test using pseudoisochromatic plates (PIP) showed that he had a mild red-green defect in his colour vision. He received his medical certificate with a Statement of Demonstrated Ability (SODA) regarding the colour-vision deficiency.

After the accident, the Safety Board requested an extensive ophthalmic evaluation to determine the extent of the first officer's deficiency. The first officer passed the FALANT screening again but failed seven additional red/green colour vision tests. The tests showed specifically that the first officer may have had difficulty interpreting red-green and white signal lights.

We believe that he would definitely have had problems discriminating the PAPIs . . . because the red lights would appear not to be red at all, but . . . more indistinguishable from white than red. . . . it would be extremely unlikely that he would be capable of seeing even the color pink on the PAPI . . . more likely a combination of whites and yellows and perhaps, not even that difference.

—From USAFSAM specialists' report,
Appendix C of the official report

An Australian study discovered the same issue: individuals with colour-vision deficiencies similar to the first officer's mistakenly identify the red light signals as white in 29% of the cases. The study concluded that the Farnsworth lantern should be replaced as a colour-vision certification test.

So the pilot flying the visual approach could not see the difference between the red and white lights of the PAPI. Meanwhile, the captain, who was pilot monitoring, was fatigued and the flight engineer was focused inside of the aircraft. Everyone was so convinced that the approach was fine, they literally couldn't see the problem.

A simulator study discovered that when pilots are focused on landing using the aircraft's heads-up display, they miss obvious issues as major as an aircraft blocking the end of a runway. Analysing the data from accidents, it is clear that illusions such as a black hole approach can also cause pilots to not comprehend visual data such as the PAPI.

Fatigue and high workload are both likely to increase the possibility of missing relevant information. If the captain and flight engineer monitored the runway environment during the final approach and if the PAPI signal was visible without obstruction, inappropriate selective attention could help explain the failure of both crewmembers to respond to the PAPI information.

—From the official report

The heavy workload and fatigue may have combined to keep the flight crew from monitoring the runway in the hurried final approach. Both flight crew must have been fixated or keeping their attention inside the cockpit, as neither recalls seeing the PAPI show as four reds and neither was aware how low the aircraft was.

3.2 Probable Cause

The National Transportation Safety Board determines that the probable cause of the accident was the captain's and first officer's failure to establish and maintain a proper glidepath during the night visual approach to landing. Contributing to the accident was a combination of the captain's and first officer's fatigue, the captain's and first officer's failure to adhere to company flight procedures, the captain's and flight engineer's failure to monitor the approach, and the first officer's color vision deficiency.

—From the official report

As a result of this accident, FedEx has revised their training and their documentation specifically in terms of runway selection and dispatching to non-tower and high-CFIT-risk airports. The lead instructor at FedEx also lobbied the airline to replace the phrase *pilot not flying* with the clearer phrase *pilot monitoring* in order to help non-flying pilots think more about the importance of their monitoring role. Since then, several air carrier operators have incorporated *pilot monitoring* into their training.

FedEx also committed to having EGPWS (Enhanced Proximity Ground Warning System) and TCAS (Traffic Collision Avoidance System) installed in all aircraft by 2004, although in this instance, the software available at the time would not have resulted in a warning based on the glidepath. The EGPWS manufacturer began work on an upgrade which *would* provide an aural warning for this type of situation and in this instance would have provided an aural warning about 19 seconds before the first sounds of impact were recorded by the CVR.

Official Documentation

- Original accident report:
  http://www.ntsb.gov/investigations/AccidentReports/Reports/
  AAR0402.pdf

Other References

- Simulated accident reconstruction:
  https://www.youtube.com/?v=fC-K3wkD6Cw

MIDAIR COLLISION

WITH SO MUCH SKY, midair collisions seem like they should be vanishingly rare. And yet, at the beginning of the millennium, we had only just begun to understand the issues that led to this particularly frightening occurrence.

A systemic weakness is when the system (rather than *a* system) fails. The weakness affects the entire system or organisation and increases the risk of breakdowns or failures throughout. This is the type of situation that is often described as "an accident waiting to happen".

Each weakness in isolation may not lead to an incident; often the weakness is easy to route around, which is exactly why it has not been treated as a priority to fix. But as the problems stack up, these deep-seated flaws swiftly become fatal. With a systemic weakness, the root cause of the incident is human error; however the systems and processes have set it up that such an error is extremely likely to occur.

The now famous Überlingen accident finally forced aviation to face the horror of midair collisions and get a grip on the causes. This accident is of particular interest because two systemic weaknesses were brought to light as a part of the crash: operations at Air Traffic Control in Zürich and the flight training systems of Bashkirian Airlines.

The terrible story of the Überlingen midair collision starts with routine maintenance.

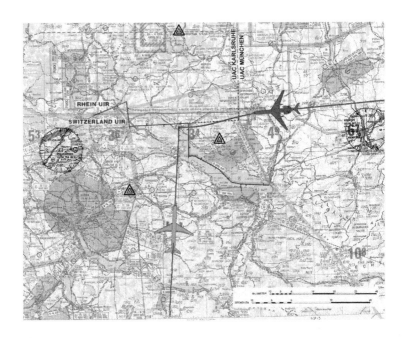

Radar data for B757-200 and TU154M

Obviously, every system needs maintenance. System works, upgrades, replacement hardware all have to be dealt with at some point. With a 24-hour operation like Air Traffic Control, this can mean disruption to services. Even for minor maintenance, it is critical that everyone understand exactly what the effects are. In July 2002, we received a tragic reminder of what happens if the communications are not clear.

The incident happened in German territory but the airspace in question was controlled by the Swiss Air Navigation Services. Swiss Air Navigation Services covered air navigation services in Swiss airspace and the airspaces of adjoining states which had been delegated to them. As a result, the sector in question was handled by Zürich Air Traffic Control.

It was a quiet night over Lake Constance. At the Zürich control centre, the night-shift controllers reported for duty at 17:50. The chief controller told them that there was scheduled work during the night, starting at 21:00 and lasting for six hours.

The work would affect the following systems:

- The radar data processing and presentation system

- The multi-radar data computer

- The flight plan processing system for Tower and Approach control

- The Departure and Arrival Traffic Management System

- The Air Traffic telephone system, which needed to be switched off to perform sectorisation changes.

Issue Number One: Understanding the Effects of the Maintenance

Information about the planned maintenance had been posted in the staff room but the notice only stated that work was scheduled, not what the consequences were. As it happens in this case, more explicit information wouldn't have made a difference as not a single member of the staff on the shift that night had actually read the notice. Or we can turn it around: the fact that the controllers did not read the notice that night didn't matter, because the document didn't explain how the scheduled work would affect them anyway.

Either way, the users of the system did not know what to expect as a result of the work planned that night.

The chief controller had been briefed in person. Somehow, it never occurred to him to talk to the staff about the details of the maintenance or, crucially, how the maintenance might affect their ability to do their jobs.

He left the building at 21:00.

Ten minutes later, the technicians entered the control room and got started on the maintenance work. The technical team included a system manager and an ATCO technical expert to assist the technicians. Both were qualified and would have recognised the effects of the maintenance on the air traffic control operation. However as the work had been scheduled for some time, they assumed that there was no need to brief anyone or that they should check.

And so it goes on. The system manager did not brief the controller on the impact of the work being done. The technical expert was prepared to work with the controller if asked, but he didn't volunteer. The controller had no idea that he had access to support from the team, so he never asked.

The maintenance started: the controller workstations were all switched to fallback mode, which meant that new radar targets weren't correlated and the optical Short Term Conflict Alert (STCA) was not available. Critical information was missing. The controller on duty had no idea that he had lost anything.

Issue Number Two: Adequate Staff on Night Shifts

Nights are quiet at Zürich Control. Night shift at the tower was covered by two air traffic controllers who each had an assistant. One controller covered the night shift sector and the other controller covered the radar. The supervisor (in this case the chief controller) and the system manager typically went off shift at 21:00 and, during the night, the more senior controller would take on the supervisory responsibility of these two roles. Most of the night traffic were transit overflights who needed little or no handling.

The original shift pattern scheduled three controllers for the night shift, which means that two controllers were always at their workstations while the third took a break. It was common practice for one controller to take a long rest break during the night and then to cover the busier early hours of the morning.

When staff shortages meant that the night shift was reduced to two controllers, the practice continued. On a typical night at ACC Zürich in 2002, one controller covered all the roles while the other controller took an extended rest break.

The second controller would return to duty refreshed in the early hours, when traffic got busy again. If an unusual situation arose, it was believed that the resting controller could simply be requested to return to the control room. However, the distance between the lounge and the control room was such that there was no means of a quick alert—the controller on duty would have to contact the other controller by phone.

Management were aware of this situation. Although it was not optimal to have only one controller in the control room at a time, staff shortages meant that they could not get a third controller for that shift. The system appeared to work and so, without a solution in sight, it was tolerated.

That night at 21:15, the second controller retired to the lounge for his rest. The on-duty controller received control slips for two aircraft which were transiting his area.

Issue Number Three: Flight Crew Training

Bashkirian Airlines Flight 2937 was a Tupolev TU154M en route from Moscow, Russia to Barcelona, Spain. The Tupolev carried sixty passengers, including forty-five Russian school children on a school trip to Spain. The commander and co-pilot were joined on the flight deck by an instructor, the chief pilot of Bashkirian Airlines, who was evaluating the captain's performance. The commander was the pilot flying under the supervision of the instructor, who was the Pilot in Command. The co-pilot had no function on this flight.

DHL Flight 611 was a Boeing 757-23APF en route from Bergamo, Italy to Brussels, Belgium. This is a twin-jet transport category aircraft. The captain and his first officer had flown together for a month and had a good working relationship. For this flight, the first officer was the pilot flying.

21:06 The DHL Flight 611 Boeing 757 departs Bergamo after refuelling to continue to Brussels.

21:10 The technicians start work in the control room at ACC Zürich.

As a result of the work, there was no further automatic correlation of new radar targets in the system. Also, the optical Short Term Conflict Alert was no longer available to the controller. The controller was not aware of these secondary effects of the work being carried out.

A technician asked the controller if it was possible to turn off the SWI-02 phone system as a part of the maintenance. The controller argued that he had immediate need of that phone system. However, a few minutes later, the system manager asked again whether the SWI-02 phone system could be switched off for maintenance. This time, the controller ceded control of the system to the technicians.

21:15 The second controller retires to the lounge for his rest.

The controllers expected that they would only have transit flights until morning. The controller's assistant left the control room about 10 minutes later. The remaining controller was now responsible for everything. He was the Radar Executive Controller, the Radar Planning Controller and the Supervisor. His assistant was there to support him with routine coordination tasks but had no responsibility or training within air traffic control.

What they didn't know was that a delayed Airbus A320 was approaching Friedrichshafen Airport, which is in the Zürich control zone. This meant that the controller was also responsible for approach, which meant using two adjacent workstations and working on two different radio frequencies.

21:16:10 Bashkirian Airlines Flight 2937, a Tupolev TU154M passenger jet, carrying 60 passengers and nine crew, enters German airspace at flight level 360 (36,000 feet).

The controller was thus responsible for three aircraft. The Boeing 757-200 was at FL 360 (36,000 feet) flying direct to the Tango VOR (VHF Omni-directional Radio Range, a type of short-range radio navigation system for aircraft). The Tupolev TU154M was at FL 360 (36,000 feet) flying direct to Trasadingen VOR. Both of these aircraft were on the same frequency.

Control slips are used in Air Traffic Control as physical representations of the flights that the controller is responsible for. Each aircraft has a control slip including flight-plan data, flight-path data and transponder code which allows for the controller to analyse the air traffic situation. Under normal circumstances, the Radar Planning Controller considers the traffic flow and intersection points. He informs the Radar Executive Controller if there's a risk that the minimum separation between aircraft might not be maintained.

On this night, the controller was covering all these roles. The control strips were available to him about 20 minutes before the aircraft entered the sector. The control slips did not indicate a crossing fix, even though both the Tupolev TU154M and the Boeing 757-200 routes intersected at FL 360. The control strips for these flights did not show the impending conflict situation.

DHX611	7524	260 ⟍⟍	360	ABE	KUD	LOK
	0463			2120	2130	2135
LIME TGO	EBBR					
B752	465 48		R360			

Control strip for B757-200

BTC2937	7520	360	350	NEG	TRA	BEN
	4125			2136	2142	2151
UUDD NINTU	LEBL					
T154	470 44		R360			

Control strip for TU154M

Control slips showing intended routing for both
aircraft

Only in conjunction with the radar display was it obvious that
they were heading for a collision point at the same height.

In his position of Radar Planning Controller, the controller
should have been continuously analysing and comparing the flight
data to the actual position of the aircraft on radar. However, the
delayed Airbus A320 coming into Friedrichshafen Airport held his
attention. The controller had to use two radar screens with
significantly different scales in order to carry out his tasks.

It is the responsibility of the supervisor to notice that there
were not enough controllers to cover the workload as required.
However, the role of supervisor was also covered by the same
controller. He never stopped reacting to the workload long enough
to recognise the problem.

The controller believed that he could safely handle the three
aircraft and did not ask for support from his colleague. He did not
know or take into account the effects of the scheduled technical
work which had already taken place.

Meanwhile, the delayed Airbus A320 approaching Friedrichshaven was on a different frequency which meant the flight crews could not hear each other, resulting in simultaneous transmissions.

21:21:50 The Pilot in Command of the Boeing contacts ACC Zürich and requests permission to climb to FL 360.

21:23 The technicians disconnect the direct telephone lines to the neighbouring ATC units as a part of their scheduled work.

The adjacent control centres should have been advised that the telephone lines were disconnected; however there was no specific person who was responsible for making sure that they were informed. No other units were warned about the outage.

Once the telephone lines were disconnected, phone communication with air traffic control centres should have continued over the bypass system. However, a technical defect occurred. The bypass system had failed.

ACC Zürich's connection to his supporting air traffic control units had just been cut off.

21:26 The DHL Boeing 757 is cleared to climb to FL 360.

21:30:11 The Bashkirian Tupolev TU154M flight crew contact ACC Zürich reporting their flight level.

The two aircraft are now on the same frequency and flying at the same level. Although the Boeing 757 heard the transmission, no position or routing was given and none of the flight crew saw it as important.

The two aircraft are now only 64 nautical miles apart and racing towards each other. If the controller had noticed, he would have instructed the Tupolev TU154M to descend 1,000 feet, which would have been enough to let them pass safely: keeping the traffic separated. The Tupolev flight plan showed that they wanted a descent after the next reporting point anyway, so they would be happy to take the thousand-foot descent now.

But at this point, the controller was focused on the Airbus A320 on approach to Friedrichshafen airport.

The controller's workload continued to increase.

The Short Term Collision Alert is the back-up system in place to ensure that a controller's eyes are drawn to two aircraft approaching each other. He was using two radar screens with different scales, which probably distorted his ability to judge the distance between the aircraft. The optical Short Term Collision Alert at Zürich would have shown multiple alerts on both screens, but it had been disabled as a part of the technical work.

The controller received no warning at all.

21:33:18 The flight crew of the Tupolev TU154M notice an airplane approaching from the left on the Traffic Collision Awareness System (TCAS).

It should have been a straightforward *see-and-avoid* situation at this point but being aware of something in the sky and seeing the approaching aircraft are two different things.

In the dark night, all the crew could see were a set of lights in the distance. There were no other references which would allow the crew to evaluate the Boeing's flight path and attitude.

It is a common optical illusion to misjudge an object which is rapidly approaching: lights coming straight towards us will appear to stay the same distance away until they are quite close.

The apparent object size of an aircraft changes in form of an exponential function during the approach of two aircraft on collision course. This means that the object stays little for a relatively long period of time before it "busts" or "explodes" optically just a few seconds prior to the collision.

—From the English translation of the official report

The two aircraft were now 27 nautical miles apart.

21:33:24 The radar controller at UAC Karlsruhe is alerted to the impending collision on his Short Term Conflict Alert (STCA). He notifies his supervisor and tries to contact the controller at ACC Zürich but is unable to get through.

The direct phone line was disconnected for the scheduled work and the bypass system had a technical defect. The Karlsruhe radar controller attempted to phone ACC Zürich eleven times, including using the priority button, but was unable to get through.

21:34:30 The Tupolev and the Boeing are now 13.6 nautical miles apart. The first officer on the Boeing, who is the pilot flying, hands over control of the aircraft to the captain, in order to go to the lavatory.

If the Boeing crew had their Traffic Collision Awareness System (TCAS) set to a range of 16 nautical miles, they would have noticed the Tupolev. Investigators were not able to determine the actual setting but one thing is clear: if the pilots had been aware of the approaching aircraft, the pilot flying would never have left his seat. They have no idea that the Tupolev is bearing down on them.

21:34:32 The aircraft are 11.97 nautical miles apart.

21:34:36 The captain of the Tupolev says, "Here, visually," followed by "Here, it is showing us zero."

The Tupolev flight crew are looking for the aircraft they saw on the TCAS. The captain is saying that he's made visual contact with the Boeing: he can see the lights of the other aircraft. He must have then looked at the TCAS again, which showed him the altitude difference, in feet, of the two aircraft. At this point, it is displaying zero because they are at the same altitude.

21:34:37 The technicians switch the phone system back on.

However, no one told the controller. UAC Karlsruhe, who were still desperately trying to notify Zürich about the conflict, phoned three more times. Friedrichshafen phoned once. The controller was speaking on the radio and completely focused on the job at hand. He knew the phone line was out. As a result, he never reacted to the sound of the phone ringing.

21:34:42 Both aircraft receive traffic advisories from their respective TCAS systems.

The Traffic Collision Awareness System offers *traffic advisories* to alert a flight crew that there is an aircraft nearby. The crew are not expected to perform avoidance manoeuvres necessarily; a traffic advisory is meant to make them aware that there is the possibility of a conflict.

If the conflict becomes imminent, the TCAS will broadcast an urgent resolution advisory (climb or descend) as an evasive manoeuvre.

The first alert, the traffic advisory, is a warning. The correct response would be to make a visual identification of the approaching aircraft and be prepared for the resolution advisory.

It's not clear that the Boeing flight crew made visual contact with the Tupolev. The CVR recording is unclear, likely because of the pilot who was still in the rear cockpit area.

The Tupolev already had visual contact with the Boeing, so they were ready and waiting for an instruction for an avoidance manoeuvre.

21:34:49 43 seconds to impact. The controller spots the conflict and instructs the Tupolev crew to descend to 35,000 feet.

His voice was calm and with no sense of urgency but even before the transmission ended, the instructor, who was Pilot Not Flying, commanded, "Descend!"

The controller should have been keeping the two aircraft *at least* seven nautical miles apart. By the end of his transmission, this minimum separation was lost.

Flying at night, under radar control, see-and-avoid has serious limitations. The Tupolev crew had identified the other aircraft but must have been relieved that the potential conflict appeared to have been solved by the air traffic controller.

However, the separation had been lost and the Traffic Collision Awareness System kicked in at that moment.

21:34:56 Both aircraft receive simultaneous resolution advisories from their respective TCAS systems.

If the TCAS determines that there is a real risk of collision, and if the other aircraft is also TCAS-equipped, the TCAS will send a coordination signal to the other aircraft in order to resolve the encounter.

In this way, the evasive manoeuvres are coordinated: one TCAS system will select an "upward sense Resolution Advisory (RA)" (instructing the pilot to climb) and the coordination signal to the second TCAS means that the second system will select a "downward sense RA" (instructing the pilot to descend), thus resolving the conflict immediately.

The resolution advisory in the Boeing was "DESCEND, DESCEND."

The resolution advisory in the Tupolev was "CLIMB, CLIMB".

At the moment that the TCAS broadcast its message, the pilot flying in the Tupolev was pushing the control column forward to descend.

The first officer interrupted to say that the TCAS said *climb*. The pilot flying pulled the control column back, reducing the descent rate. The instructor, who was monitoring, snapped back. "He (the controller) is guiding us down!"

The first officer sounded dubious and commented that TCAS has priority over ATC but no one listened.

The Boeing responded to the TCAS advisory by initiating a descent.

The flight crew conversation in the Tupolev stopped and the thrust levers were retracted, which the investigators believe was done by the instructor. The pilot flying held the control column in place for about two more seconds before pushing it forward to increase the rate of descent.

The ATC command had come too late: The Tupolev could not have achieved 1,000 feet below the Boeing unless they'd finished descending by 31:34:56, which is when they started. They needed the ATC instruction at least one full minute earlier to achieve separation.

However, if there had been no TCAS resolution advisory, the fast descent of the Tupolev would have at least avoided the collision.

The controller had no idea that the Boeing was now also descending.

> The ATCO considered he could handle the situation in which he found himself. He did not express doubt as to whether he was able to work in the environment that was developing around him. He concentrated his efforts on functioning as an ATCO but did not stop to fully consider whether he had the resources to cope. He was now at the heart of a system that was more exposed to undetected error and was not supported by the well-maintained sociotechnical system he was accustomed to.
>
> —From the English translation of the official report

21:35:05 The first officer of the Boeing, returning from the lavatory, says, "Traffic right there." The captain says, "Yes," in acknowledgement. The first officer puts his headset on ready to resume his role as pilot flying. The TCAS system sounds a further advisory: INCREASE DESCENT. INCREASE DESCENT.

The Boeing's rate of descent increased to 2,600 feet per minute.

21:35:13 The controller is unaware that the aircraft are now racing towards each other. He says to the Tupolev, "Ja, we have traffic at your 2 o'clock now at 360."

This was wrong. The Boeing was in the Tupolev's 10 o'clock position: the controller had reported a mirror image. The Boeing had already descended to 35,600 feet; however the radar image didn't renew until 21:35:24, so the controller did not see the Boeing's descent.

As a result of the call stating that traffic was at 2 o'clock, the flight crew of the Tupolev became unsettled. The instructor searched the airspace in front and to the right but could not find the traffic. Meanwhile, the controller believed that his instruction had averted the danger of a collision and the situation was resolved.

At this moment, the crew of the Airbus A320 coming into Friedrichshafen called again regarding their approach.

21:35:19 Both pilots on the Boeing transmit simultaneously that they have initiated a TCAS descent.

They had waited while the controller spoke to the Tupolev and once the frequency was clear, both tried to call at the same time. The first part of the Boeing was garbled as a result. The rest of the message was clear but was at the same moment as the transmission by the Airbus on the other frequency. The Boeing crew couldn't hear the transmission so had no idea that it had overlapped their call.

Meanwhile, the controller turned his attention back to Friedrichshafen approach. The controller never heard the Boeing's broadcast that they were descending; he was listening to the Airbus.

The telephone work and the defective bypass meant that the controller couldn't get through to Friedrichshafen by the internal phone system. He asked his assistant to find another number but still couldn't get through. They discussed options, including contacting Munich Air Traffic Control to ask them to relay the message or to talk to the technicians in the other room to find out what other options there were as the phones were not working. In the end, the controller decided to ask the Airbus to contact Friedrichshafen directly.

The radar controller at UAC Karlsruhe had given up on trying to get through to the controller although he could see that the aircraft were on a collision course. Regulations prohibited him from talking to the two aircraft directly, as direct interactions with flights outside of his responsibility required him to coordinate with the responsible controller, who wasn't answering his phone. There was nothing he could do.

Finally, the controller was able to hand off the delayed flight into Friedrichshafen. He was free to concentrate on the rest of the airspace. But it was too late.

At this point, every safety net was gone. Now that both the Tupolev and the Boeing were descending steeply at close range, there was nothing left that the controller could do to avert the collision.

21:35:24 The distance between the aircraft is now 1.54 nautical miles. In the Tupolev, the TCAS generates a resolution advisory to increase climb. The first officer calls out "It says climb!" He receives no response from the other two pilots.

5 seconds before impact The captain (pilot not flying) in the Boeing shouts, "Descend! [Expletive]. Descend hard!"

The captain (pilot flying) in the Tupolev begins pulling the control column back to transition back to level flight. They are at 35,100 feet at that moment.

2 seconds before impact The control column in the Boeing is pushed forward to the limit, putting the aircraft into a dive. The first officer can see the Tupolev and is desperately trying to avoid it. It's too late.

1 second before impact The control column in the Tupolev is pulled back hard, a sudden attempt by the captain to avoid the collision with the Boeing which must have appeared right in front of them.

Bashkirian Airlines Flight 2937 DHL Flight 611
moments before the collision *(Re-creation by*
Anynobody)

The Radar Controller at UAC Karlsruhe watched the aircraft
collide on his radar monitor. The Tupolev turned red, indicating that
radar signal has been lost. The Boeing disappeared.

21:36:01 Having asked the Airbus to contact Friedrichshafen
directly, the controller turned his attention back to the situation in the upper airspace. The Tupolev displayed as a red
dot on his display.

21:36:01 The controller attempts to contact the Tupolev crew and
receives no response.

21:36:23 The controller attempts to contact the Tupolev crew and
receives no response.

21:37:17 The controller attempts to contact the Tupolev crew and
receives no response.

The Boeing was no longer displayed on his radar monitor. He made no attempt to contact the aircraft.

The first official report of the accident was a man standing outside in Überlingen, who heard "explosive sounds" and rang emergency services to report it.

Eyewitnesses said they heard roaring and rumbling and saw pieces of burning debris falling from the sky.

The wreckage of both planes was found north of Lake Constance, scattered over seven sites. The ground impact of the Boeing caused an extensive forest fire.

It's hard to avoid thinking about how this could have gone differently. If both controllers had been on-duty and at their workstations, the accident would almost certainly have been prevented.

If the visual Short Term Conflict Alert had been available—or at least visibly not in service with an error display—then the controller would likely have noticed the conflict, just as the controllers at Munich and Karlsruhe did, and kept the prescribed separation.

If the controller had not misjudged the situation and made a quick decision to increase separation, the Tupolev would not have descended against the TCAS.

If the phone system were working, the traffic controllers from other units would have been able to warn ACC Zürich about the impending conflict. Furthermore, the controller on duty would not have been focused on repeated calls to Friedrichshafen that couldn't get through.

If the prescribed separation of 7 nautical miles had been adhered to, the accident would have been prevented.

If both aircraft had responded correctly to the resolution advisory as it was broadcast, the accident would have been prevented.

If only.

The following immediate causes have been identified:

- The imminent separation infringement was not noticed by ATC in time. The instruction for the TU154M to descend was given at a time when the prescribed separation to the B757-200 could not be ensured anymore.

  Altogether the BFU considers the issued instruction to the TU154M crew as too late and the resulting separation infringement as one of the immediate causal factors having led to the accident.

  The BFU assumes, however, that the TU154M crew would have followed TCAS if the controller had not earlier instructed an avoidance manoeuvre in the form of a descent.

- The TU154M crew followed the ATC instruction to descend and continued to do so even after TCAS advised them to climb. This manoeuvre was performed contrary to the generated TCAS RA.

  It is to be assumed that the crew considered the instruction to descend to FL 350 more as a manoeuvre to avoid an imminent collision than a normal manoeuvre to re-establish the prescribed separation. This fits the picture of the swift initiated and carried out descent which was not finished early enough to level off at FL 350.

  After the crew initiated a descent contrary to the RA, the outcome was left to chance.

> **The BFU considers the accomplishment of the ma-
> noeuvre contrary to the RA to be one of the immedi-
> ate causal factors having led to the accident.**
>
> —From the English translation of the official report

It was the controller's job to be aware of the situation in his airspace and keep the aircraft separated by the legal minimums. The Tupolev crew, having just received a traffic advisory, were waiting for an instruction to climb or descend. When the air traffic controller asked them to descend, it was treated as an urgent command to avoid crashing into the other aircraft, which they had in sight. Once the TCAS resolution advisory kicked in, they had conflicting instructions. The most senior crew member, the flight instructor, decided to continue with the controller's instruction, despite the fact that a TCAS resolution advisory should take precedence.

There was no time to think about it, but clearly the instructor—and presumably the captain—did not understand that if they were advised by the TCAS to climb, then the other aircraft would be receiving an advisory to descend, thus acting against the TCAS advisories was the worst possible option.

When given conflicting instructions by an air traffic controller and TCAS, there is one key consideration: the air traffic control systems have *already failed*. If you are flying in controlled airspace and the TCAS sounds a resolution advisory, then minimum separation has been already been lost.

The following **systemic causes** have been identified:

- The integration of ACAS/TCAS II into the system aviation was insufficient and did not correspond in all points with the system philosophy.

- The regulations concerning ACAS/TCAS published by ICAO and as a result the regulations of national aviation authorities, operational and procedural instructions of the TCAS manufacturer and the operators were not standardised, incomplete and partially contradictory.

With ACAS/TCAS an additional safety system was introduced into aviation. It works independently of ground equipment and is installed in airplanes. ACAS/TCAS is a system of last resort and works independently of ATC units. Collision avoidance is one of the common tasks of the two systems. The instructions of both systems may command opposite directions. Yet, in case of an RA ACAS/TCAS takes priority, there is no contradiction.

ACAS/TCAS as actually implemented apparently comes short of its intended purpose:

The Integration of ACAS/TCAS II into the system aviation was insufficient and did not in all points correspond with the system philosophy. The regulations concerning ACAS/TCAS II published by ICAO and as a result the regulations of national aeronautical authorities, operational and procedural instructions of the TCAS manufacturer and the operators were not standardised, incomplete and partially contradictory.

> **The BFU considers these deficiencies as systemic causal factors having led to the accident.**
>
> - Management and quality assurance of the air navigation service company did not ensure that during the night all open workstations were continuously staffed by controllers.
>
> - Management and quality assurance of the air navigation service company tolerated for years that during times of low traffic flow at night only one controller worked and the other one retired to rest.
>
> —From the English translation of the official report

When the systems are weak, the risk of breakdowns and failures become high. Two aircraft colliding can only happen when multiple systems all break down, like a pile of dominoes.

The investigators discovered that in May 2001, the same controller was involved in an incident where minimum separation had been infringed. The Swiss BFU investigated the incident and came to the conclusion that it was an error in judgement by the controller which had been compounded by the lack of a second controller on shift. A computer-generated "range scale bar" was introduced on the radar monitor as a result of that incident; however the night of the midair collision, the range scale bar was not available as a result of the scheduled work.

This shows clearly the tragedy of a systemic weakness waiting to lead to failure: the near miss happened when a controller was alone covering multiple roles, with no human redundancy and inadequate radar aids. And a year later, the same situation led to a horrific midair collision.

Also, the controller was covering the position of Supervisor as one of his many roles, but he was not trained to deal with supervisory decisions. That night, he was focused on the direct operations, which is what he was trained for and most comfortable with. He did not have the experience or the training to back off and recognise the continuously increasing workload. The team doing the work included a technical expert, but the controller did not know that this person was available to support him, he considered the technical expert to be just another technician working on the systems.

He was not able to balance the requirements of the scheduled work against his own ability to perform his job. A supervisor would be expected to prioritise the full operational and personnel requirements. The controller, on his own, did not recognise that the efficient operation of the system had a higher priority than any single task demanding his attention.

He simply knuckled under and got on with it.

As the situation deteriorated, the controller's environment became less error-tolerant and the risk factors increased. The technical team never evaluated the air traffic control situation, nor had they been trained to recognise the deteriorating conditions. It did not occur to them that the controller required their support to deal with the unfolding situation.

It's clear that under the circumstances, with the radar system in fallback mode, telephones unavailable and an unexpected late arrival, both controllers were required to be on duty and at their work stations. But neither the controller nor the technical team recognised the deteriorating situation.

The other systemic failure involved the training of the Tupolev crew.

> The TU154M crew has attentively observed the development on the TCAS display showing the conflicting traffic and discussed it internally. When the distance between the airplanes was still approximately 10 NM, the commander of the TU154M visually identified the other airplane.
>
> Thus the TA was no surprise for the crew. When they received the instruction of the controller to descend to FL 350 and the explicit information about the conflicting traffic it was clear to them that the controller had also realized the situation and had made a decision to solve the problem.
>
> They followed this instruction very swiftly because they were in a situation of uncertainty, which now could be considered as settled. After TCAS issued an RA to climb the crew stuck to their decision to follow the controller's instruction. The decision to follow the controller's instruction was even confirmed to be "correct" by the repeated instruction to descend and the information of the controller about the other airplane being at FL 360.
>
> —From the English translation of the official report

Although all the flight crew except the flight engineer had received TCAS training, the airline did not have TCAS equipped flight simulators to offer them practical training. TCAS is not mandatory in the Russian Federation, so only aircraft flying into regions where TCAS is mandatory have the equipment installed. As a result, the crew of the Tupolev, including the chief pilot, had only marginal practical TCAS experience.

Worse, investigators discovered that the instructions in the flight operations manual implied clearly that it wasn't mandatory to follow a resolution advisory. The manual specifically describes it as a *recommendation to the crew*, which clearly led the chief pilot and commander to make the decision that it was better to follow the ATC advisory instead.

Here's where we uncover the systemic weakness within the airline. This lack of practical experience and bad Cockpit Resource Management (CRM) made it easy for this mistake to be made. The instructor, who was also the chief pilot of the company and the pilot-in-command of the aircraft, made a bad decision. His position within the company made it difficult to argue. Only the first officer spoke up, but when he didn't receive a reaction, he gave up. This is exactly what CRM is about: teaching everyone on the flight deck to work together to avoid these accidents where an obviously bad decision has fatal consequences.

However, the Russian Federation, in response to the accident investigation, made a strong argument that it was unreasonable to expect the Russian pilots to climb, because they were at 35,500 feet and the controller, incorrectly, stated that the conflicting traffic was above them at 36,000 feet.

If the flight crew had completely ignored the air traffic controller, who, after all, had already failed in his duty to ensure minimum separation, then the TCAS resolution advisories would have separated the aircraft and avoided the collision.

And that's the key reason, right there, why TCAS resolution advisories must take precedence over Air Traffic Control. As we saw in the 2001 near-miss incident over Tokyo and again here, the air traffic control unit had already failed in their duty and the controllers were not clear on the current situation. As such, they simply can't be trusted to be advising over the collision system.

How can we avoid such tragic accidents in the future? By focusing on the roots of the causes rather than the final actions.

It's clear that the works at Zürich should have been explained better, that people need to be kept in the know. Two controllers need to be on active duty at all times, with additional controllers assigned to manage breaks. An attitude of "we'll just make do with what we've got" was clearly an issue.

After the near-miss incident over Tokyo (covered in Why Planes Crash: 2001), it was already obvious that TCAS procedure needs to be crystal clear and pilots must understand that if a resolution advisory is given, they must follow it unless in the most extreme circumstances and certainly they must never manoeuvre in the opposite direction to the resolution advisory. They should be aware that the other conflicting aircraft is being given an advisory based on the presumption that both aircraft will follow the advisory immediately.

The Short Term Conflict Alert should include an indication of failure and availability, so that the controller is at least aware that he may not be given the alerts as expected. In addition, the audio alert should sound permanently until acknowledged.

Nothing here is new: better training for staff, safe staff levels, better communication, better CRM. Slowly but surely, this is becoming reality as we learn from tragic mistakes.

In a sad footnote to this accident, the controller on duty that night was murdered a few years later by a man who had lost his wife and two children in the air crash.

Official Documentation

- Original Accident Report:
  *http://www.bfu
  web.de/DE/Publikationen/Untersuchungsberichte/
  2002/Bericht_02_AX001-1-2.html*

Other References

- Accident report translated into English: AX001-1-2/02—
  *http://www.bfu-web.de/EN/Publications/
  Investigation Report/2002/Report_02_AX001-1-2_
  Ueberlingen_Report.pdf?__blob=publicationFile*

Photography

- Unattributed photographs are taken directly from the accident
  report.

- CGI image of *Bashkirian Airlines Flight 2937* final moments
  re-created by Anynobody:
  https://de.wikipedia.org//Datei:.png

Thank You for Reading

IF YOU ENJOYED this book, please sign up to the notification mailing list, so I can let you know when the next one is out. You can mail me at *sylvia@planecra.sh* or sign up at *http://planecra.sh/notify/*.

As a thank you for subscribing to the mailing list, you will receive a free copy of "Mobile Phone Interfering with Flight," an excerpt from *Why Planes Crash Case Files: 2003*.

I also post accident analyses and aviation news on my website every Friday. You can join in at *http://www.fearoflanding.com/* or receive the posts in your inbox once a week by subscribing to the email updates.

ABOUT THE AUTHOR

SYLVIA WRIGLEY is a pilot and aviation writer who has been obsessing about aviation safety for over a decade.

- Her non-fiction has appeared in publications all over the world, including *The Guardian, Piper Flyer* and *Forbes*.

- She has appeared as an aviation expert on the BBC as well as for the Discovery Channel series *Air Crash Confidential* (Series 2, Episodes 3 and 5), the Russian Channel 1 news, French Channel M6 "Disparition du vol MH370" and ntv.ru Central Television program.

- Her aviation website *http://fearoflanding.com/* received 145,000 visits in 2014 and continues to grow.

- *You Fly Like a Woman,* her short memoir about learning to fly, has had over 12,000 downloads in the first quarter and remains in the Amazon top 50 aviation books.

- Her series, *Why Planes Crash,* was launched in May 2013. The first book of the series covers eleven accidents and incidents in 2001, including the disastrous runway incursion at Linate, the near-miss over Tokyo, the Avjet crash at Aspen, the Twin Towers and American Airlines Flight 587 disintegrating over Queens. Find out more at *http://planecra.sh*

Made in the USA
Middletown, DE
05 June 2020